The Orpheus C. Kerr Papers

Also from Westphalia Press

westphaliapress.org

The
Orpheus C. Kerr
Papers

by Robert Henry Newell

WESTPHALIA PRESS
An imprint of Policy Studies Organization

Westphalia Press
An imprint of Policy Studies Organization
1527 New Hampshire Ave., NW
Washington, D.C. 20036
info@ipsonet.org

ISBN-13: 978-1-63391-118-5
ISBN-10: 1633911187

Cover design by Taillefer Long at Illuminated Stories:
www.illuminatedstories.com

Daniel Gutierrez-Sandoval, Executive Director
PSO and Westphalia Press

Rahima Schwenkbeck, Director of Marketing and Media
PSO and Westphalia Press

Updated material and comments on this edition
can be found at the Westphalia Press website:
www.westphaliapress.org

THE

ORPHEUS C. KERR PAPERS.

———————

NEW YORK:

BLAKEMAN & MASON,

21 MURRAY STREET.

1862.

CONTENTS.

LETTER I.

SHOWING HOW OUR CORRESPONDENT CAME INTO THE WORLD: WITH
SOME PARTICULARS CONCERNING HIS EARLY CHILDHOOD.

WASHINGTON, D. C., March 20th, 1861.

JUDGE not by appearances, my boy ; for appearances are very deceptive, as the old lady cholerically
remarked when one, who was really a virgin on to
forty, blushingly informed her that she was "just
twenty-five this month."

Though you find me in Washington now, I was
born of respectable parents, and gave every indication, in my satchel and apron days, of coming to
something better than this,—much better, my boy.

Slightly northward of the Connecticut river, where
a pleasant little conservative village mediates between two opposition hills, you may behold the land-
scape on which my infantile New England eyes first
traced the courses of future railroads.

Near the centre of this village in the valley, my
boy, and a little back from its principal road, stood
the residence of my worthy sire—and a very pretty
residence it was. From the frequent addition of a

new upper-room here, a new dormer window there, and an innovating skylight elsewhere, the roof of the mansion had gradually assumed an Alpine variety of juts and peaks somewhat confusing to behold. Local tradition related that, on a certain showery occasion, a streak of lightning was seen to descend upon that roof, skip vaguely about from one peak to another, and finally slink ignominiously down the water-pipe, as though utterly disgusted with its own inability to determine, where there are so many, which peak it should particularly perforate.

Years afterwards, my boy, this strange tale was told me by a venerable chap of the village, and I might have believed it, had he not outraged the probability of the meteorological narrative with a sequel.

"And when that streak came down the pipe," says the aged chap, thoughtfully, "it struck a man who was leaning against the house, ran down to his feet, and went into the ground without hurting him a mite !"

With the natural ingenuousness of childhood I closed one eye, my boy, and says I :

"Do you mean to tell me, old man, that he was struck by lightning, and yet wasn't hurt ?"

"Yes," says the venerable chap, abstractedly cutting a small log from the door-frame of the grocery store with his jack-knife ; "the streak passed off from him, because he was a conductor."

" A conductor ?" says I, picking up another stone
to throw at the same dog.

" Yes," says the chap confidentially, " he was a
conductor—on a railroad."

The human mind, my boy, when long affected by
country air, tends naturally to the marvellous, and
affiliates with the German in normal transcendent-
alism.

Such was the house in which I came to life a certain number of years ago, entering the world, like a
human exclamation point, between two of the an-
griest sentences of a September storm, and adding
materially to the uproar prevailing at the time.

Next to my parents, of whom I shall say little at
present, the person I can best remember, as I look
back, was our family physician. A very obese man
was he, my boy, with certain sweet-oiliness of manner, and never out of patients. I think I can see
him still, as he arose from his chair after a profound
study of the case before him, and wrote a prescrip-
tion so circumlocutory in its effect, that it sent a
servant half a mile to his friend, the druggist, for
articles she might have found in her own kitchen,
aqua pumpaginis and sugar being the sole ingredients
required.

The doctor had started business in our village as a
veterinary surgeon, my boy ; but, as the entire extent
of his practice for six months in that line was a call

to mend one of Colt's revolvers, he finally turned his attention to the ailings of his fellows, and wrought many cures with sugar and water Latinized.

At first, my father did not patronize the new doctor, having very little faith in the efficacy of sugar and water without the addition of a certain other composite often seen in bottles; but the doctor's neat speech at a Sunday school festival won his heart at last. The festival was held near a series of small waterfalls just out of the village, my boy, and the doctor, who was an invited guest, was called upon for a few appropriate remarks. In compliance with the demand he made a speech of some compass, ending with a peroration that is still quoted in my native place. He pointed impressively to the waterfalls, and says he :

" All the works of nature is somewhat beautiful, with a good moral. Even them cataracts," says he, sagely, " have a moral, and seem eternally whispering to the young, that ' Those what err falls'."

The effect of this happy illustration was very pleasing, my boy ; especially with those who prefer morality to grammar ; and after that, the physician had the run of all the pious families—our own included.

It was a handsome compliment this worthy man paid me when I was about six months old.

Having just received from my father the amount

of his last bill, he was complacent to the last degree, and felt inclined to do the handsome thing. He patted my head as I sat upon my mother's lap, and says he :

"How beautiful is babes ! So small, and yet so much like human beings, only not so large. This boy," says he, fatly, looking down at me, "will make a noise in the world yet. He has a long head, a very long head."

"Do you think so ?" says my father.

"Indeed I do," says the doctor. "The little fellow," says he, in a sudden fit of abstraction, "has a long head, a very long head—and it's as thick as it is long."

There was some coolness between the doctor and my father after that, my boy ; and, on the following Sunday, my mother refused to look at his wife's new bonnet in church.

I might cover many pages with further account of childhood's sunny hours ; but enough has been given already to establish the respectability of my birth, despite my present location ; and there I let the matter rest, my boy, for the time being.

Yours, retrospectively,
ORPHEUS C. KERR.

LETTER II.

SHOWING HOW THE WRITER INCREASED IN YEARS AND INDISCRETION, AND HOW HE WAS SAVED FROM MATRIMONY BY THE LAMENTABLE EXAMPLE OF JED SMITH.

WASHINGTON, D. C., March 25th, 1861.

To continue from where I left off, my boy : between the interesting ages of ten and eighteen I went to school at the village academy, working through the English branches and the Accidence, with a lively sense of a preponderance of birch in the former, and occasional class-sickness in the latter.

Those were my happiest days, my boy ; and as I look back to them now, for a moment all my flippancy leaves me, and I forget that I am an American and a politician. Those dear old days ! those short, unreal days ! Only long in being long past.

It was just after the eternal " *Bonus—Bona—Bonum*" of the master had ceased to ring in my ears, that I commenced to be a young man. I knew that I was becoming a young man, my boy ; for it was then that I began to regard the unmarried women of America with sheepish bashfulness, and stumbled awkwardly as I entered my father's pew in church.

Then it was that the sound of a young female giggle threw me into a cold perspiration, and a looking-glass deluded me into gesticulating in solitude before it, and extemporizing the speeches I was to make when called upon to justify the report of fame by admiring populaces.

Do you remember the asinine time in your own life, my boy,—do you remember it ? I know that you do, my boy, for I can feel your blush on my own cheeks.

Of the few women of America who looked upon me with favor, there was one—Ellen—whom I really loved, I think ; for of all the girls, the mention of her name, alone, gave me that peculiar feeling in which instinctive impulse blends undefinably and perpetually with a sense of reverent respect ; or, rather, with a sense of some unworthiness of self. Ellen died before I had known her a year. I thought afterwards, like any other youngster, that I loved half-a-dozen different girls ; but, even in maturer years, second love is a poor imitation. Say what you will about second love, my boy, in the breast of him truly a man, it is but an *imperium in imperio*—a flower on the grave of the first.

There was one young woman of America in our village, my boy, about whom the chaps teased me not a little ; and I might, perhaps, have been teased into matrimony, like many another unfortunate, but for the example of a Salsbury chap I met one night in one of the village stores. He was a Yankee chap with much southwestern experience, my boy, and when he heard the lads teasing me about a woman, he hoisted his heels upon the counter, and says he :

"Anybody'd think that creation was born with a frock on, to hear the way you younkers talk woman. Darn the she-critters !" says he, shutting his jack-knife with a clash. "I'd rayther be as lonesome as a borryed pup, than see a piece of caliker as big as a pancake. What's wimmen but a tarnation bundle of gammon and petticoats. Powerful ! Be you married folks, stranger ?"

"Not yet," says I.

"Don't never be then," says he. "My name's Smith—one of the Smithses down to Salsbury, that's guaranteed to put away as much provender and carry as big a turkey as ever set on critters down in that deestrict. And whilst my name's Smith, there'll never be a younker to call me 'daddy,' ef a gal was to have Jerusalem tantrums after me. You'rn a stranger, and ain't married folks ; but I don't mind tellin' ye about a golfired rumpus I got into down in Salsbury when I took to a gal that stuck out all around like a hay-stack, an' was a screamer at choir-meetin' and such like. Her name was Sal Green—one of the Greenses down in Pegtown—and the first time I took a notion to her was down to the old shingle meetin'-house, when Sam Spooner had a buryin'. When the parson gets out a hymn, she straightened up like a rooster at six o'clock of daybreak, and let out a string of screams that set all the babies to yelping as though big pins was goin' clean through their insides. Geewhillikins ! how the critter did squawk and squeal, and turn up her eyes like a sick duck in a shower. I was jest fool enough to think it pooty ; and when my old man says, says he, ' Jed, you're took all of a heap with that pooty creeter,' I felt as ef chills an' fever was givin' me partikiler agony. Says I, ' She's an armful fur the printze of Wales, and ef that Bob Tompkins don't stop makin' eyes at her over there, I'll give him sech a lacing that he won't comb his hair for six weeks.'

" The old man put a chaw into his meat-safe, and shut one eye ; and, sez he : ' Jed, you're a fool ef you don't hook that gal's dress fur her before next harvestin'. She's a mighty scrumptious creetur, and just about ripe for the altar. Jest tell her there's more Smithses wanted an' she'll leave the Greenses 'thout a snicker.' I rayther liked the idee : but I told the old man that his punkin-pie was all squash ; because it wouldn't do to let on too soon. When the folks was startin' from the church, I went up to Sal, and sez I, ' Miss, I s'pose you wouldn't mind lettin' me see you tu hum.' She blushed like a biled lobster, and sez she : ' I don'ᵗ know your folks.' I felt

sorter streaked ; but I gev my collar a hitch, and sez
I : ' I'm Mister Smith : one of the Smithses of this
deestrict, an' always willin' for a female in distress.'
Then she made a curtesy, an' was goin' to say somethin', when Bob Tompkins steps up, and sez he :
' There's a-goin' to be another buryin' in this settle-
ment, ef some folks don't mind their own chores, an'
quit foolin' with other folkses company !'   This riled
me rite up, and sez I : ' There's a feller in this
deestrict that hain't had a spell of layin' on his back
for some time : but he's in immediate danger of
ketchin' the disease bad.'   Bob took a squint at the
width of my chist, and then he turned to Sal, who
was shakin' like a cabbage leaf in a summer gale, and
sez he : ' Sal, let's marvel out of bad company before
it spiles our morials.'   With that he crooked one of
his smashin' machines, and Sal was jest hookin' on,
when I put the weight of about one hundred pounds
under his car, an' sez I : ' Jest lay there, Bob Tompkins, until your parients comes out to look fur your
body.'   He went down as ef he'd been took with a
suddint desire to examine the roots of the grass, and
Sal screamed out that I'd murdered the rantankerous
critter.   Sez I : ' The tombstun that's fur his head
ain't cut yet : but I calkilate it'll be took out of
the quarry ef he comes smellin' around my heels
ag'in.'   Jest as I made this feelin' remark, the varmint began to scratch earth as ef he had a mind to

see how it would feel to be on his pins ag'in, and I
crooked my elbow to Sal and thought it was about
time to marvel. She layed up to me like a pig to a
rough post, and we peregrinated along for some distance until we were pretty nigh hum. I was askin'
her ef it hurt her much when she sung, an' she was
sayin' ' not partikeler;' when all of a suddint somethin'
knocked Fourth-o'-July fireworks out of my eyes,
and I went to grass with my heels up. It was Bob
Tompkins, and sez he : ' Lay there, Mr. Smith, and
let us here from you by the next mail.' For a minute, I thought I was bound for glory, but pooty soon
I come to my oats, and then I rolled over and seen
Bob a-squeezing Sal's hand. All right, my prooshian
blue, thinks I, there'll be a 'pothecary's bill for some
family in this here deestrict : but I won't say who's
to pay it at present. I jest waited to see the feller
try to put his nose into Sal's face, and then I stretched
to my feet, and sez I : ' This here pasture wants a
little mashin' down to make it fruitful, and it's my
impreshun that I can do it.' Sal see that I was
bound to make somebody smell agony, so she jist
ripped away from Bob, and marveled for the house,
screaming ' fire,' like a scrumptious fire-department.
Bob looked after her for a minit, and then he turned
to me, and sez he : ' I hope your folks have got some
crape to hum ; because there's goin' to be a job fur
our wirtuous sexton.' I kinder smiled outer one eye,

and sez I : ' When Sal and I is married, we'll drop a
tear fur the early decease of an individual who never
would hev been born if it hadn't been for your parients.' This riled Bob up awful, and he came right
at me, like a mad bull at a red shawl. I felt somethin' drop on the bridge of my nose, and see a hull
nest of sky rockets all at onct ; but I only keeled for
the shake of a tail, and then I piled in like a mad
buffalo with the cholic. It was give and take for
about five minutes ; and, I tell you, Bob played
away on my nose like a Trojan. The blood flu some,
and I was sorry I hadn't said good-bye to the folks
before I left them ; but I gave Bob some happy
evidences of youthful Christianity around his goggles,
and pooty soon he looked as ef he'd been brought up
to the charcoal business. We was makin' pooty
good time round the lot, when, all of a suddint, Sal
came running up with her father and mother ; and,
sez the old feller : ' Ef you two members of the church
don't stop your religious exercises, there'll be some
preachin' from the book of John.'

"With that, Bob took his paw out of my hair,
and sez he : 'Smithses son hit me the first whack.'
I jest promenaded up to the old man, and sez I : ' If
you'll jest show me a good buryin'-place, I'll take
pleasure in makin' a funeral for the Tompkinses.'
The old man looked kinder queerious at Sally, and
she commenced to snicker ; and sez she : ' What are
you two fellers rumpussin' about ?' I looked lovin'

at her, and sez I : ' It's to see who shall hev the poot-
iest gal of all the Greenses.' When I said this, the
old man bust into a larf like a wild hyenner ; and the
old woman, she put her hands across her stummik
and begin to larf like mad, and Sal she snickered
right eout in my countenance, and sez she : ' Why,
I'm engaged to Sam Slocum !'

"Strannger, there's no use of talkin'. My hair riz
right up like a blackin'-brush, and Bob's eyes came
out like peas out of a yaller pod. There was speechless silence for two minits, and then says Bob :
' There's a couple of golfired fools somewheres in this
country, and it's a pity their dads ever seen their
mothers.' I see he felt powerful mean, so I walked
up to him, and sez I : ' Suppose we go and look for
the New Jerusalem ?' He jest hooked to my elbow,
and without sayin' another word, we marveled for hum.

"Sence that, I hain't held no communion with
petticoats, and ef I ever get married, you shall hev
an invite to the funeral."

As I went home that night, my boy, after hearing
the story of that rude, unlettered man, I made up
my mind to have nothing more to do with the uncer-
tain women of America, until my position should be
such that they would not dare to "fool" me. The
women of America, my boy, are equally apt at making a fool of a man in his own estimation, and a man
of a fool in *their* own. Yours, for celibacy,

ORPHEUS C. KERR.

LETTER III.

OUR CORRESPONDENT BECOMES LITERARY, AND FATHOMS CERTAIN MYS-
TERIES OF JOURNALISM. HE PRODUCES A DISTINCTIVE AMERICAN
POEM, AND GAINS THE USUAL REWARD OF YOUTHFUL GENIUS.

WASHINGTON, D. C., March 31st, 1861.

As far I can trace back, my boy, we never· had a
literary character in our family, save a venerable aunt
of mine, on my mother's side, who commenced her
writing career by refusing to contribute to the Sunday
papers, and subsequently won much fame as the au-
thoress of a set of copy-books. When this gifted relative found herself acquiring a reputation, she came
in state to visit us, and so disgusted my very practical
father by wearing slip-shod gaiters, inking her right
hand thumb nail every morning, calling all things by
European names, and insisting upon giving our old-
est plough horse the romantic and literary title of
"Lord Byron," that my exasperated parent incurred
a most tremendous prejudice against authorship, my
boy, and vowed, when she went away, that he never
would invite her presence again.

I was only twenty years old at that time, and the
novelty of my aunt's conduct had rather an infatu-

ating effect upon me. With that perversity often observable in youngsters before they have seen much of the world, I became deeply interested in my literary relative as soon as my father commenced to speak contemptuously of her pursuits, and it took very little time to invest me with a longing and determination to be a writer.

Thenceforth I wore negligent linen; frequently rested my head upon the forefinger of my right hand, with a lofty and abstracted air; assumed an expression of settled and mysterious gloom when at church, and suffered my hair to grow long and uncombed.

Speaking of the masculine literary habit of wearing the hair in this way, my boy, I find myself impressed with a profound metaphysical idea. You have probably noticed that writers following this fashion will frequently scratch their heads when inspiration plays the laggard. It is also true that wearers of long and uncombed hair who are *not* writers, will scratch their heads in the same way, occasionally. The action being the same in both cases, can it be that physiological inspection would develope an affinity between the natural causes thereof?

I have often thought of this, my boy,—I've often thought of this.

My bearing during this period of infatuation could hardly fail to attract considerable attention in our village, and there were two opinions about me. One

was that I had been jilted ; the other, that I was
about to become a vagabond and an actor.   My
father inclined to the former, and left me, as he
thought, to get over my disappointment in the natural way.

My peripatetic spell had lasted about six weeks, my
boy, when I formed the acquaintance of the editor of
the *Lily of the Valley*, who permitted me to mope in
his office now and then, and soothed my literary in-
flammation by permitting me to write "puffs" for
the village milliner.

Oh !. the fierce and tremendous ecstasy of that
moment when I first saw my own words in print,
with not more than six typographical errors in each
line :—" QUEEN VICTORIA, it is said, is comind to
this coontry for the xpress purpose of obtoining
one of these beautiful spring bunnets at Madame
Smith's."

I noticed as I went home on the day of publication,
that all whom I passed paused to look after me.   I
was already famous.   The discovery, on reaching our
house, that one of my temples was somewhat fingered
with printers' ink, did not shake me in this belief, my
boy ; I was too far gone for that.

The editor of the *Lily* treated me considerately,
and even asked me at times to accompany him to the
place where he daily sipped inspiration, gaining thereby a fresh flow of ideas and the qualified immortality

of certain additional chalk-marks on the back of a door. I refer to a spirituous establishment.

Finding that the editorial treasury did not redeem its verbal promissory notes, my boy, the proprietor of this establishment suddenly put forth a new sign, conspicuously reading :—

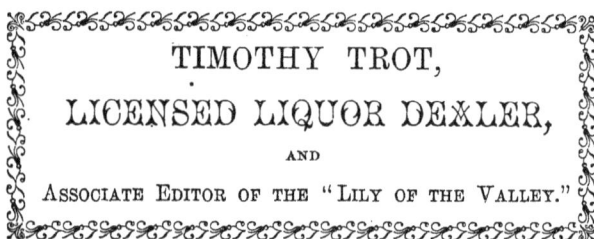

> TIMOTHY TROT,
>
> LICENSED LIQUOR DEALER,
>
> AND
>
> ASSOCIATE EDITOR OF THE "LILY OF THE VALLEY."

The editor went to him, and says he :

"What do you mean by this impertinence, Timothy ?"

The liquor chap stuck his hands into his pockets, my boy, and says he :

"If I furnish inspiration for nothing, I may as well have some literary credit. The village swallows what you furnish," says the chap, reasoningly, "and you swallow what I furnish, and so I'm the head editor after all."

But he took down the sign, my boy, when the editor dissolved the partnership by paying his score.

What are called Spirited Editorials in the New York papers, my boy, very often involve two swallows as well as a spread-eagle.

While looking over some old magazines in the *Lily* office one day, I found in an ancient British periodical a raking article upon American literature, wherein the critic affirmed that all our writers were but weak imitators of English authors, and that such a thing even as a Distinctively American Poem *sui generis*, had not yet been produced.

This radical sneer at the United States of America fired my Yankee blood, my boy, and I vowed within myself to write a poem, not only distinctively American, but of such a character that only America could have produced it. In the solitude of my room, that night, I wooed the aboriginal muse, and two days thereafter the *Lily of the Valley* contained my distinctive American poem of

THE AMERICAN TRAVELER.

To Lake Aghmoogenegamook,
    All in the State of Maine,
A man from Wittequergaugaum came
    One evening in the rain.

"I am a traveler," said he,
    "Just started on a tour,
And go to Nomjamskillicook
    To-morrow morn at four."

He took a tavern bed that night,
    And with the morrow's sun,
By way of Sekledobskus went,
    With carpet-bag and gun.

A week passed on; and next we find
  Our native tourist come
To that sequestered village called
  Genasagarnagum.

From thence he went to Absequoit,
  And there—quite tired of Maine—
He sought the mountains of Vermont,
  Upon a railroad train.

Dog Hollow, in the Green Mount State,
  Was his first stopping-place,
And then Skunk's Misery displayed
  Its sweetness and its grace.

By easy stages then he went
  To visit Devil's Den;
And Scrabble Hollow, by the way,
  Did come within his ken.

Then, *via* Nine Holes and Goose Green,
  He traveled through the State,
And to Virginia, finally,
  Was guided by his fate.

Within the Old Dominion's bounds,
  He wandered up and down,
To-day, at Buzzard Roost ensconced,
  To-morrow, at Hell Town.

At Pole Cat, too, he spent a week,
  Till friends from Bull Ring came,
And made him spend a day with them
  In hunting forest game.

Then, with his carpet-bag in hand,
  To Dog Town next he went;
Though stopping at Free Negro Town,
  Where half a day he spent.

From thence, into Negationburg
　　His route of travel lay,
Which having gained, he left the State
　　And took a southward way.

North Carolina's friendly soil
　　He trod at fall of night,
And, on a bed of softest down,
　　He slept at Hell's Delight.

Morn found him on the road again,
　　To Lousy Level bound;
At Bull's Tail, and Lick Lizzard, too,
　　Good provender he found.

The country all about Pinch Gut
　　So beautiful did seem,
That the beholder thought it like
　　A picture in a dream.

But the plantations near Burnt Coat
　　Were even finer still,
And made the wond'ring tourist feel
　　A soft, delicious thrill.

At Tear Shirt too, the scenery
　　Most charming did appear,
With Snatch It in the distance far,
　　And Purgatory near.

But spite of all these pleasant scenes,
　　The tourist stoutly swore,
That home is brightest, after all,
　　And travel is a bore.

So back he went to Maine, straightway,
　　A little wife he took;
And now is making nutmegs at
　　Moosehicmagunticook.

In his note, introductory of this poem, my boy, the editor of the *Lily* affirmed (which is strictly true) that I had named none but veritable localities ; and ventured the belief that the composition would remind his readers of Goldsmith.   Upon which his scorpion contemporary in the next village observed, that there was rather more smith than gold about the poem.   Genius, my boy, is never appreciated until its possessor is dead ; and even the useless praise it then obtains is chiefly due to the pleasure that is experienced in burying the poor wretch.

Up to the time when this poem appeared in print, I had succeeded in concealing from my father the nature of my incidental occupation ; but now he must know all.

He did know all, my boy ; and the result was, that he gave me ten dollars, and sent me to New York to look out for myself.

" It's the only thing that will save him," says he to my mother, " and I must either send him off, or expect to see him sink by degrees to editorship, and commence to wear disgraceful clothes."

I went to New York ; I became private secretary and speech-scribe to an unscrupulous and, therefore, rising politician ; and now—I am in Washington.

Thus, my boy, have I answered your desire for an outline of my personal history ; and henceforth let me devote my attention to other and more important

inhabitants of our distracted country. I had a certain postmastership in my eye when I first came
hither ; but war's alarms indicate that I may do
better as an amateur hero.

Yours inconoclastically,

ORPHEUS C. KERR.

LETTER IV.

DESCRIBING THE SOUTH IN TWELVE LINES, DEFINING THE CITIZEN'S
FIRST DUTY, AND RECITING A PARODY.

WASHINGTON, D. C., April —, 1861.

THE chivalrous South, my boy, has taken Fort
Sumter, and only wants to be "let alone." Some
things of a Southern sort I like, my boy ; Southdown
mutton is fit for the gods, and Southside particular
is liquid sunshine for the heart ; but the whole country was growing tired of new South wails before this,
and my present comprehensive estimate of all there
is of Dixie may be summed up in twelve straight
lines, under the general heading of

REPUDIATION.

'Neath a ragged palmetto a Southerner sat,
A-twisting the band of his Panama hat,
And trying to lighten his mind of a load
By humming the words of the following ode:
   "Oh! for a nigger, and oh! for a whip;
   Oh! for a cocktail, and oh! for a nip;
   Oh! for a shot at old Greeley and Beecher;
   Oh! for a crack at a Yankee school-teacher;
   Oh! for a captain, and oh! for a ship;
   Oh! for a cargo of niggers each trip."
And so he kept oh-ing for all he had not,
Not contented with owing for all that he'd got.

In view of the impending conflict, it is the duty of every American citizen, who has nothing else to do, to take up his abode in the capital of this agonized Republic, and give the Cabinet the sanction of his presence. Some base child of treason may intimate that Washington is not quite large enough to hold every American citizen ; but I'm satisfied that, if all the democrats could have one good washing, they would shrink so that you might put the whole blessed party into an ordinary custom house. Some of the republicans are pretty large chaps for their size, but Jeff Davis thinks they can be " taken in" easily enough ; and I know that the new tariff will be enough to make them contract like sponges out of water. The city is full of Western chaps, at present, who look as if they had just walked out of a charity-hospital, and had not got beyond gruel diet yet. Every soul of them knew old Abe when he was a child, and one old boy can even remember going for a doctor when his mother was born. I met one of them the other day (he is after the Moosehicmagunticook post-office), and his anecdotes of the President's boyhood brought tears to my eyes, and several tumblers to my lips. He says, that when Abe was an infant of sixteen, he split so many rails that his whole county looked like a wholesale lumber-yard for a week ; and that when he took to flat-boating, he was so tall and straight, that a fellow once took

him for a smoke-stack on a steamboat, and didn't
find out his mistake until he tried to kindle a fire
under him.   Once, while Abe was practising as a
lawyer, he defended a man for stealing a horse, and
was so eloquent in proving that his client was an
honest victim of false suspicion, that the deeply-
affected victim made him a present of the horse as
soon as he was acquitted.   I tell you what, my boy,
if Abe pays a post-office for every story of his childhood that's told, the mail department of this glorious
nation will be so large that a letter smaller than a
two-story house would get lost in it.

Of all the vile and damning deeds that ever rendered a city eternally infamous, my boy—of all the
infernal sins of dark-browed treachery that ever made
open-faced treason seem holy, the crime of Baltimore
is the blackest and worst.   All that April day we
were waiting with bated breath and beating hearts
for the devoted men who had pledged their lives to
their country at the first call of the President, and
were known to be marching to the defence of the
nation's capital.   That night was one of terror : at
any moment the hosts of the rebels might pour upon
the city from the mountains of guilty Virginia, and
grasp the very throat of the Republic.   And with

the first dim light of morning came the news that our soldiers had been basely beset in the streets of Baltimore, and ruthlessly shot down by a treacherous mob! Those whom they had trusted as brothers, my boy—whose country they were marching to defend with their lives—assassinating them in cold blood!

I was sitting in my room at Willard's, when a serious chap from New Haven, who had just paused long enough at the door to send a waiter for the same that he had yesterday, came rushing into the apartment with a long, fluttering paper in his hand.

"Listen to this," says he, in wild agitation, and read :

BALTIMORE.

Midnight shadows, dark, appalling, round the Capitol were falling,
And its dome and pillars glimmered spectral from Potomac's shore;
All the great had gone to slumber, and of all the busy number
That had moved the State by day within its walls, as erst before,
None there were but dreamed of heroes thither sent ere day was o'er—
        Thither sent through BALTIMORE.

But within a chamber solemn, barred aloft with many a column,
And with windows tow'rd Mount Vernon, windows tow'rd Potomac's
      shore,
Sat a figure, stern and awful; Chief, but not the Chieftain lawful
Of the land whose grateful millions Washington's great name
      adore—
Sat the form—a shade majestic of a Chieftain gone before,
      Thine to honor, Baltimore!

There he sat in silence, gazing, by a single planet's blazing,
At a map outspread before him wide upon the marble floor;
And if 'twere for mortal proving that those reverend lips were moving,
While the eyes were closely scanning one mapped city o'er and o'er—
While he saw but one great city on that map upon the floor—
      They were whispering—" BALTIMORE."

Thus he sat, nor word did utter, till there came a sudden flutter,
And the sound of beating wings was heard upon the carvéd door.
In a trice the bolts were broken; by those lips no word was spoken,
As an Eagle, torn and bloody, dim of eye, and wounded sore,
Fluttered down upon the map, and trailed a wing all wet with gore
      O'er the name of BALTIMORE!

Then that noble form uprising, with a gesture of surprising,
Bent with look of keenest sorrow tow'rd the bird that drooped be-
    fore;
" Emblem of my country!" said he, " are thy pinions stained already
In a tide whose blending waters never ran so red before?
Is it with the blood of kinsmen? Tell me quickly, I implore!"
      Croaked the eagle—" BALTIMORE!"

" Eagle," said the Shade, advancing, " tell me by what dread mis-
    chancing
Thou, the symbol of my people, bear'st thy plumes erect no more?
Why dost thou desert mine army, sent against the foes that harm me,
Through my country, with a Treason worlds to come shall e'er de-
    plore?"
And the Eagle on the map, with bleeding wing, as just before,
      Blurred the name of BALTIMORE!

" Can it be?" the spectre muttered. " Can it be?" those pale lips ut-
    tered;
" Is the blood Columbia treasures spilt upon its native shore?
Is there in the land so cherished, land for whom the great have per-
    ished,
Men to shed a brother's blood as tyrant's blood was shed before?
Where are they who murder Peace before the breaking out of war?"
      Croaked the Eagle—" BALTIMORE."

At the word, of sound so mournful, came a frown, half sad, half scornful,
O'er the grand, majestic face where frown had never been before;
And the hands to Heaven uplifted, with an awful pow'r seemed gifted
To plant curses on a head, and hold them there forevermore—
To rain curses on a land, and bid them grow forevermore—
> Woe art thou, O Baltimore!

Then the sacred spirit, fading, left upon the floor a shading,
As of one with arms uplifted, from a distance bending o'er;
And the vail of night grew thicker, and the death-watch beat the
> quicker
For a death within a death, and sadder than the death before!
And a whispering of woe was heard upon Potomac's shore—
> Hear it not, O Baltimore!

And the Eagle, never dying, still is trying, still is trying,
With its wings upon the map to hide a city with its gore;
But the name is there forever, and it shall be hidden never,
While the awful brand of murder points the Avenger to its shore;
While the blood of peaceful brothers God's dread vengeance doth im-
> plore,
> Thou art doomed, O Baltimore!

" There !" says the serious New Haven chap, as he finished reading, stirring something softly with a spoon, " what do you suppose Poe would think, if he were alive now and could read that ?"

" I think," says I, striving to appear calm, " that he would be ' Raven ' mad about it."

" Oh—ah—yes," says the serious chap, vaguely, " what will *you* take ?"

Doubtless I shall become hardened to the horrors of war in time, my boy ; but at present these things unhinge me.   Yours, unforgivingly,

> ORPHEUS C. KERR.

LETTER V.

CONCERNING THE GREAT CROWD AT THE CAPITAL, OWING TO THE VAST
INFLUX OF TROOPS, AND TOUCHING UPON FIRE-ZOUAVE PECULIARI-
TIES AND OTHER MATTERS.

WASHINGTON, D. C., May 24th, 1861.

I AM living luxuriously, at present, on the top of
a very respectable fence, and fare sumptuously on
three granite biscuit a day, and a glass of water,
weakened with brandy. A high private in the
Twenty-second Regiment has promised to let me
have one of his spare pocket-handkerchiefs for a
sheet on the first rainy night, and I never go to bed
on my comfortable window-brush without thinking
how many poor creatures there are in this world who
have to sleep on hair mattresses and feather-beds all
their lives. Before the great rush of the Fire Zouaves
and the rest of the menagerie commenced, I boarded
exclusively on a front stoop on Pennsylvania Avenue,
and used to slumber, regardless of expense, in a well-
conducted ash-box ; but the military monopolize all
such accommodation now, and I give way for the sake
of my country.

I tell you, my boy, we're having high old times

here just now, and if they get any higher, I shan't be able to afford to stay. The city is in "danger" every other hour, and as a veteran in the Fire Zouaves remarked, there seems to be enough danger laying around loose on Arlington Heights to make a very good blood-and-thunder fiction in numerous pages. If the vigilant and well-educated sentinels happen to see an old nigger on the other side of the Potomac, they sing out, "Here they come!" and the whole blessed army is snapping caps in less than a minute. Then all the cheap reporters telegraph to their papers in New York and Philadelphia, that "Jeff. Davis is within two minutes' walk of the Capital, with a few millions of men," and all the free states send six more regiments a piece to crowd us a little more. I sha'n't stand much more crowding, for my fence is full now, and there were six applications yesterday to rent an improved knot-hole. My landlord says that, if more than three chaps set up housekeeping on one post, he'll be obliged to raise the rent.

Those Fire Zouaves are fellows of awful suction, I tell you. Just for greens, I asked one of them, yesterday, what he came here for? "Hah!" says he, shutting one eye, "we came here to strike for your altars and your fires—especially your *fires*." General Scott says that if he wanted to make these chaps break through the army of a foe, he'd have a fire-bell rung for some district on the other side of the rebels.

He says that half a million of the traitors couldn't keep the Fire Zouaves out of that district five minutes. I believe him, my boy!

The weather here is highly favorable to the free development of perspiration and mint-juleps, and I have enjoyed the melancholy satisfaction of losing ten pounds of flesh in three days. One of the lieutenants of the Eighth has a gutter about half an inch deep worn down the bridge of his nose by the stream of perspiration since Wednesday; and a chap from Vermont melted so awfully the other day, that they had to put him in a refrigerator to keep enough of him to send home to his rich but pious family.

In fact, this weather makes the Northern boys fall away awfully; one of the Fire Zouaves fell away tremendously yesterday; he fell away from Washington to Annapolis, and then somebody had to put him in a guard-house to keep him from perspiring all the way back to New York. The chap that boards on the next front stoop to me now, was so fat when he came here that his captain refused to use him as a sentinel, because he could not see far enough over his stomach to detect any one approaching him. Well, my boy, that chap has fallen away to such an extent that it took me half an hour last night to find out what part of his uniform he lived in. He blew down three or four times while we were walking up Pennsylvania avenue; and while I was helping him up the last time, a passer-by asked me "What I would take for that ere flag-staff?"

By-the-by, you ought to have heard Honest Old Abe's speech, on Wednesday, when we raised the Star-spangled particular on the Post-office. Says he: "On this present occasion, I feel that it will not be out of place to make a few remarks which were not applicable at a former period. Yesterday, the flag hung on the staff throughout the Union, and in consequence of the scarcity of a breeze, there was not much wind blowing at the time. On the present happy occasion, however, the presence of numerous zephyrs causes the atmosphere to agitate for our glorious Union, and this flag, which now unfolds itself to the sight, is observed, upon closer inspection, to present a star-spangled appearance."

Mr. Seward's speech, which was also received with frantic enthusiasm, sounded equally well. He said: "I trust that this glorious spectacle will make a deep impression upon all present, notwithstanding the fact that I am still convinced that peace may yet put an end to this unhappy conflict by means of a convention of all the States on the Fourth of July, 2776, which I have always advocated. As the President has remarked, the breeze which has just arisen in the bay of Naples, causes the Star-Spangled Banner to arouse a far prouder feeling in every American breast, than if a vessel should come in with a palmetto flag at her peak, and upon being asked where it came from, should reply : ' Oh, from one of the petty republics of America.' I have nothing more to say."

I know this report is correct, for I copied both the speeches from a phonographic reporter's copy, and the phonographic reporter had only taken six glasses of old peach and honey before he went to work.

Yours, hastily,

ORPHEUS C. KERR.

LETTER VI.

INTRODUCING THE MACKEREL BRIGADE, DILATING ON HAVELOCKS AS
FIRST MADE BY THE WOMEN OF AMERICA, ILLUSTRATING THE
STRENGTH OF HABIT AND WEAKNESS OF "SHODDY," AND SHOWING
HOW OUR CORRESPONDENT INDULGED IN A HUGE CANARD, AFTER
THE MANNER OF AN ENLIGHTENED DAILY PRESS.

WASHINGTON, D. C., June 15th, 1861.

THE members of the Mackerel Brigade, now sta-
tioned on Arlington Heights to watch the movements
of the Potomac, which is expected to rise shortly,
desire me to thank the women of America for supplies
of Havelocks and other delicacies of the season just
received. The Havelocks, my boy, are rather roomy,
and we took them for shirts at first ; and the shirts
are so narrow-minded, that we took them for Havelocks. If the women of America could manage to get
a little less linen in the collars of the latter article,
and a little more into the other departments of the
graceful garment, there would be fewer colds in this
division of the Grand Army.

The Havelocks, as I have said before, are roomy—
very roomy, my boy. Villiam Brown, of Company
3, Regiment 5, put one on last night, when he went

on sentry-duty, and looked like a broomstick in a pillow-case, for all the world. When the officer of the night came round and caught sight of Villiam in his Havelock, he was struck dumb with admiration for a moment. Then he ejaculated :

" What a splendid moonbeam !"

Villiam made a movement, and the sergeant came up.

" What's that white object ?" says the officer to the sergeant.

" The young man which is Villiam Brown," says the sergeant.

" Thunder !" roars the officer, " tell him to go to his tent, and take off that night-gown !"

" You're mistaken," says the sergeant. " The sentry is Villiam Brown, in his Havelock, which was made by the wimmen of America."

. The officer was so justly exasperated at his· mistake, that he went immediately to his head-quarters, and took the Oath three times running, with a little sugar.

The Oath is very popular, my boy, and comes in bottles. I take it medicinally myself.

The shirts made by the women of America are noble articles, as far down as the collar ; but would not do to use as an only garment. Captain Mortimer de Montague, one of the skirmish squad, put one on when he went to the President's Reception, and the

collar stood up so high, that he couldn't put his cap
on, while the other departments didn't quite reach to
his waist. His appearance at the White House was
picturesque and interesting, and as he entered the
drawing-room, General Scott remarked, very feelingly :

"Ah ! here comes one of our wounded heroes."

" He's not wounded, general," remarked an officer,
standing by.

" Then, why is his head bandaged up so ?" asked
the venerable veteran.

" Oh !" says the officer, " that's only one of the
shirts made by the patriotic wimmen of America."

In about five minutes after this conversation, I
saw the venerable veteran, the wounded hero, and the
officer taking the Oath together.

The Seventy-ninth, Highlanders, came to town
early last week, and are the finest body of Scotchmen
that were ever half *kilt* by uniform alone. My heart
warmed to them when I first saw them ; and, with
arms outspread, I greeted the gallant fellow nearest
to me. With a tear of gratified pride in his eye, he
exclaimed :

" Auld lang syne and Scots who ha'e ; but gang
awa' wi' Heeland laddie thegither o' John Anderson
my Jo ; and, moreover, we'll tak' a right gude willie
wacht for muckle twa and braw chiel."

I told him I thought so myself.

I'm sorry to say, my boy, that some members of this splendid regiment are badly off for trowsers, and shock my modesty tremendously. They probably forgot them in their hurry to get to the war, and the Union Pretence Committee ought to send them out an assortment of peg-tops at once. "Not that I hobject to the hinnocent hamusements of the Highlanders, but that decency and propriety *must* be preserved within the limits of the army"—as the British showman observed.

I took a trip down to Alexandria the other night, to see how the Fire Zouaves were getting along, and came pretty near getting into trouble with one of Five's screamers. He was on guard ; and when he challenged me, the pass-word slipped my memory.

"Drop that ere butt," says he, bringing his musket to a charge, " or I'll give yer a taste of the old masheen. Who-wha-what are yer coughin' at— sa-a-ay ?"

I was frightened, my boy, and had just commenced the appropriate prayer of " Now I lay me down to sleep," when suddenly an idea struck me, and I acted on it immediately.

" Hello !" says I, " Johnny, didn't you hear the old Hall kettle strike for the Fourth District ? Come along with me and help to get the old dog-cart on a jump, or Nine's roosters will get the rail-road track and have the old butt in Christie street before we can swing the old masheen over a pig's whisker."

"Bully for you!" says he, dropping his musket, all in a quiver, and commencing to roll up his pantaloons. "I've got a bet on that ere fire ; and ef I don't take the starch out of that ere Nine's feller what wears good clothes and don't do nothing—you may just take my boots."

It was all the force of habit, you see ; and if I hadn't stopped that Zouave, I really believe he'd have run clean into the bosom of all the first families, looking for the Fourth District and Nine's feller !

The Mackerel brigade have got their new uniforms, and they are not the martial garments it would do to get fat in. High private Samivel Green put his on, partially, yesterday ; but, it's a positive fact, my boy, that by the time he got his coat buttoned, his pantaloons were all worn out. I managed to get on one of the uniforms myself, and the first time I went into the open air all the buttons blew off.

I've just returned from visiting the most mournful sight that ever made a man feel as though he'd been peeling onions all the week, and grating horse-radish on Sunday. It was the first dying scene of one of the " Pet Lammers," down at Alexandria, and, as one of Five's chaps remarks, it was enough to make the eye of a darning-needle weep, and bring tears to the cheek of the Greek slave. Jim was the only name of the sufferer, and if he ever had any other, it had slipped his memory, though his affectionate relatives sometimes called him " Shorty," by way of endearment. He was out on picket-guard the night before, when the Southern Confederacy attempted to pass him. He challenged the intruder, and called to his comrades for help ; but, before the latter could arrive, the Southern Confederacy drew a masked battery from his pocket, and fired six heavy balls through the head of the unfortunate Zouave, nearly fracturing his skull, and breaking several panes of glass. The cowardly miscreant then fled to an adjacent fence, closely followed by Sherman's Artillery.

Upon discovering that he was wounded, Mr. Shorty examined the cap on his musket, and stood it carefully against a tree, buttoned his jacket to his neck, and asked a comrade for a chew of tobacco. Too full of emotion to speak, the comrade handed a gentlemanly plug to the dying man, who cut about half an ounce from it, placed it thoughtfully in his mouth, and then stuffed his handkerchief carefully in the hole in his forehead made by the balls.

" Is any of my brains hanging out ?" he asked of another of his comrades.

"No, Shorty," answered the other, bursting into tears; "you never had any to hang out."

After this response, the dying man paused for a moment to spit in the eyes of a dog that was smelling around his heels, and then proceeded with his comrades in the direction of the hospital, or the house used for that purpose.

As they were passing the quarters of the officer with whom I was spending the night, the expiring Zouave stopped to twist the tail of an old darkey's cat, which made such a noise that the officer's attention was attracted, and he called the whole party into his room. I at once noticed that the top of Mr. Shorty's head was completely gone, and that one of his eyes was half-way down the back of his neck. Upon entering the room he took a pipe from the mantel and commenced to smoke it, giving us, at the same time, a history of Nine's Engine and the first "muss" he was ever engaged in. After finishing the pipe, and requesting me to wrap him up in the American flag, he spit on one of my boots, and then died. I append a short biographical sketch.

THE LATE PRIVATE SHORTY.

Mr. James Shorty, the gallant Zouave who was shot last night by the Southern Confederacy, was born some years ago in a place I am not aware of, and graduated with high honors in the New York

Fire Department. He was universally beloved for his genial manner of taking the butt, and never hit a feller bigger than himself. In the year 1861, he entered the United States army as a private Zouave, and was in it when the fate of war deprived the country of his beloved presence. His remains will be taken to the first fire that occurs.

Poor Shorty! I knew him well, my boy, and shall never forget how ready he always was to take a cigar from

Yours, mournfully,

ORPHEUS C. KERR.

P. S.—Since writing the above, I have heard that no such occurrence took place at Alexandria. The alarm was occasioned by the fall of a bag of hay in one of the officers' quarters, the noise being mistaken for the firing of a battery. Mr. Shorty, it seems, does not belong to the Zouaves, at all, and is still in New York.

O. C. K.

LETTER VII.

RECORDING THE FIRST SANGUINARY EXPLOIT OF THE MACKEREL
BRIGADE, AND ITS VICTORIOUS ISSUE.

WASHINGTON, D. C., June 20th, 1861.

I HAVE just returned, my boy, with my fellow-
mercenaries and several mudsills from a carnival of
gore. I am wounded—my sensibilities are wounded,
and my irrepressibles reek with the blood of the slain.
These hands, that once opened the oysters of peace
and toyed with the bivalves of tranquillity, are now
sanguinary with the *red juice of battle* (gushing idea!),
and linger in horrid ecstacy about the gloomy neck of
a bottle holding about a quart. Eagle of my country,
proud bird of the menagerie! thou art avenged!

At a late hour last evening, the Brigadier-General
of the Mackerel Brigade (formerly a practitioner in
the Asylum for Idiots) received intelligence from a
messenger that a strong force of chickens were intrenched near Fairfax Court-House under the command of a rabid secessionist named Binks. The
brigade was at once ordered over the bridge at a
double-quick, the general throwing a strong force of
skirmishers into the Potomac, and waving his sword

repeatedly to show that he was a stranger to fear.
Shortly after touching Virginia soil, the orderly
sergeant reported an engagement, on the left flank,
between private Villiam Brown and the man that puts
his hair in papers. A consultation of officers was immediately called, and the order "About face" was given.
So excited was our general by the event, that when
the order to march was given he forgot all about the
"About face" business, and we didn't know that we
were going the wrong way until we suddenly found
ourselves at the bridge again. A consultation of
officers was immediately called, and it was determined that, in consequence of the well-known revolution of the world on its axis, the part with the
bridge on it had taken a turn while we were halting,
and we were ordered to counterbalance the singular
phenomena by marching the other way immediately.
We had proceeded about one mile, when a scout reported that a shower was coming up. A consultation
of officers was immediately called, and it was determined that a squad should search a neighboring farm-
house for an umbrella for the Brigadier-General. The
umbrella being obtained without loss of life, we pushed
on toward Fairfax, and soon found ourselves before
the works of the enemy. A consultation of officers
was immediately called, and it was decided that the
Brigadier-General should climb a tree, in order to be
able to direct the assault effectively, and prevent the

appearance of a widow in his family at home. The first regiment, Watch Guards, were ordered to reconnoitre the works, and private Villiam Brown had almost succeeded in surrounding a very fat pullet, when Colonel Binks put his head out of the window of his fortress, and discharged a ten-inch boot-jack at our centre.

The Man that puts his hair in papers was wounded severely on one of his corns, and the Brigadier-General slid hastily down from the tree, and retired to the rear of an adjacent barn. A consultation of officers was immediately called, and it was determined to form our brigade into a square, and receive the charge of the enemy, who speedily appeared before the breastworks with a pair of tongs in his hands. Reaching forward with the horrid weapon, he pulled the nose of our returned Brigadier-General with it. A consultation of officers was immediately called, and it was determined that death was preferable to defeat. Accordingly, the brigade was ordered to advance cautiously upon the enemy, while the orderly sergeant was sent to harass his rear, and turn his flank, if possible. Our brigadier-general attempted to lead the charge, but made a mistake about the direction again, and had galloped half a mile toward where we came from before he could be convinced of his mistake. Seeing us descending upon him, at last, like an avalanche, the enemy deployed to the right, and poured in a volley of "cusses," throwing our right column into confusion, and wounding the delicacy of our chaplain. A consultation of officers was immediately called, and it was determined to make one more dash. We were formed into the shape of a bunch of radishes, the brigadier-general retired a distance of two miles to encourage us, and we poured down upon the foe with irresistible force. His ranks were broken by the impetuosity of our charge, and he scattered and fled in dismay.

The engagement then became general, and in a little while we were on our victorious way to Washington again, with 150 rebel prisoners. Our captives were chickens, in excellent condition for dressing, and their appearance so delighted our brigadier-general— whom we found sharpening his sword on the bottom of his boot, some miles away—that a consultation of officers was immediately called, and it was determined to cook and eat them immediately, lest the President should administer the oath of allegiance to them, and discharge them in the morning.

Yours, victoriously,

ORPHEUS C. KERR.

LETTER. VIII.

THE REJECTED "NATIONAL HYMNS."

WASHINGTON, D. C., June 30th, 1861.

IMMEDIATELY after mailing my last to you, I se-
cured a short furlough, and proceeded to New York,
to examine into the affairs of that venerable Committee which had offered a prize of $500 for the best
National Hymn.

Upon going into literary circles, my boy, no less
than fifty acknowledged poets confidentially informed
me, that the idea of bribing the muse to be solemnly
patriotic was altogether too vulgar to be tolerated for
a moment by writers of reputation ; and a whole
swarm of poets, never acknowledged by anybody,
were human enough to say that $500 was not a
small sum in these times ; but they hadn't "come to
that yet, you know."

One very poor Bohemian, my boy (whose scathing
sarcasm at the expense of those degraded creatures
who prefer wealth to intellect, has often delighted
and improved the public mind), was so rash as to
intimate that the importunities of his laundress

might drive him to the desperate resource of com-
peting for the prize ; but he was quickly made to
blush for the unworthy thought, by the undisguised
contempt for his "dem'd lowness" displayed by a
decayed young gentleman in a dirty collar and very
new neck-tie, who lives in a two-pair back in
Wooster street (fish balls and a roll twice a day), and
writes graphic sketches of fashionable life for the
wholesale market.

And yet, notwithstanding all this high-mindedness,
my boy, there is an immense amount of some sort of
genius insidiously pitted against the contemptible
$500.   Astounding and distracting to relate, the
committee announces the reception of no less than
eleven hundred and fifty "anthems" !

The magnitude of eleven hundred and fifty "anthems" is almost more than one human mind can
grasp.   Allowing that each "anthem" is a quarter
of a yard long, we have a grand total of two hundred
and eighty-seven and a half yards of "anthem" ;
allowing that each "anthem" weighs half a pound
(intellectually and materially), I find a gross weight
of five hundred and seventy-five pounds of "anthem" !

Let the reflective mind consider these figures for a
moment, and it will be stricken with a sense of the
singular resemblance between Genius and other mar-
ketable commodities.   Eleven hundred and fifty an-

thems are enough to prove that Genius has its private
mercenary weaknesses as well as Trade, my boy, and
that brains can be bought by the yard as well as calico. Genius may carry with it a seeming contempt
for the yellow dross of common humanity ; but—it
has to pay its occasional washerwoman.

And all these " anthems" are rejected by the venerable committee ! But must they *all*, therefore, be
lost to the world ? I hope not, my boy,—I hope
not. Having some acquaintance with the discriminating rag-merchant to whom they were turned over
as rejected, I have procured some of the best, from
which to quote for your special edification.

Imprimis, my boy, observe this

NATIONAL ANTHEM.

BY H. W. L———, OF CAMBRIDGE.

Back in the years when Phlagstaff, the Dane, was monarch
    Over the sea-ribbed land of the fleet-footed Norsemen,
Once there went forth young Ursa to gaze at the heavens—
    Ursa, the noblest of all the Vikings and horsemen.

Musing, he sat in his stirrups and viewed the horizon,
    Where the Aurora lapt stars in a North-polar manner,
Wildly he started—for there in the heavens before him
    Fluttered and flew the original Star-Spangled Banner.

The committee have two objections to this : in the
first place, it is not an " anthem" at all ; secondly,
it is a gross plagiarism from an old Scandinavian war-
song of the primeval ages.

Next, I present a

NATIONAL ANTHEM.

BY THE HON. EDWARD E———, OF BOSTON.

Ponderous projectiles, hurled by heavy hands,
    Fell on our Liberty's poor infant head,
Ere she a stadium had well advanced
    On the great path that to her greatness led;
Her temple's propylon was shattered;
    Yet, thanks to saving Grace and Washington,
Her incubus was from her bosom hurled;
    And, rising like a cloud-dispelling sun,
She took the oil, with which her hair was curled,
To grease the "Hub" round which revolves the world.

This fine production is rather heavy for an "anthem," and contains too much of Boston to be considered strictly national. To set such an "anthem" to music would require a Wagner; and even were it really accomodated to a tune, it could only be whistled by the populace.

We now come to a

NATIONAL ANTHEM.

BY JOHN GREENLEAF W———.

My native land, thy Puritanic stock
Still finds its roots firm-bound in Plymouth Rock,
And all thy sons unite in one grand wish—
To keep the virtues of Preserv-éd Fish.

Preserv-éd Fish, the Deacon stern and true,
Told our New England what her sons should do,
And should they swerve from loyalty and right,
Then the whole land were lost indeed in night.

The sectional bias of this "anthem" renders it unsuitable for use in that small margin of the world situated outside of New England. Hence the above must be rejected.

Here we have a very curious

NATIONAL ANTHEM.

BY DR. OLIVER WENDELL H———.

A diagnosis of our hist'ry proves
Our native land a land its native loves;
Its birth a deed obstetric without peer,
Its growth a source of wonder far and near.

To love it more behold how foreign shores
Sink into nothingness beside its stores;
Hyde Park at best—though counted ultra-grand—
The "Boston Common" of Victoria's land—

The committee must not be blamed for rejecting the above, after reading thus far ; for such an "anthem" could only be sung by a college of surgeons or a Beacon-street tea-party.

Turn we now to a

NATIONAL ANTHEM.

BY RALPH WALDO E———.

Source immaterial of material naught,
    Focus of light infinitesimal,
Sum of all things by sleepless Nature wrought,
    Of which abnormal man is decimal.

Refract, in prism immortal, from thy stars
    To the stars blent incipient on our flag,
The beam translucent, neutrifying death;
    And raise to immortality the rag.

This "anthem" was greatly praised by a celebrated German scholar; but the committee felt obliged to reject it on account of its too childish simplicity.

Here we have a

NATIONAL ANTHEM

BY WILLIAM CULLEN B———.

The sun sinks softly to his evening post,
   The sun swells grandly to his morning crown;
Yet not a star our flag of Heav'n has lost,
   And not a sunset stripe with him goes down.

So thrones may fall; and from the dust of those,.
   New thrones may rise, to totter like the last;
But still our country's nobler planet glows
   While the eternal stars of Heaven are fast.

Upon finding that this did not go well to the air of "Yankee Doodle," the committee felt justified in declining it; being furthermore prejudiced against it by a suspicion that the poet has crowded an advertisement of a paper which he edits into the first line.

Next we quote from a

NATIONAL ANTHEM

BY GEN. GEORGE P. M———.

In the days that tried our fathers
   Many years ago,
Our fair land achieved her freedom,
   Blood-bought, you know.
Shall we not defend her ever
   As we'd defend
That fair maiden, kind and tender,
   Calling us friend?

> Yes! Let all the echoes answer,
>   From hill and vale;
> Yes! Let other nations, hearing,
>   Joy in the tale.
> Our Columbia is a lady,
>   High-born and fair;
> We have sworn allegiance to her—
>   Touch her who dare.

The tone of this "anthem" not being devotional enough to suit the committee, it should be printed on an edition of linen-cambric handkerchiefs, for ladies especially.

Observe this

NATIONAL ANTHEM

BY N. P. W——.

> One hue of our flag is taken
>   From the cheeks of my blushing Pet,
> And its stars beat time and sparkle
>   Like the studs on her chemisette.
>
> Its blue is the ocean shadow
>   That hides in her dreamy eyes,
> It conquers all men, like her,
>   And still for a Union flies.

Several members of the committee being pious, it is not strange that this "anthem" has too much of the Anacreon spice to suit them.

We next peruse a

NATIONAL ANTHEM

BY THOMAS BAILEY A———.

> The little brown squirrel hops in the corn,
>   The cricket quaintly sings;

The emerald pigeon nods his head,
  And the shad in the river springs,
The dainty sunflower hangs its head
  On the shore of the summer sea;
And better far that I were dead,
  If Maud did not love me.

I love the squirrel that hops in the corn,
  And the cricket that quaintly sings;
And the emerald pigeon that nods his head,
  And the shad that gayly springs.
I love the dainty sunflower, too,
  And Maud with her snowy breast;
I love them all;—but I love—I love—
  I love my country best.

This is certainly very beautiful, and sounds somewhat like Tennyson. Though it was rejected by the Committee, it can never lose its value as a piece of excellent reading for children. It is calculated to fill the youthful mind with patriotism and natural history, besides touching the youthful heart with an emotion palpitating for all.

Notice the following

NATIONAL ANTHEM

BY R. H. STOD——.

Behold the flag! Is it not a flag?
  Deny it, man, if you dare;
And midway spread, 'twixt earth and sky,
  It hangs like a written prayer.

Would impious hand of foe disturb
  Its memories' holy spell,
And blight it with a dew of blood?
  Ha, tr-r-aitor! ! * * * It is well.

And this is the last of the rejected anthems I can quote from at present, my boy, though several hundred pounds yet remain untouched.

Yours, questioningly,

ORPHEUS C. KERR.

LETTER IX.

IN WHICH OUR CORRESPONDENT TEMPORARILY DIGRESSES FROM WAR
MATTERS TO ROMANTIC LITERATURE, AND INTRODUCES A WOMAN'S
NOVEL.

WASHINGTON, D. C., July —, 1861.

WHILE the Grand Army is making its preparations
for an advance upon the Southern Confederacy, my
boy, and the celebrated fowl of our distracted country is getting ready his spurs, let me distract your
attention for a moment to the subject of harrowing
Romance as inflicted by the intellectual women of
America.

To soothe and instruct me in my leisure and more
ebrious moments, one of the ink-comparable women
of America has sent me her new novel to read ; and
before I allow *you* to enjoy its green leaves, my boy,
you must permit me to make a few remarks concerning the generality of such works.

Long and patient study of womanly works teaches
me that woman's genius, as displayed in gushing
fiction, is a power of creating an unnatural and un-
mitigated ruffian for a hero, my boy, at whose shrine
all created crinoline and immense delegations of infe-

rior broadcloth are impelled to bow. Such a one was
that old humbug, Rochester, the beloved of "Jane
Eyre." The character has been done-over scores of
times since poor Charlotte Bronté gave her famous
novel to the world, and is still "much used in
respectable families."

The great difficulty with the intellectual women
of America is, that they will persist in attempting to
delineate a phase of manly character which attracts
them above all others, but which they do not comprehend. Woman entertains a natural fondness for
that which she can not understand, and hence it is
that we very seldom find her without a wildly-vague
admiration of Emerson.

There is in this world, my boy, a noble type of
manhood which unites dignified reserve with the most
loyal integrity, relentless pride of manner with the
kindest humility of heart, rigid indifference to the
applause of the world with the finest regard for its
honest respect, and carelessness of woman's mere
frivolous liking with the most profound and chivalrous reverence for her virtues and her love.

This is the type which, without comprehending
it, the intellectual women of America are continually
striving to depict in their novels ; and a pretty mess
they make of it, my boy,—a pretty mess they make
of it.

Their "Rochester" hero is harder to understand

than Hamlet, when he falls into the hands of our
school-girl authoresses. He looms rakishly upon us,
my boy, a horridly misanthropic wretch, despising
the world with all the dreadful malignity of chronic
dyspepsia, and displaying a degree of moral bilious-
ness truly horrifying to members of the church. His
behavior to the poor little heroine is a perpetual outrage. Alternately he caresses and snubs her. He
never fails to make her read to him when he traps her
in the library ; and when she says, " Good night" to
him he is too deep in a " fit of gloomy abstraction"
to answer her civilly. If he calls her a " little fool,"
her fondness for him becomes ecstatic ; and at the
first hint of his having murdered a noble brother and.
two beautiful sisters in early life, she is led to fear
that her adoration of him will exceed the love she
owes to her Maker !

This unprincipled ruffian may be separated from the
virtuous little heroine for years, and be flirting con-
sumedly with half a dozen crinolines when next she
sees him ; yet is he loved dearly by the virtuous little
heroine all the time, and when last we hear of him,
she is resting peacefully upon his vest-pattern.

What makes the inconsistency of the whole story
still more apparent, is the intense and double-refined
piety of the heroine, as contrasted with an utter stag-
nation of all morality in the breast of the ruffian.
How the two can assimilate, I do not understand ;

and my misunderstanding is wofully augmented by the heroine's frequent expressions of churchliness, and the ruffian's equally frequent outbursts of waggish infidelity.

And now, my boy, let me transcribe for you the new novel, sent to me with such kind intent by one of the young and intellectual women of America. You will find much lusciousness of sentiment, my boy, in

HIGGINS.

AN AUTOBIOGRAPHY.
BY GUSHALINA CRUSHIT.

PREFACE.

In writing the ensuing pages, I have been guided by no motives other than those which lead the mind, in its leisure hours, to scatter the germs of the beautiful. It may be urged that the character of my hero is unnatural ; but I am sure there are many of my sex who will discover in Mr. Higgins a counterpart of the ideal of days when life still knew the odors of its first spring, and the soul of man seemed to the eye of innocence an elysium of virtue into which no gangrene of mere worldliness intruded. I have done.

CHAPTER I.

It was on the eve of a day in the happy month of June, that my great grandfather's carriage, drawn by six hundred and twenty-two white horses, drew up under the tall palm trees before the gates of the venerable Higgins' Lodge, and I was lifted almost fainting from the wearied vehicle. As my grandfather supported my trembling steps into the spacious hall of the lodge, I noticed that another figure had been added to our party. It was that of a man six feet high, and broad in proportion, whose majestic and spacious brow betokened realms of elysian thought and excrescent ideality. His pallid tresses hung in curls down his back, and an American flag floated from his Herculean shoulders. Fixed by a fascination only to be realized by those who have felt so, I cast my piercing glance at him, and my inmost soul knew all his sublimity. It was as though an angel's wing had swept my temples, and left a glittering pinion there.

"Mr. Higgins," said my grandfather, "here is your ward, Galushianna."

For an instant silence prevailed.

Then Mr. Higgins said, in tones of exquisitely modulated thunder :

"What did you bring the d—d girl *here* for, you old cuss you ?"

It was as when one sees a strain of music. I remembered the prayers of my dear departed mother when she sought to enlighten my speechless infancy with divine grace, and I felt that I loved this Higgins.

Such is life. We wander through the bowers of love without a thought of the morrow, while the dread vulture of predestination eats into our souls, and cries, wo ! wo ! Truly, earthly happiness is a mockery.

CHAPTER II.

Scarcely had I taken my seat in the library after my grandfather had left us, when Mr. Higgins ordered me to black his boots. This I proceeded to do with a haughty air, scarcely daring to hope, but wishing that he would conquer his freezing reserve, and speak to me again. For I was but a child, and my young heart yearned for sympathy.

Presently, Mr. Higgins turned his large gray eyes on me, and said :

" Ha !"

After this, he remained in a thoughtful reverie for two hours, and then turning to me, asked :

" Galushiana, what do you think of me ?"

" I think," replied I, carefully putting the blacking-brush in its place, " that your nature is naturally a noble one, but has been warped and shadowed by a misconceived impression of the great arcana of the universe. You permit the genuflexions of human sin to bias your mind in its estimate of the true economy of creation ; thus blighting, as it were, the fructifying evidences of your own abstract being—"

I blushed, and feared I had gone too far.

"Very true," responded Mr. Higgins, after a moment's pause ; "Schiller says nearly the same thing. It was a sense of man's utter nothingness that led me to kill my grandmother, and poison the helpless offspring of my elder brother."

Here Mr. Higgins held down his head and quivered with emotions, as the ocean quakes under the shrieking howl of the blast.

I felt my whole being convulsed, and could not endure the spectacle. I stole softly to the door, and stammered through my tears, "Good-night, Mr. Higgins, I will pray for you."

He did not turn his noble head, but said, in firm tones : "Poor little beast, good night."

I went to my room, but could not sleep. Shortly after half-past two o'clock I crawled noiselessly down to the library-door and looked in. Mr. Higgins still sat before the fire in the same thoughtful position. "Poor little beast !" I heard him murmur softly to himself—"poor little beast !"

CHAPTER III.

Let the reader transport himself to a small stone cottage on the Hudson, and he will behold me as I was at the age of twenty-one. I had reached that acme of woman's career when common sense is to her as nothing, and the world with all its follies bursts upon her ravished ears with ten-fold succulence. My grandfather had been dead some fifty years, and I was even thinking of him, when the door opened, and Mr. Higgins entered. I felt my heart palpitate, and was about to quit the room, when he cast a searching glance at me, and said :

" Well, girl—are you as big a fool as ever ?"

I hung my head, for the tell-tale blush *would* bloom.

" Come," said Mr. Higgins, " don't speak like a donkey. I'm no priestly confessor. Curse the priests ! Curse the world ! Curse everybody ! Curse everything !" And he placed his feet upon the mantel-piece, and gazed meditatively into the fire.

I could hear the beatings of my own heart, and all the warmth of my nature went forth to meet this sublime embodiment of human majesty ; yet I dared not speak.

After a short silence, Mr. Higgins took a chew of tobacco, and placing his hand on my shoulder, exclaimed :

" Why should I deceive you, girl ? Last night I poisoned my only remaining sister because she would have wed a circus-keeper, and scarcely an hour ago I lost two millions at faro. Your priests would say this was wrong—hey ?"

I stifled my sobs and said, as calmly as I could :

"Our Church looks at the motive, not the deed. If a high sense of honor compelled you to poison all your relatives and play faro, the sin was rather the effect of vice in others than in your own noble heart, and I doubt not you may be called innocent."

He glanced into the fire a few hours, and then said :

" Go, Galushianna !—I would be alone ! Go, innocent young scorpion."

Oh, Higgins, Higgins, if I could have died for thee then, I don't know but I should have done it !

CHAPTER IV.

Seventy-five years have rolled by since last I met the reader, and I am still a thoughtless girl. But oh, how changed ! The raven of despair has flapped his hideous brood over the halls of my ancestors, and taken from them all that once made them beautiful. When I look back I can see nothing before me, and when I look forward I can see nothing behind me. Thus it is with life. We fancy that each hour is a butterfly made to play with, and all is gall and bitterness.

I was chastened by misfortune, and occupied a secluded cavern in the city of New Orleans, when my faithful old nurse entered my dressing-room, and burst into a fit of hysterical laughter.

" Sassafrina !" I exclaimed, half angrily.

" Please don't be angry, miss," responded the tried old creature ; " but I knew it would come all right at last. I told you Sir Claude Higgins hadn't married his youngest sister, but you wouldn't believe me. Now he's down stairs in the parlor waiting for you."

And the attached domestic fell dead at my feet.

After hastily putting on a pair of clean stockings and reading a chapter in my mother's family Bible, I left the room, murmuring to myself, " Be still, my throbbing heart, be still."

CHAPTER V.

When I entered the parlor, Mr. Higgins sat gazing into the fire in an attitude of deep reflection, and did not note my entrance until I had touched him. His dishevelled hair hung from his massive temples in majestic discomposure, and an extinguished torch lay smouldering at his glorious feet.

O my soul's idol ! I can see thee now as I saw thee then, with the firelight glowing over thee, like a smile from the cerulean skies !

As I touched him, he awoke.

" Miserable girl !" he exclaimed, in those old familiar tones, drawing me towards him, while a delicious tremor shook my every nerve. " Wretched little serpent ! And is it thus we meet ? Poor idiot, you are but a woman, and I—alas ! what am I ? Two hours ago, I set fire to three churches, and crushed a sexton 'neath my iron heel. Do you not shrink? 'Tis well. Then hear me, viper, *I lovest thee.*"

Was it the music of a higher sphere that I smelt, or was I still in this world of folly and sin? And were all my toils, my cares, my heart-breathings, my hope-sobbings, my soul-writhings to end thus gloriously at last in the adoration of a being on whom I lavished all the spirit's purest gloatings?

My bliss was more than I could endure. Tearing all the hair-pins from my hair and tying my pocket handkerchief about my heaving neck, I flung myself upon his steaming chest.

"*My* Higgins !"

" Your Higgins ! !"

" OUR Higgins ! ! !"

The Blissful Finis.

The intellectual women of America draw it rather tempestuously when they try to reproduce gorgeous manhood ; but they mean well, my boy,—they mean well. Yours, in a brown study,

Orpheus C. Kerr.

LETTER X.

MAKING CONSERVATIVE MENTION OF THE BATTLE OF BULL RUN AND
ITS EVENTS.   THE FIRE-ZOUAVE'S VERSION OF THE AFFAIR, AND
SO ON.

WASHINGTON, D. C., July 28th, 1861.

We have met the enemy at last, my boy ; but I
don't see that he's ours.   We went after him with
flying banners, and I noticed when we came back
that they were flying still !   Honor to the brave who
fell on that bloody field ! and may we kill enough
secessionists to give each of them a monument of
Southern skulls !

I was present at the great battle, my boy, and appointed myself a special guard of one of the baggage-
wagons in the extreme rear.   The driver saw me
coming, and says he :

" You can't cut behind this here wehicle, my fine
little boy."

I looked at him for a moment, after the manner of
the late great actor, Mr. Kirby, and says I :

" Soldier, hast thou a wife ?"

Says he :

" I reckon."

" And sixteen small children ?"

Says he :

" There was only fifteen when last heard from."

" Soldier," says I, " were you to die before to-morrow, what would be your last request ?"

Here I shed two tears.

" It would be," says he, " that some kind friend would take the job of walloping my offspring for a year on contract, and finding my beloved wife in subjects to jaw about."

" Soldier," says I, " I'm your friend and brother. Let me occupy a seat by your side."

And he didn't let me do it.

Just at this moment, something burst, and I found myself going up at the rate of two steeples and a shot-tower a second. I met a Fire Zouave on the way down, and says he :

" Towhead, if you see any of our boys up where you're goin' to, just tell them to hurry down ; fur there's goin' to be a row, and Nine's fellers 'll take that ere four-gun hydrant from the seceshers in less time than you can reel two yards of hose."

As I was *very* tired I did not go all the way up ; but turned back at the first cloud, and returned hastily to the scene of strife. I happened to light on a very fat secesher, who was doing a little running for exercise. Down he went, with me on top of him. He was dreadfully scared ; but says he to me : " I've seen you before, by the gods !" I winked at him, and commenced to sharpen my sword on a stone.

" Tell me," says he, " had you a female mother ?"

" I had," says I.

" And a masculine father ?"

" He wore breeches."

" Then you *are* my long lost grandfather !" says the secesher, endeavoring to embrace me.

" It won't do," says I ; " I've been to the Bowery Theatre myself ;" and with that I took off his necktie and wiped my nose with it. This action was so repugnant to the feelings of a Southern gentleman, that he immediately died on my hands ; and there I left him.

It was my first personal victory in this unnatural war, my boy, and as I walked away I thought sadly of the domestic circle in the Southern Confederacy that might be waiting anxiously, tearfully, for the husband and father—him whom I had morally assassinated. And there he sprawled, denied even the simple privilege of extending a parting blessing to his children. Under ordinary circumstances, my boy, there's something deeply affecting in

THE DYING SOUTHERNER'S FAREWELL TO HIS SON.

> My boy, my lion-hearted boy,
>   Your father's end draws near ;
> Already is your loss begun,
>   And, curse it, there's a tear.

I've sought to bring you up, my son,
  A credit to the South,
And all your poker games have been
  An honor to us both.

Though scarcely sixteen years of age,
  Your bowie 's tickled more
Than many Southerners I know
  At fifty and three score.

You've whipped your nigger handsomely,
  And chewed your plug a day;
And when I hear you swear, my son,
  What pride my eyes betray!

And now, that I must leave the world,
  My dying words attend;
But first, a chew of niggerhead,
  And cut it near the end.

To you the old plantation goes,
  With mortgage, tax, and all,
Though compound interest on that first,
  Will make the profit small.

The niggers to your mother go;
  And if she wants to sell,
You might contrive to buy her out,
  Should all the crops grow well.

I leave you all my debts, my son,
  To Yankees chiefly due;
But—curse the black republicans!
  That needn't trouble you.

A true-born Southern gentleman
  Disdains the vulgar thought
Of paying, like a Yankee clerk,
  For what is sold and bought.

Leave that to storekeepers and fools
  Who never banked a card;
We pay our " debts of honor," boy,
  Though pressed however hard.

Last summer at the North I bought,
  Some nigger hats and shoes,
And gave my note for ninety days;
  Forget it if you choose.

The Yankee mudsills would not have
  Such articles to sell,
If Southern liberality
  · Had fattened them less well.

The Northern dun we hung last week
  Had twenty dollars clear,
And that, my son, is all the cash
  I have to give you here.

But that's enough to make a start,
  And, if you pick your boat,
A Mississippi trip or two
  Will set you all afloat.

You play a screaming hand, my son,
  And push an ugly cue;
Oh! these are thoughts that make me feel
  As dying Christians do!

Keep cool, my lion-hearted boy,
  Till second ace is played,
And then call out for brandy sour
  As though your pile was made.

The other chaps will think you've got
  The tiger by the tail;
And when you see them looking glum,
  Just call for brandy pale !

I never knew it fail to make
  Some green one go it blind;
And when the first slip-up is made,
  It's all your own, you'll find.

My breath comes hard—I'm euchred, boy—
  First Families must die;
I leave you in your innocence,
  And here's a last good-bye.

Shortly after the event I have recorded, I was examining the back of a house near the battle-field, to
see if it corresponded with the front, when another
Fire Zouave came along, and says he :

"It's my opine that you're sticking rather too
thick to the rear of that house to be much punkins
in a muss. Why don't you go to the front like a
man ?"

" My boy," says I, " this is the house of a pre-
dominant rebel, and I'm detailed to watch the back
door."

With that the Zouave was taken with such a dreadful fit of coughing that he had to move on to get his
breath, and I was left alone once more.

These Fire Zouaves, my boy, have a perversity
about them not to be repressed. They were neck-
and-neck with the rest of us in our stampede back to
to this city ; and yet, my boy, they refuse to consider
the United States of America worsted. Here is the
version of

BULL RUN,

BY A FIRE ZOUAVE.

Oh, it's all very well for you fellers
    That don't know a fire from the sun,
To curl your moustaches, and tell us
    Just how the thing *oughter* be done;
But when twenty wake up ninety thousand,
    There's nothin' can follow but rout;
We didn't give in till we had to;
    And what are yer coughin' about?

The crowd that was with them ere rebels
    Had ten to our every man;
But a fireman's a fireman, me covey,
    And he'll put out a fire if he can:
So we run the masheen at a gallop,
    As easy as open and shut,
And as fast as one feller went under,
    Another kept takin' der butt.

You oughter seen Farnham, that mornin'!
    In spite of the shot and the shell
His orders kept ringing around us
    As clear as the City Hall bell.
He said all he could to encourage
    And lighten the hearts of the men,
Until he was bleeding and wounded,
    And nary dried up on it then.

While two rifle regiments fought us,
    And batteries tumbled us down,
Them cursed Black-Horse fellers charged us,
    Like all the Dead Rabbits in town.
And that's just the way with them rebels,
    It's ten upon one, or no fair;
But we emptied a few of their saddles—
    You may bet all your soap on that air!

"Double up!" says our colonel, quite coolly,
    When he saw them come riding like mad,
And we did double up in a hurry,
    And let them have all that we had.
They came at us counting a hundred,
    And scarcely two dozen went back;
So you see, if they bluffed us on aces,
    We made a big thing with the Jack.

We fought till red shirts were as plenty
    As blackberries, strewing the grass,
And then we fell back for a breathing,
    To let Sixty-nine's fellers pass.
Perhaps Sixty-nine didn't peg them,
    And give them uncommon cheroots?
Well—I've just got to say, if they didn't
    You fellers can smell of my boots!

The Brooklyn Fourteenth was another,
    And those Minnesota chaps too;
But the odds were too heavy against us,
    And but one thing was left us to do:
We had to make tracks for our quarters,
    And finished it up pretty rough;
But if any chap says that they licked us,
    I'd just like to polish him off!

With the remembrance of the many heroic souls who sacrificed themselves for their country that day, I have not the heart, my boy, to continue the subject. I was routed at about five o'clock in the afternoon, and fell back on Washington, where I am now receiving my rations. I don't take the oath with any spirit since then; and a skeleton with nothing on but a havelock is all that is left of

Yours, emaciatedly,   ORPHEUS C. KERR.

LETTER XI.

GIVING AN EFFECT OF THE NEW BUGLE DRILL IN THE MACKEREL
BRIGADE, AND MAKING SOME NOTE OF THE LATEST IMPROVEMENTS
IN ARTILLERY, ETC.

WASHINGTON, D. C., August —, 1861.

The Mackerel Brigade, of which I have the honor
to be a member, was about the worst demoralized of
all the brigades that covered themselves with glory
and perspiration at the skrimmage of Bull Run. In
the first place, it never had much morals, and when
it came to be demoralized, it hadn't any ; so that
ever since the disaster, the peasantry in the neighborhood of the camp have been in constant mourning
for departed pullets ; and one venerable rustic com-
plains that the Mackerel pickets milk all his cows
every night, and come to borrow his churn in the
morning. When one of the colonels heard the venerable rustic make this accusation, he says to him :

"Would you like to be revenged on the men who
milk your animiles ?" The venerable rustic took a
chew of tobacco, and says he : "I wouldn't like anything better." The colonel looked at him sadly for a
moment, and then remarked : "Aged stranger, you

are already revenged. The men who milked your animiles are all from New York, where they had been accustomed to drink milk composed principally of Croton water. Upon drinking the pure article furnished by your gentle beastesses, they were all taken violently sick, and are now lying at the point of illness, expecting every moment to be their first." The venerable rustic was so affected by this intelligence, that he immediately went home in tears.

The new bugle drill is a very good idea, my boy, and our lads will probably become accustomed to it by the time they get used to it. The colonel of Regiment Five likes it so much that he has substituted the bugle for the drum, even. The other morning, when he tried it on for the first time, I was just entering the tent of one of the captains, to take the Oath with him, when the bugle sounded the order to turn out.

" Ah !" says the captain, when he heard it, " we're going to have fish for breakfast at last. I hope its porgies," says he : " for I'm uncommon fond of porgies."

" Why, what are you talking about ?" says I.

" You innocent lamb," says he, " didn't you hear that ere fish-horn. It said 'porgies,' as plain as could be."

" Why, that's the bugle," says I, " and it sounded the order to turn out."

He took his disappointment very severely, my boy, for he was really very fond of porgies.

By invitation of a well-known official, I visited the Navy-Yard yesterday, and witnessed the trial of some newly-invented rifled cannon. The trial was of short duration, and the jury brought in a verdict of "innocent of any intent to kill."

The first gun tried was similar to those used in the Revolution, except that it had a larger touch-hole, and the carriage was painted green, instead of blue. This novel and ingenious weapon was pointed at a target about sixty yards distant. It didn't hit it, and as nobody saw any ball, there was much perplexity expressed. A midshipman did say that he thought the ball must have run out of the touch-hole when they loaded up—for which he was instantly expelled from the service. After a long search without finding the ball, there was some thought of summoning the Naval Retiring Board to decide on the matter, when somebody happened to look into the mouth of the cannon, and discovered that the ball hadn't gone out at all. The inventor said this would happen sometimes, especially if you didn't put a brick over the touch-hole when you fired the gun. The Government was so pleased with this explanation, that it ordered forty of the guns on the spot, at two hundred thousand dollars apiece. The guns to be furnished as soon as the war is over.

The next weapon tried was Jink's double back-action revolving cannon for ferry-boats. It consists of a heavy bronze tube, revolving on a pivot, with both ends open, and a touch-hole in the middle. While one gunner puts a load in at one end, another puts in a load at the other end, and one touch-hole serves for both. Upon applying the match, the gun is whirled swiftly round on a pivot, and both balls fly out in circles, causing great slaughter on both sides. This terrible engine was aimed at the target with great accuracy ; but as the gunner has a large family dependent on him for support, he refused to apply the match. The Government was satisfied without firing, and ordered six of the guns at a million of dollars apiece. The guns to be furnished in time for our next war.

The last weapon subjected to trial was a mountain howitzer of a new pattern. The inventor explained that its great advantage was, that it required no powder. In battle it is placed on the top of a high mountain, and a ball slipped loosely into it. As the enemy passes the foot of the mountain, the gunner in charge tips over the howitzer, and the ball rolls down the side of the mountain into the midst of the doomed foe. The range of this terrible weapon depends greatly on the height of the mountain and the distance to its base. The Government ordered forty of these mountain howitzers at a hundred thousand dollars apiece, to be planted on the first mountains discovered in the enemy's country.

These are great times for gunsmiths, my boy ; and if you find any old cannon around the junk-shops, just send them along.

There is much sensation in nautical circles arising from the immoral conduct of the rebel privateers ; but public feeling has been somewhat easier since the invention of a craft for capturing the pirates, by an ingenious Connecticut chap. Yesterday he exhibited a small model of it at a cabinet meeting, and explained it thus :

"You will perceive," says he to the President, "that the machine itself will only be four times the size of the Great Eastern, and need not cost over a few millions of dollars. I have only got to discover one thing before I can make it perfect. You will observe that it has a steam-engine on board. This engine works a pair of immense iron clamps, which are let down into the water from the extreme end of a very lengthy horizontal spar. Upon approaching the pirate, the captain orders the engineer to put on steam. Instantly the clamps descend from the end of the spar and clutch the privateer athwartships. Then the engine is reversed, the privateer is lifted bodily out of the water, the spar swings around over the deck, and the pirate ship is let down into the hold by the run. Then shut your hatches, and you have ship and pirates safe and sound."

The President's gothic features lighted up beautifully at the words of the great inventor ; but in a moment they assumed an expression of doubt, and says he :

" But how are you going to manage, if the privateer fires upon you while you are doing this ?"

" My dear sir," says the inventor, " I told you I had only one thing to discover before I could make the machine perfect, and that's it."

So you see, my boy, there's a prospect of our doing something on the ocean next century, and there's only one thing in the way of our taking in pirates by the cargo.

Last evening a new brigadier-general, aged ninety-four years, made a speech to Regiment Five, Mackerel Brigade, and then furnished each man with a lead-pencil. He said that, as the Government was disappointed about receiving some provisions it had ordered for the troops, those pencils were intended to enable them to draw their rations as usual. I got a very big pencil, my boy, and have lived on a sheet of paper ever since.   Yours, pensively,

ORPHEUS C. KERR.

LETTER XII.

GIVING AN ABSTRACT OF A GREAT ORATOR'S FLAGGING SPEECH, AND
RECORDING A DEATHLESS EXPLOIT OF THE MACKEREL BRIGADE.

WASHINGTON, D. C., September 8th, 1861.

THE weather in the neighborhood of Chain Bridge
still continues to bear hard on fat men, my boy, and
the man who carries a big stomach around with him
will be a person in reduced circumstances before he
gets to be a colonel. The Brigadier-General of the
Mackerel Brigade observed, the other day, that he had
been in hot water four weeks running, and ordered me
to work six hours in the trenches for not laughing
at the joke ; he said that old Abe had people expressly to laugh at his jokes, and had selected his
Cabinet officers because they all had large mouths,
and could laugh easily ; he said that he was resolved
to have his own jokes appreciated, and if he didn't,
he'd be perditionized. It's my impression—I say it's
my impression, my boy, that the general got off his
best joke when he promised the Mackerel Brigade to
look after their interests as though they were his
brothers. He may look after them, my boy, but it's

after they're out of sight. I don't say that he takes
advantage of us : but I know that just after a basket
of champagne was sent to the camp, directed to me,
yesterday, I saw him sitting on an empty basket in
his tent, trying to wind up his watch with a cork-
screw. I asked him what time it was, and he said
the Conzstorshun must and shall be blockade-dade-
did. I told him I thought so myself, and he immediately burst into tears, and said he should never see
his mother again.

On Tuesday, there was a rumor that the Southern
Confederacy had attacked at regiment at Alexandria,
for the purpose of creating a confusion, so that it
might pick the colonel's pockets, and Regiment 5,
Mackerel Brigade, was ordered to go instantly to the
rescue. Just as we were ready to march, a distinguished citizen of Washington presented a sword to
the colonel from the ladies of the Capital, and made
an eloquent speech. He spoke of the wonderful
manner in which the world was called out of chaos at
the creation, and spoke feelingly of the Garden of
Eden, and the fall of our first parents ; he then went
on to review the many changes the earth had experienced since it was first created, and described the
method of the ancients to cook bread before stoves
were invented ; he then spoke of the glories of Greece
and Rome, giving a full history of them from the
beginning to the present time ; he then went on to

describe the origin of the republican and democratic parties,. reading both platforms, and giving his ideas of Jackson's policy ; he then gave an account of the war of the Roses in England, and the cholera in Persia, attributing the latter to a sudden change in the atmosphere ; he then went on to speak of the difficulties encountered by Columbus in discovering this country, and gave a history of his subsequent career and death in Europe ; he then read an extract from Washington's Farewell Address ; in conclusion, he said that the ladies of Washington had empowered him to present this here sword to that ere gallant colonel, in the presence of these here brave defenders of their country. ·

At the conclusion of this speech, starvation commenced to make great ravages in the regiment, and the colonel was so weak, for want of sleep, that he had to be carried to his tent.   A private remarked to me, that, if we could only have one more such presentation speech as that, the regiment would be competent to start a grave-yard before it was finished.   I believe him, my boy !

When the presentation was finished, the colonel announced from his camp-bedstead that the rumor of· a fight at Alexandria was all a hum, and ordered us back to our tents.   We hadn't been to our tents for such a long time, that some of us-couldn't find them, and one of our boys actually wandered around until ·he found himself ·at home in New York.

The Mackerel Brigade, my boy, had a great engage-. ment yesterday, and came very near repulsing the enemy. We were ordered to march forward in three columns, until we came within five miles of the enemy, Colonel Wobbles leading the first ; Mr. Wobbles, the second ; and Wobbles, the third. In the advance our lines presented the shape of a clam-shell, but as we neared the point of danger, they gradually assumed more of the form of a cone, the rear-guard being several times as thick as the advance guard. When within six miles of the seceshers, we planted our battery of four six pounders, and opened a horrible fire of shot and shell on the adjacent country. The seceshers replied with a hail of canister and shrapnell, and for eight hours the battle raged fearfully, but without hurting anybody, as the hostile forces were too far apart to reach each other with shot. Finally, Colonel Wobbles sent a messenger, by railroad, to ask the seceshers what they wanted, and they said they only wanted to be let alone. On receiving this reply, Colonel Wobbles was much affected, and ordered us to march back to camp, which we did.

This affair was really a great victory for the Union, my boy, and I cannot refrain from giving short biographical sketches of the leaders concerned in it, commencing with

COLONEL WOBBLES.

This gallant officer, on whom the eyes of the whole world are now turned, was born at an exceedingly early age, in the place of his nativity. When but a mere boy, he evinced a fondness for the law, and his father, who was his mother's husband, placed him in the office of the late Daniel Webster. He practised law for some years, but failed to find any clients, and finally started a grocery store under Jackson's administration. At this time, Calhoun's peculiar views were agitating Christendom, and Mr. Wobbles married a daughter of the late John Thomas, by whom he had no children. When the war broke out in Mexico, he left the grocery business, and opened a liquor store on the estate of the late J. Smith, and accumulated sufficient money to send his family into the country. Colonel Wobbles is now about eighty-five years old.

MR. WOBBLES.

This heroic young officer, now attracting so much attention, drew his first breath among the peaceful scenes of home, from which the captious might have augured anything but a soldier's destiny for him. While yet very young, he was remarkable for his proficiency in making dirt-pies, and went to school with the sons of the late Mr. Jones. In 1846, he did not graduate at West Point ; but when the war broke

out between Mexico and the United States, he married a niece of the late Daniel Webster. It was also
at this period of his eventful career that he first became a husband, and shortly after the birth of his
eldest child, it was rumored that he had also become
a father. He entered the present war as a military
man. He is now but forty years old.

WOBBLES.

This noble patriot soldier, whose name is now a
household word all over the world, was reared from
infancy in the village of his birth, and took a promi-
nent part in the meals of his family. While yet a
youth, the Florida war broke out, and he attended
the high-school of the late Mr. Brown. On arriving
of age, he was just twenty-one years old, and was not
a student at West Point. Shortly after this event,
he married a cousin of the late Daniel Webster, and
during the Mexican War he had one child, who still
bears his father's name. Wobbles is now sixty years
old.

You will observe, my boy, that these noble officers
have merited the commissions of brigadier-generals,.
and if they don't get them they'll resign. Colonel
Wobbles told me this morning, that if he resigned
the army would all go to pieces. I believe him, my
boy !—field pieces. Yours, biographically,
ORPHEUS C. KERR.

LETTER XIII.

SUBMITTING VARIOUS RUMORS CONCERNING THE CONDITION OF THINGS
AT THE SOUTH, WITH A SKETCH OF A LIGHT SKELETON REGIMENT
AND A NOTE OF VILLIAM BROWN'S RECRUITING EXPLOIT.

WASHINGTON, D. C., September 20th, 1861.

THERE is every indication that something is about
to occur, which, when it does transpire, my boy, will
undoubtedly give rise to the rumor that a certain
thing has happened. It was observed in military circles yesterday, that General McClellan ordered a new
pair of boots to be forwarded immediately from New
York, and from this it is justly inferred that the
Chain Bridge will be attacked by the rebels in force
very shortly.

A gentleman who has just arrived from the South
to purchase some postage-stamps, states that the rebel
army is in an awful condition, and will starve to death
as soon as Beauregard gives the order. At Richmond,
ice-cream was selling for a hundred dollars a quart,
gum-drops at sixty dollars an ounce, Brandreth's Pills
at forty-two dollars and a half a box, Spaulding's
Prepared Glue at twenty dollars a pint, and Mrs.
Winslow's Soothing Syrup at four hundred dollars a

bottle. In consequence of the sudden approach of fall and the renewed stringency of the blockade, there are no strawberries to be had, and the First Families are subsisting entirely upon persimmons. Should the winter prove cold, the Southerners to a man will be compelled to wear much thicker clothing, and it is anticipated that many of them will take cold. *De lunatico inquirendo* has broken out among the rebel troops at Manassas Junction, in consequence of insufficient accommodation, and the hospitals are so full of patients that numerous sufferers may be seen bulging out of the windows.

The same gentleman thinks that Beauregard will be obliged to attack Washington at once, or resign his commission and go to the Dry Tortugas with his whole army. They are called the *Dry* Tortugas, my boy, because not a cocktail was ever known to be raised there.

A perfectly reliable but respectable person arrived here yesterday from Paris, and brings highly important intelligence from North Carolina. He has been permitted to sleep with a gentleman formerly residing in that State, and his report is credited by the Administration. Nearly all the people of North Carolina are devoted Union men at heart, and would gladly rally around the old flag, if it were not for the fact that nearly all the rest of the people of the State are secessionists and won't let them. In a town of

750 inhabitants, 748 and a half (one small boy)'are determined Unionists ; but the remainder, who are brutal traitors, have seized all the arms in the place, and threaten all who oppose them with instant death. At Raleigh, a mob consisting of three secessionists, has seized the post-office and all the letters of marque found in it. Marque has fled from the State. Since the victory of Hatteras Inlet, the Union men have taken courage, and say, that if the Government will send two hundred thousand men to their. assistance, and seventy-five rifled cannon, they can expel their oppressors in a few years. These true patriots must be instantly assisted, or a decimated and infuriated people will demand the expulsion of the entire Cabinet, and an entirely new issue of contracts for shoddy. In the interior of North Carolina there has been a rising of slaves. In fact, they rise every morning very early. From this the *Tribune* report of a negro insurrection originated.

I formed a new acquaintance the other day, my boy, in the shape of the Calcium Light Regiment, which is now ready to receive a few more recruits. The Calcium Light Regiment was born in Boston, near Bunker Hill Monument, and is now about sixty-five years old. He has become greatly demoralized from going without his. rations for some days past, and is what may be called a skeleton regiment. He says that if he goes without them much longer, he'll soon be as light as a 12-inch comet, and won't need much calcium to blind the enemy to his presence. He's *very* light, my boy, and his features are so sharp that he might be used to spike a cannon with. The Calcium Light Regiment was recruited at great expense in New York, and went into camp on Riker's Island, until Secretary Cameron ordered his colonel to bring him on immediately for the defence of Washington. The regiment has three officers, and will elect the others as soon as his voice is strong enough. He says that he is a regiment of 1,000 men; he says that 1,000 is simply the figure 1 and three ciphers, and that he represents the 1, and his three officers the three ciphers.

I believe him, my boy!

Villiam Brown, of Regiment 5, Mackerel Brigade, asked his colonel last week for leave to go to New York on recruiting service, and got it. He came back to-day, and says the colonel to him :

" Where's your recruits ?"

Villiam smiled sweetly, and remarked that he didn't see it.

" Why, you went to New York on recruiting service, didn't you ?" exclaimed the colonel.

" Yes," says Villiam, " I went to recruit my health."

The colonel immediately administered the Oath to

him. The Oath, my boy, tastes well with lemon in it.

The women of America, my boy, are noble creatures, and do not forget the brave soldiers· of the Union. They have just sent the Mackerel Brigade a case of umbrellas, and we expect a gross of hair-pins by the next train.   Yours, meditatively,

ORPHEUS C. KERR.

LETTER XIV.

SHOWING HOW OUR CORRESPONDENT MADE A SPEECH OF VAGUE
CONTINUITY, AFTER THE MODEL OF THE LATEST APPROVED STUMP
ORATORY.

WASHINGTON, D. C., September 30th, 1861.

ANOTHER week has fled swiftly by, my boy, on
those wings which poets and other long-haired creatures suppose to be eternally flapping through the
imaginary atmosphere of time ; yet the high old
battle so long expected has not got any further than
"heavy firing near the Chain Bridge," which takes
place every afternoon punctually at three o'clock—just
in time for the evening papers. I have been thinking, my boy, that if this heavy firing in the vicinity
of Chain Bridge lasts a few years longer, it will finally
become a nuisance to the First Families living in that '
vicinity. But sometimes what is thought to be
heavy firing is not that exactly ; the other day, a
series of loud explosions were heard on Arlington
Heights, and twenty-four reporters immediately tele-
graphed to twenty-four papers that five hundred
thousand rebels had attacked our lines with two
thousand rifled cannon, and had been repulsed with

a loss of fourteen thousand killed. Federal loss—
one killed, and two committed suicide. But when
General McClellan came to inquire into the cause of
the explosions, this report was somewhat modified :

"What was that firing for ?" he asked an orderly,
who had just come over the river.

"If you please, sir," responded the sagacious animal, "there was no firing at all. It was Villiam
Brown, of Regiment 5, Mackerel Brigade, which has
a horrible cold, and sneezes in that way."

Villiam has since been ordered to telegraph to the
War Department whenever he sneezes, so that no
more of these harrowing mistakes may be made.

Last night, my boy, an old rooster from Cattarau-
gus, who wants a one-horse post-office, and thinks
I've got some influence with Abe the Venerable,
brought six big Dutchmen to serenade me ; and, as
soon I opened the window to damn them, he called
unanimously for a speech. At this time, my boy, an
immense crowd, consisting of two policemen and a
hackman, were drawn to the spot, and greeted me with
great applause. Feeling that their intentions were
honorable, I could not bear to disappoint my fellow-citizens, and so I was constrained to make the
following

SPEECH.

Men of America :—It is with feelings akin to emotion that I regard this vast assemblage of Nature's

noblemen, and reflect that it comes to do honor to
, me, who have only performed my duty. Gentlemen,
my heart is full ; as the poet says :

> " The night shall be filled with burglars,
> And the chaps that infest the day
> Shall pack up their duds like peddlers,
> And carry the spoons away."

It seems scarcely five minutes ago that this vast
and otherwise large country sprung from chaos at
the call of Columbus, and immediately commenced
to produce wooden nutmegs for a foreign shore. It
seems but three seconds ago that all this beautiful
scene was a savage wild, and echoed the axe-falls of
the sanguinary pioneer, and the footfalls of the Last
of the Mohicans. Now what do I see before me ?
A numerous assembly of respectable Dutchmen, and·
other Americans, all ready to prove to the world that

> " Truth crushed to earth shall rise again,
> The immortal ears of jack are hers ;
> But Sarah languishes in pain
> And dyes, amid her worshipers."

I am convinced, fellow-citizens, that the present
outrageous war is no ordinary row, and that·it cannot
be brought to a successful termination· without some
action on the part of the Government. If to believe
that a war cannot rage without being prosecuted, is
abolitionism, then I am an abolitionist ; if to believe
that a good article of black ink can be made out of

black men, is republicanism, then I am a republican; but we are all brothers now, except that fat Dutchman, who has gone to sleep on his drum, and I pronounce him an accursed secessionist:

> "How doth the little busy bee
>   Improve each shining hour,
>   And gathers beeswax all the day,
>   From every opening flower."

Men of America, shall these things longer be ?—I address myself particularly to that artist with the accordeon, who don't understand a word of English— shall these things longer be ? That's what I want to know. The majestic shade of Washington listens for an answer, and I intend to send it by mail as soon as I receive it. Fellow citizens, it can no longer be denied that there is treason at our very hearthstones. Treason—merciful Heavens !

> "Come rest in this bosom, my own little dear,
>   The Honourable R. M. T. Hunter is here ;
> I know not, I care not, if jilt's in that heart,
>   I but know that I love thee, whatever thou art."

And now the question arises, is Morrill's tariff really a benefit to the country ? Gentlemen, it would be unbecoming in me to answer this question, and you would be incapable of understanding what I might say on the subject. The present is no time to think about tariffs : our glorious country is in danger, and there is a tax of three per cent. on all incomes over

ORPHEUS C. KERR PAPERS.103

eight hundred dollars. Let each man ask himself in Dutch : " Am I prepared to shoulder my musket if I am drafted, or to procure a reprobate to take my place ?" In other words :

> " The minstrel returned from the war,
>   With insects at large in his hair,
>   And having a tuneful catarrh,
>   He sung through his nose to his fair."

Therefore, it is simply useless to talk reason to those traitors, who forget the words of Jackson—words, let me add, which I myself do not remember. Animated by an unholy lust for arsenals, rifled cannon, and mints, and driven to desperation by the thought that Everett is preparing a new Oration on Washington, and Morris a new song on a young woman living up the Hudson River, they are overturning the altars of their country and issuing treasury bonds, which cannot be justly called objects of interest. What words can express the horrors of such unnatural crime ?

> " Oft in the chilly night,
>   When slumber's chains have bound me,
>   Soft Mary brings a light,
>   And puts a shawl around me."

Such, fellow-citizens, is the condition of our unhappy country at present, and as soon as it gets any better I will let you know. An Indian once asked a white man for a drink of whisky. " No !" said the man, " you red skins are just ignorant enough to ruin yourselves with liquor." The sachem looked calmly into the eyes of the insulter, as he retorted : " You say I am ignorant. How can that be when I am a well-red man ?"

And so it is, fellow-citizens, with this Union at present, though I am not able to show exactly where the parallel is. Therefore,

> "Let us then be up and wooing,
>   With a heart for any mate,
> Still proposing, still pursuing,
>   Learn to court her, and to wait."

At the conclusion of this unassuming speech, my boy, I was waited upon by a young man, who asked me if I did not want to purchase some poetry ; he had several yards to sell, and warranted it to wash.

Yours, particularly,

ORPHEUS C. KERR.

LETTER XV.

WHEREIN WILL BE FOUND THE PARTICULARS OF A VISIT TO A SUS-
PECTED NEWSPAPER OFFICE, AND SO ON.

WASHINGTON, D. C., October 2d, 1861.

THIS is a time, my boy, when it is the duty of
every American citizen to make himself into a committee of safety, for the good of the republic, and
make traitors smell the particular thunder of national
vengeance. The eagle, my boy, has spread his sanguinary wings for a descent upon the bantams of
secession ; and if we permit his sublime pinions to
be burthened with the shackles of domestic sedition,
we are guilty of that which we do, and are otherwise
liable to the charge of committing that which we perform. These thoughts came to me yesterday, after I
had taken the Oath six times, and so overpowered me
that I again took the Oath, with a straw in it. Just
then it struck me that the *Daily Union,* published
near Alexandria, ought to be suppressed for its treason ; and I immediately started for the office, with
an intention to offer personal violence to the editor.
I found him examining a cigar through the bottom

of a tumbler, whilst on the desk beside him lay the first "proof" of

THE EDITOR'S WOOING.

We love thee, Ann Maria Smith,
  And in thy condescension,
We see a future full of joys
  Too numerous to mention.

There 's Cupid's arrow in thy glance,
  That by thy love's coercion
Has reached our melting heart of hearts,
  And asked for one insertion.

With joy we feel the blissful smart,
  And ere our passion ranges,
We freely place thy love upon
  The list of our exchanges.

There's music in thy lowest tone,
  And silver in thy laughter;
And truth—but we will give the full
  Particulars hereafter.

Oh! we could tell thee of our plans
  All obstacles to scatter;
But we [illegible] full just now, and have
  A press of other matter.

Then let us marry, Queen of Smiths,
  Without more hesitation;
The very thought doth give our blood
  A larger circulation!

When the editor noticed my presence, he scowled so that his spectacles dropped off.

"Ha, my fine little fellow," says he, hastily ; "I don't want to buy any poetry to-day."

"Don't fret yourself, my venerable cherub," says I ; "I don't deal in poetry at present. I just came here to tell you that if you don't stop writing treason, I'll suppress you in the name of the United States."

"You're a mudsill mob," says he ; "and I don't allow no violent mobs around this office. I am an American citizen, and I won't stand no mobs. What does the Constitution say about newspapers ? Why, the Constitution don't say anything about them ; so you've got no Constitutional authority for mobbing me."

"Then take the Oath," says I.

He looked at me for a moment, and then passed me a small black bottle. I held it up over my eyes for some time, to see if it was perfectly straight, and he remarked that if all Northerners took the Oath as freely as I did, they must be a water-proof conglomeration of patriots. I believe him, my boy!

The Mackerel Brigade has established a cookery department for itself, and is using a stove recently patented by the colonel of Regiment 5. This stove is a miraculous invention, and has already made fortunes for six cooks and a scullion. You put a shilling's worth of wood into it, which first cooks your meat and then turns into two shilling's worth of charcoal ; so you make a shilling every time you kindle a fire.

Yesterday, a gentleman, brought up to the oyster-trade, and who has made several voyages on the Brooklyn ferry-boats, exhibited the model of a new gun-boat to the Secretary of the Navy. He said its great advantage was that it could easily be taken to pieces ; and the Secretary was just going to order seventy-five for use in Central Park, when it leaked out that when once the gun-boat was taken to pieces there was no way of putting it together again. Only for this, my boy, we might have a gun-boat in every cistern.   Yours, nautically,

ORPHEUS C. KERR.

LETTER XVI.

INTRODUCING THE GOTHIC STEED, PEGASUS, AND THE REMARKABLE GERMAN CAVALRY FROM THE WEST.

WASHINGTON, D. C., October 6th, 1861.

THE horse, my boy, is an animal in which I have taken a deep interest ever since the day on the Union Course, when I bet ten dollars that the " Pride of the Canal " would beat " Lady Clamcart," and was compelled to leave my watch with Mr. Simpson on the following morning. The horse, my boy, is the swarthy Arab's bosom friend, the red Indian's solitary companion, and the circus proprietor's salvation. One of these noble animals was presented to me last week, by an old-maid relative whose age I once guessed to be "about nineteen." The glorious gift was accompanied by a touching letter, my boy ; she honored my patriotism, and the self-sacrificing spirit that had led me to join the gallant Mackerel Brigade, and get a furlough as soon as a rebel picket appeared ; she loved me for my mother's sake, and as she happened to have ten shillings about her, she thought she would buy a horse with it for me. Mine, affectionately, Tabitha Turnips.

Ah, woman! glorious woman! what should we do
without thee? All our patriotism is but the inspiration of thy proud love, and all our money is but the
few shillings left after thou hast got through buying
new bonnets. Oh! woman—thoughtful woman! the
soldier thanks thee for sending him pies and cakes
that turn sour before they leave New York; but, for
heaven's sake don't send any more havelocks, or
there'll be a crisis in the linen market. It's a common thing for a sentry to report "eighty thousand
more havelocks from the women of America;" and
then you ought to hear the Brigadier of the Mackerel
Brigade cuss! "Jerusalem!" says he, "if any more
havelocks come this afternoon, tell them that I've
gone out and won't be back for three weeks. Thunder!" says he, "there's enough havelocks in this here
deadly tented field to open a brisk trade with Europe,
and if the women of America keep on sending them,
I'm d—d if I don't start a night-cap shop." The
general is a profane patriarch, my boy, and takes the
Oath hot. The Oath, my boy, is improved by nutmeg and a spoon.

But to return to the horse which woman's generosity has made me own—me be-yuteous steed. The
beast, my boy, is fourteen hands high, fourteen hands
long, and his sagacious head is shaped like an old-
fashioned pick-axe. Viewed from the rear, his style
of architecture is gothic, and he has a gable-end, to

which his tail is attached. His eyes, my boy, are two pearls, set in mahogany, and before he lost his sight, they were said to be brilliant. I rode down to the Patent Office, the other day, and left him leaning against a post, while I went inside to transact some business. Pretty soon the Commissioner of Patents came tearing in like mad, and says he :

" I'd like to know whether this is a public building belonging to the United States, or a second-hand auction-shop."

" What mean you, sirrah ?" I asked majestically.

" I mean," says he, " that some enemy to his country has gone and stood an old mahogany umbrella-stand right in front of this office."

To the disgrace of his species be it said, my boy, he referred to the spirited and fiery animal for which I am indebted to woman's generosity. I admit that when seen at a distance, the steed somewhat resembles an umbrella-stand ; but a single look into his pearly eyes is enough to prove his relations with the animal kingdom.

I have named him Pegasus, in honor of Tupper, and when I mount him, Villiam Brown, of Company 3, Regiment 5, Mackerel Brigade, says that I remind him of Santa Claus sitting astride the roof of a small gothic cottage, holding on by the chimney.

Villiam is becoming rather too familiar, my boy, and I hope he'll be shot at an early day.

Yesterday the army here was reënforced with a regiment of fat German cavalry from the West, under the command of Colonel Wobert Wobinson, who has had great experience in keeping a livery-stable. Their animals are well calculated to turn the point of a sword, and are of the high-backed fluted pattern, very glossy at the joints. I saw one of the dragoons cracking nuts on the backbone of the Arabian he rode, and asked him about how much such an animal was worth without the fur? He considered for a moment and then remarked that nix fustay and dampfnoodle, though many believed that swei glass und sweitzer-kase; but upon the whole, it was nix cumarouse and apple-dumplings, notwithstanding the fact that yawpy, yawpy, betterish. Singular to relate, my boy, I had arrived at the very same conclusion before I asked him the question.

Colonel Wobert Wobinson reviewed the regiment near Chain Bridge this morning, and each horse used about an acre to turn around in. Just before the order to "charge" was given, the orderly sergeant kindled a fire under each horse, and when the charge commenced, only about six of the animals laid down. Colonel Wobinson remarked that these six horses were in favor of peace, and refused to fight against their

Southern brethren. I told him I thought that the peace breed had longer ears ; and he said that that kind had been very scarce since the Government commenced appointing its foreign consuls.

Yours, hoarsely,
ORPHEUS C. KERR.

LETTER XVII.

NOTING A NEW VICTORY OF THE MACKEREL BRIGADE IN VIRGINIA,
AND ILLUSTRATING THE PECULIAR THEOLOGY OF VILLIAM BROWN;
WITH SOME MENTION OF THE SHARP-SHOOTERS.

WASHINGTON, D. C., October 18th, 1861.

At an early hour yesterday morning, while yet the
dew was on the grass, and on everything else green
enough to be out at that matinal hour, my boy, I
saddled my gothic steed Pegasus, and took a trot for
the benefit of my health. Having eaten a whole
straw bed and a piece of an Irishman's shoulder during the night, my architectural beast was in great
spirits, my boy, and as he snuffed the fresh air and
unfurled the remnants of his warlike tail to the breeze
of heaven, I was reminded of that celebrated Arabian
steed which had such a contempt for the speed of all
other horses that he never would run with them—in
fact, my boy, he never would run at all.

Having struck a match on that rib of Pegasus which
was most convenient to my hand, I lit a cigar, and
dropped the match, still burning, into the right ear
of my fiery charger. Something of this kind is always
necessary to make the sagacious animal start ; but

when once I get his mettle up he never stops, unless he happens to hear some crows cawing in the air just above his venerable head. I am frequently glad that Pegasus has lost his eyesight, my boy ; for could he see the expression on the faces of some of these same crows, when they get near enough to squint along his backbone, it would wound his sensibilities fearfully.

On this occasion he carried me, at a speed of 2.40 hours a mile, to a point just this side of Alexandria, where the sound of heavy cannonading and cursing made me pause. At first, my boy, I remembered an engagement I had in Washington, and was about to hasten back ; but while I was pressing the lighted end of my cigar to the side of Pegasus, to make him turn, Colonel Wobert Wobinson, of the Western Cavalry, came walking toward me from a piece of woods on my right, and informed me that ten of his men had just been attacked by fourteen thousand rebels, with twenty columbiads. " The odds," says he, " is rather heavy ; but our cause is the noblest the world ever knew, and if my brave boys do not vanquish the un-natural foe, an indignant and decimated people will at once call upon the Cabinet to resign."

I told him that I thought I had read something like that in the *Tribune ;* but he didn't seem to hear me.

By this time the cannonading had commenced to subside, and as I trotted alongside of Colonel Wobinson toward the field of battle, I asked him what he had done with his horse. He replied, that while on his way to the field, his sagacious beast had observed a hay-stack, and was so entranced with the vision that he refused to go a step further ; so he had to leave him there.

Upon reaching the scene of strife, my boy, we discovered that the ten Western Cavalry men had routed the rebels, killing four regiments, which were all carried away by their comrades, and capturing six columbiads, which were also carried away. On our side nobody was killed nor wounded. In fact, two of our men, who went into the fight sick with the measles, were entirely cured, and captured four good surgeons. I must state, however, my boy, that although nobody was killed or wounded on our side, there was one man missing. It seems that when he found the balls flying pretty thickly about his ears, he formed himself into a hollow-square, my boy, and retreated in good order into the neighboring bushes. He formed himself into a hollow-square by bending gently forward until his hands touched the ground, and made his retrograde movement on all-fours. Colonel Wobinson remarked that this style of forming a hollow-square was an intensely-immense thing on Hardee.

I believe him, my boy !

The women of America, my boy, are a credit to

the America eagle, and a great expense to their hus-
bands and fathers, but they don't exactly understand
the most pressing wants of the soldier. For instance,
a young girl, about seventy-five years of age, has
been sending ten thousand pious tracts to the Mackerel Brigade, and the consequence is, that the air
around the camp has been full of spit-balls for a
week. These tracts, my boy, are very good for dying
sinners and other Southerners, but I'd rather have
Bulwer's novels for general reading. Villiam Brown,
of Company 3, Regiment 5, got one of them the other
day, headed, "Who is your Father?" The noble
youth read the question over once or twice, and then
dashed the publication to the ground, and took some
tobacco to check his emotions. (That brave youth's
father, my boy, is a disgrace to his species; he has
been sinking deeper and deeper in shame for some
months past, until at last his name has got on the
Mozart Hall ticket.) I saw that Villiam didn't understand what the tract really meant, and so I explained to him that it was intended to signify that
God was his Father. The gifted young soldier looked
at me dreamily for a moment, and then says he:

"God is my Father!" says he. "Well, now I
am hanged if that ain't funny; for, whenever mother
spoke of dad, she always called him 'the old devil!'"

Villiam never went to Sabbath-school, my boy, and

his knowledge of theology wouldn't start a country-church.

Wishing to find out if he knew anything about catechism, I asked him, last Sunday afternoon, if he knew who Moses was.

" Yes," says he, " I know him very well ; he sells old clothes in Chatham street."

I went over to Virginia the other day to review Berdan's Sharpshooters, and was much astonished, my boy, at their wonderful skill with the rifle. The target is a little smaller than the side of a barn, with a hole through the centre exactly the size of a bullet. They set this up, my boy, just six hundred yards away, and fire at it in turn. After sixty of them had fired, I went with them to the target, but couldn't see that it had been hit by a single bullet. I remarked this to the captain, whereupon he looked pityingly at me, and says he :

" Do you see that hole in the bull's eye, just the size of a bullet ?"

I allowed that I did.

" Well," says he, "the bullets all went through that hole."

Now I don't mean to say that the captain lied, my boy ; but it's my opinion—my private opinion, my boy, that if he ever writes a work of fiction, it will sell !

La Mountain has been up in his balloon, and went

so high that he could see all the way to the Gulf of Mexico, and observe what they had for dinner at Fort Pickens. He made discoveries of an important character, my boy, and says that the rebels have concentrated several troops at Manassas. A reporter of the *Tribune* asked him if he could see any negro insurrections, and he said that he *did* see some black spots moving around near South Carolina, but found out afterward that they were some ants which had got into his telescope.

The Prince de Joinville's two sons, my boy, are admirable additions to General McClellan's staff, and speak English so well that I can almost understand what they say. Two Arabs are expected here to-morrow to take command of Irish brigades, and General Blenker will probably have two Aztecs to assist him in his German division.

Yours, musingly,

ORPHEUS C. KERR.

LETTER XVIII.

DESCRIBING THE TERRIBLE DEATH AND MYSTERIOUS DISAPPEARANCE
OF A CONFEDERATE PICKET, WITH A TRIBUTE TO HIS MEMORY.

WASHINGTON, D. C., October 28th, 1861.

My head swells with patriotic pride when I casually
remark that the Mackerel Brigade occupy the post of
honor to the left of Bull Run, which they also left
on the day we celebrated. The banner which was
presented to us by the women of America, and which
it took the orator of the day six hours and forty minutes to describe to us, we are using in the shape of
blazing neck-ties ; and when the hard-up sun of Virginia shines upon the glorious red bands around the
sagacious necks of our veterans, they all look as
though they had just cut their throats. The effect is
gory, my boy—extremely gory and respectable.

At the special request of Secretary Seward, who
wrote six letters about it to the Governors of all the
States, I have been appointed a picket of the army of
the Upper Potomac. In your natural ignorance, my
boy, you may not know why a man is called a picket.
He is called a picket, my boy, because, if anybody
drops a pocket-book or a watch anywhere, his natural

gifts would cause him to pick-it up. If he saw a pocket, he would not pick-it—oh, no ! But pick-it—picket.

The Picket, my boy, has been an institution ever since wars began, and his perils are spoken of by some of the high old poets in these beautiful lines :

> "The chap thy tactics doom to bleed to-day—
> Had he thy reasons, would he poker play?
> Pleased to the last, he does a deal of good,
> And licks the man just sent to shed his blood."

I am weeping, my boy.

While on my lonely beat, about an hour ago, a light tread attracted my attention, and looking up, I beheld one of secesh's pickets standing before me.

" Soldier," says he, " you remind me of my grandmother, who expired before I was born ; but this unnatural war has made us enemies, and I must shoot you. Give me a chaw terbacker."

He was a young man, my boy, in the prime of life, and descended from the First Families of Virginia.

I looked at him, and says I :

" Let's compromise, my brother."

" Never !" says he. " The South is fighting for her liberty, her firesides, and the pursuit of happiness, and I desire most respectfully to welcome you with bloody hands to a hospitable grave."

" Stand off ten paces," says I, " and let's see whose name shall come before the coroner first."

He took his place, and we fired simultaneously. I heard a ball go whistling by a barn about a quarter of a mile on my right ; and, when the smoke cleared away, I saw the secesh picket approaching me with an awful expression of woe on his otherwise dirty countenance.

"Soldier," says he, "was there anything in my head before you fired ?"

"Nothing," says I, "save a few harmless insects."

"I speak not of them," says he. "Was there anything *inside* of my head ?"

"Nothing !" says I.

"Well," says he, "just listen now."

He shook his head mournfully, and I heard something rattle in it.

"What's that ?" I exclaimed.

"That," says he, "is your bullet, which has penetrated my skull, and is rolling about in my brain. I die happy, and with an empty stomach ; but there is one thing I should like to see before I perish for my country. Have you a quarter about you ?"

Too much affected to speak, I drew the coin from my pocket and handed it to him.

The dying man clutched it convulsively, and stared at it feverishly.

"This," said he, "is the first quarter I've seen since the fall of Sumter ; and, had I wounded you, I should have been totally unable to give you any quar-

ter. Ah ! how beautiful it is ! how bright, how exquisite, and good for four drinks ! But I have not
time to say all I feel."

The expiring soldier then laid down his gun, hung
his cap and overcoat on a branch of a tree, and blew
his nose.

He then died.

And there I stood, my boy, on that lonely beat,
looking down on that fallen type of manhood, and
thinking how singular it was he had forgotten to give
me back my quarter.

As I looked upon him there, I could not help thinking to myself, " here is another whose home shall
know him no more."

The sight and the thought so affected me, that I
was obliged to turn my back on the corpse and walk
a little way from it. When I returned to the spot,
the body was gone ! Had it gone to Heaven ?
Perhaps so, my boy—perhaps so ; but I hav'n't seen
my quarter since.

Your own picket,
ORPHEUS C. KERR.

LETTER XIX.

NOTICING THE ARRIVAL OF A SOLID BOSTON MAN WITH AN UNPRE-
CEDENTED LITERARY PRIZE, AND SHOWING HOW VILLIAM BROWN
WAS TRIUMPHANTLY PROMOTED.

WASHINGTON, D. C., November —, 1861.

HAVING just made a luscious breakfast, my boy,
on some biscuit discovered amid the ruins of Herculaneum, and purchased expressly for the grand army
by a contracting agent for the Government, I take a
sip of coffee from the very boot in which it was
warmed, and hasten to pen my dispatch.

On Wednesday morning, my boy, the army here was
reënforced by a very fat man from Boston, who said
he'd been used to Beacon street all the days of his life,
and considered the State House somewhat superior to
St. Peter's at Rome. He was a very fat man, my boy:
eight hands high, six and a half hands thick, and his
head looked like a full moon sinking in the west at
five o'clock in the morning. He said he joined the
army to fight for the Union, and cure his asthma, and
Colonel Wobert Wobinson thoughtfully remarked,
that he thought he could grease a pretty long bayonet
without feeling uncomfortable. This fat man, my

boy, was leaning down to clean his boots just outside of a tent, when the General of the Mackerel Brigade happened to come along, and got a back view of him.

" Thunder !" says the general, stopping short ; " who's been sending artillery into camp ?"

" There's no artillery here, my boy," says I.

" Well," says he, " then what's the gun-carriage doing here ?"

I explained to him that what he took for a gun-carriage was a fat patriot blacking his boots ; and he said that he be dam.

Soon after the arrival of this solid Boston man, my boy, I noticed that he always carried about with him, suspended by a strap under his right arm, something carefully wrapped in oilskin. He was sitting with me in my room at Willard's the other evening, and says I to him :

" What's that you hug so much, my Plymouth Rocker ?"

He nervously clutched his treasure, and says he :

" It's an unpublished poem of the Honorable Edward, which I found in a very old album in Beacon street. It's an immortal and unpublished poem," says he, fondly taking a roll of manuscript from the oilskin wrapper,—" by the greatest and most silent statesman of the age. You'll recognize the style at once.—Listen—

ADVICE TO A MAID.

Perennial maiden, thou art no less fair
Than those whose fairness barely equals thine;
And like a cloud on Athos is thy hair,
Touched with Promethean fire to make it shine
Above the temple of a soul divine;
And yet, methinks, it doth resemble, too,
The strands Berenice 'mid the stars doth twine,
As Mitchell's small Astronomy doth show;
Procure the book, dear maid, when to the town you go

Young as thou art, thou might'st be younger still,
If divers years were taken from thy life:
And who shall say, if marry man you will,
You may not prove some man's own wedded wife?
Such things do happen in this worldly strife,
If they take place—that is, if they are done;
For with warm love this earthly dream is rife—
And where love shines there always is a sun—
As I remark in my Oration upon Washington.

Supposing thou dost marry, thou wilt yearn
For that which thou dost want; in fact, desire—
The wisdom shaped for older heads to learn,
And well designed to tame Youth's giddy fire:
The wisdom, conflicts with the world inspire,
Such as, perchance, I may myself possess,
Though I am but a man, as was my sire,
And own not wisdom such as gods may bless;
For man is naught, and naught is nothingness.

Still, I may tell thee all that I do know,
And telling that, tell all I comprehend;
Since all man hath is all that he can show,
And what he hath not, is not his to lend.
Therefore, young maid, if you will but attend,
You shall hear that which shall salute your ear;
But if you list not, I my breath shall spend
Upon the zephyrs wandering there and here,
The far-off hearing less, perhaps, than those more near.

Remember this : thou art thy husband's wife,
And he the mortal thou art married to ;
Else, thou fore'er hadst led a single life,
And he had never come thy heart to woo.
Rememb'ring this, do thou remember, too,
He is thy bridegroom, thou his chosen bride;
And if unto his side thou provest true,
Then thou wilt be for ever at his side;
As Tacitus observes, with some degree of pride.

See that his buttons to his shirts adhere,
As Trojan Hector to the walls of Troy ;
And see that not, Achilles-like, appear
Rents in his stocking-heels; but be your joy
To have his wardrobe all your thoughts employ,
Save such deep thought as may, in duty given,
Suit to his tastes his dinners; nor annoy
Digestion's tenor in its progress even ;
Then his the joy of Harvard, Boston, and high Heaven .

If a bread-pudding thou wouldst fondly make—
A thing nutritious, but no costly meal—
Of bread that's stale a due proportion take,
And soak in water warm enough to feel;
Then add a strip or two of lemon-peel,
With curdled milk and raisins to your taste,
And stir the whole with ordinary zeal,
Until the mass becomes a luscious paste.
Such pudding strengthens man, and doth involve no waste.

See thou thy husband's feet are never wet—
For wet brings cold, and colds such direful aches
As old Parrhasius never felt when set
On cruel racks or slow impaling stakes.
Make him abstain, if sick, from griddle-cakes—
They, being rich, his stomach might derange—
And if in thin-soled shoes a walk he takes,
See that his stockings he doth quickly change.
Thus should thy woman's love through woman's duties range.

And now, fair maiden, all the stars grow pale,
And teeming Nature drinks the morning dews;
And I must hasten to my Orient vale,
And quick put on a pair of over-shoes.
If from my words your woman's heart may choose
To find a guidance for a future way,
The Olympian impulse and the lyric muse
In such approval shall accept their pay.
And so, good-day, young girl—ah me! oh my! good-day.
EDWARD EVERDEVOURED.

As the solid Boston man finished reading this useful poem, he looked impressively at me, and says he :
" There's domestic eloquence for you ! The Honorable Edward is liberal in his views," says he, en-
thusiastically, " and treats his subject with some lati-
tude."

" Yes," says I, thoughtfully, " but they call it
Platitude, sometimes."

He didn't hear me, my boy.

It is with raptures, my boy, that I record the pro-
motion of Villiam Brown, Company 3, Regiment 5,
Mackerel Brigade, to the rank of Captain, with the
privilege of spending half his time in New York, and
the rest of it on Broadway. Villiam left the army
of the Upper Potomac to pass his examination here,
and the Board of Examiners report that he reminded
them of Napoleon, and made them feel sorry for the
Duke of Wellington. One of the questions they
asked him was :

" Suppose your company was suddenly surrounded

by a regiment of the enemy, and you had a precipice in your rear, and twenty-seven hostile batteries in front—what would you do ?"

Villiam thought a moment, and then says he :

" I'd resign my commission, and write to my mother that I was coming home to die in the spring-time."

"Sensible patriot," says the Board. "Are you familiar with the history of General Scott ?"

" You can bet on it," says Villiam, smiling like a sagacious angel ; " General Scott was born in Virginia when he was quite young, and discovered Scotland at an early age. He licked the British in 1812, wrote the Waverly Novels, and his son Whahae bled with Wallace. Now, old hoss, trot out your commission and let's liquor."

" Pause, fair youth," says the Board. " What makes you think that General Scott had a son named ' Whahae' ? We never heard that before."

" Ha !" says Villiam, agreeably, " that's because you don't know poickry. Why," says Villiam, "if you'll just turn to Burns' works, you'll learn that

" 'Scot's wha' ha'e wi' Wallace bled,'

and if that ain't good authority, where's your Shakspeare ?"

The Board was so pleased with Villiam's learning, my boy, that it gave him his commission, presented him with two gun-boats and a cannon, and recom-

mended him for President of the New York Histor-
ical Society.

It was rumored in camp last night, that the army
would go into winter-quarters, and I asked Colonel
Wobinson if he couldn't lend me a few of the quarters
in advance, as I felt like going in right away. He
explained to me that winter-quarters would only be
taken in exchange for Treasury Notes, and I withdrew my proposition for a popular loan.

Yours, speculatively,
ORPHEUS C. KERR.

LETTER XX.

CONCERNING A SIGNIFICANT BRITISH OUTRAGE, AND THE CAPTURE OF
MASON AND SLIDELL.

WASHINGTON, D. C., November 24th, 1861.

MR. SEWARD, my boy, who takes the Oath with
much sugar in it, and is likewise Secretary of State,
will probably write twenty-four letters to all the
Governors this week, in consequence of a recent outrage committed by Great Britain. I may remark
with great indignation, that Great Britain is a member of one of the New York regiments, my boy, and
enlisted for the express purpose of stretching his legs.
He is shaped something like a barrel of ale, and has a
chin that looks like an apple-dumpling with a stitch
in its side. As I rode slowly along near Fort Corcoran, on my Gothic steed Pegasus, about an hour ago,
admiring the beauties of Nature, and smoking a pipe
which was presented to me by the Women of America, I espied Great Britain seated by the roadside,
contemplating an army biscuit. These biscuit, my
boy, as I stated last week, were discovered amid the
ruins of Herculaneum, and were at first taken for
meteoric stones.

"Good morning, old Neutrality," says I, affably, "You appear to be lost in religious meditation."

"Ah !" says he, sighing like the great behemoth of the Scriptures, "I was thinking of the way of the transgressor. If the hinspired writers," says he, "thought the way of the transgressor was 'ard, I wonder what they'd think about this 'ere biscuit."

"You're jealous of America," says I, "and it will be the painful duty of the Union, the Constitution, and the Enforcement of the Law to capture Canada, if you continue your abolition harangues against the best, the most beneficent and powerful bread in the civilized world."

"Bread !" says he, with a groan in three syllables, "do you call this ere biscuit bread ? Why," says he, "this ere biscuit is Geology, and if it were in old Hingland, it would be taken for one of the Elgin marbles, and placed in the British Museum."

I need scarcely inform you, my boy, that after this ungenerous remark of Great Britain, I left him contemptuously, and at once proceeded to blockade a place where the Oath is furnished in every style. We have borne with Great Britain a great while, my boy ; but it is now time for us to take Canada, and wipe every vestige of British tyranny from the face of the Globe. The American eagle, my boy, flaps his dark wings over the red-head of battle, and as his scarlet eyes rest for a moment on the English

Custom House, he softly whispers—he simply remarks
—he merely ejaculates—GORE !

Americans ! fellow-citizens ! foreigners ! and people
of Boston ! Shall we longer allow the bloated British
aristocracy to blight us with base abolition procliv-
ities, while Mr. Seward is capable of holding a pen ?

> " Hail, blood and thunder ! welcome, gentle Gore !
>   Let the loud hewgag shatter every shore !
>   High to the zenith let our eagle fly,
>   Ten thousand battles blazing in his eye !
>   Nail our proud standard to the Northern Pole,
>   Plant patent earthquakes in each foreign hole !
>   Shout havoc, murder, victory, and spoils,
>   Till all creation crouches in our toils !
>   Then, when the world to our behest is bent,
>   And takes the *Herald* for its punishment,
>   We'll pin our banner to a comet's tail,
>   And shake the Heavens with a big ' ALL HAIL !' "

That's the spirit of America, my boy, taken with
nutmeg on top, and a hollow straw. Very good for
invalids.

Next to the question concerning the capacity of
gunboats for the sweet-potato trade, my boy, the
great topic of the day is the capture of Slidell and
Mason, whose arrest so pleased the colonel of the
Mackerel Brigade, that he got up at nine o'clock in
the morning to tell the President about it.

In the year 1776, my boy, this Slidell sold candles
in New York, and was born about two years after the
marriage of the elder Slidell. While he was yet a

young man, he went much into female society, and at
length offered his hand to a lady. Her father being a
male, gave his consent to the match, and on the day
of the wedding, there was a fire in the Seventh Ward.
Since that time, Slidell has been a married man, and
was much respected until he got into the Senate. I
get these facts from a friend of the family, who has
a set of silver spoons engraved with the name of
Slidell.

The rebel Mason was born and bred in the United
States, and has always been a First Family. He says
he was going to Europe on account of his health.

The capture of these men, my boy, cannot fail to
produce a great sensation in diplomatic circles, and I
am informed by a reliable gentleman from Weehawken,
that Mr. Seward is preparing a letter to Lord Lyons
on the subject. This letter, I learn, will contain some
such passages as this :

"I have the honor to say to your lordship, that
your lordship must be aware of your lordship's important duty as a Minister to the United States, and
I trust that your lordship will pay a little attention
to your lordship's grammar when next your lordship
addresses your lordship's most obedient servant. Your
lordship will permit me to say to your lordship, that
your lordship is in no way capable of interpreting the
Constitution to your lordship's American friends ;
and I trust your lordship will not be offended when I

state to your lordship, that your lordship will find nothing in the Constitution to compel your lordship to demand your lordship's passport on account of the recent capture of State prisoners from one of your lordship's government's vessels, your lordship."

I read this extract to Colonel Wobert Wobinson, of the Western Cavalry, my boy, and he said its only fault was, that it hadn't enough lordships in it.

"Lordships," says he, "lend an easy grace to State documents, and are as aristocratic as a rooster's tail at sunrise."

The colonel is a natural poet, my boy, and abounds in pleasing comparisons.

The review of seventy thousand troops near Munson's Hill, on Thursday, was one of those stirring events, my boy, which we have been upon the eve of for the past year. A new cavalry company, for the Mackerel Brigade, excited great attention as it went past, and I understand the President said that, with the exception of the horses and the men, it was one of the finest cavalry mobs he ever saw. The horses are a new pattern; fluted sides, polished knobs on the haunches, and a hand-rail all the way down the back. A rebel caught sight of one of these fine animals, the other day, and immediately fainted. It was afterward ascertained that he owned a field of oats in the neighborhood.

Yours, variously,   ORPHEUS C. KERR.

LETTER XXI.

DESCRIBING CAPTAIN VILLIAM BROWN'S GREAT EXPEDITION TO ACCO-
MAC, AND ITS MARVELLOUS SUCCESS.

WASHINGTON, D. C., December 1st, 1861.

'TWAS early morn, my boy. The sun rushed up
the eastern sky in a state of patriotic combustion, and
as the dew fell upon the grassy hill-sides, the mountains lifted up their heads and were rather green.
Far on the horizon six rainbows appeared, with an
American Eagle at roost on the top one, and as the
translucent pearl of the dawn shone between them,
and a small pattern of blue sky with thirty-four stars
broke out at one end, I saw—I beheld—yes, it ees !
it ees ! our Banger in the Skee yi !

The reason why the heavens took such an interest
in the United States of America was the fact, that
Captain Villiam Brown, of Company 3, Regiment 5,
Mackerel Brigade, was to make a Great Expedition
to Accomac County on that morning. Twelve years
was the period originally assigned, my boy, for the
preparation of this Expedition ; but, when the government heard that the Accomac rebels were making
candles of all the fat Boston men they took prisoners, it

concluded to do something during the present century.
Villiam Brown was assigned to the command of the
Expedition, and when I asked the General of the
Mackerel Brigade how such selection happened to be
made, he said that Villiam was assigned because there
were so many signs of an ass about him.

The General is much given to classical metaphors,
my boy, and ought to write for the new American
Encyclopedia.

Previous to starting, Villiam Brown called a meeting of his staff, for the purpose of selecting such
officers only who had slept with Hardee, and knew
beans.

"Gentlemen," said Villiam, seating himself at a
table, on which stood the Oath and a clean tumbler ;
"I wish to know which of you is the greatest shakes
in a sacred skrimmage."

A respectable leftenant stepped forward with his
hand upon his boozum.

"Being a native of Philadelphia," says he, "I am
naturally modest ; but only yesterday, when two
rebels pitched into me, I knocked them both over,
and am here to tell the tale."

Villiam Brown gave the speaker a piercing look,
my boy, and says he :

"Impostor ! beware how you insult the United
States of America. I fathom your falsehood," says
he, "by my knowledge of Matthew Maticks. You

say that two chivalries pitched into you, and you
knocked them both over. Now Matthew Maticks
distinctly says that two into one goes *no times*, and
nothing over. Speaker of the House, remove this
leftenant to the donjon keep. He's Ananias Number 2."

The officer from Philadelphia being removed to the
guard-house, where there is weeping and wailing, and
picking of teeth, another leftenant stepped forward :

"I deal in technicalities," says he, "and can post
you in law."

"Ha!" says Villiam, softly sipping the Oath,
"then I will try you with an abstract question, my
beautiful Belvideary. Supposing Mason and Slidell
were your friends, how would you work it to get them
out of Fort Warren?"

"Why," said the leftenant, pleasantly, "I'd sue
out a writ of Habeas Jackass, and get the *New York
Herald* to advise the Government not to let them
out."

"Yes," says Villiam, meditatively, "that would
be sure to do it. I'll use you to help me get up my
Proclamation."

"And now," says Villiam, dropping a lump of
sugar into the Oath, and stirring it with a comb,
"who is that air melancholy chap with a tall hat on,
who looks like Hamlet with a panic?".

The melancholy chap came to the front, shook his long locks like Banquo, and says he :

"I'm the Press. I'm the Palladium of our Liberties—

> " 'Here shall the Press the People's rights maintain,
> Unawed by affluence and inspired by gain.'

I'm the best advertising medium in the country, and have reptile cotemporaries. I won't be suppressed. No, sir !—no, sir !—I refuse to be suppressed."

" You're a giant intellek," says Villiam, looking at him through the bottom of a tumbler ; " but I can't stand the press. Speaker of the House, remove him to the bath and send for a barber. Now, gentlemen, I will say a few words to the troops, and then we will march according to Hardee."

The section of the Mackerel Brigade being mustered in line against a rail fence, my boy, Captain Villiam Brown shut one eye, balanced himself on one foot, and thus addressed them :

" FELLOW-SOLDATS ! (which is French.) It was originally intended to present you with a stand of colors ; but the fellow-citizen who was to present it has only got as far as the hundred and fifty-second page of the few remarks he intended to make on the occasion, and it is a military necessity not to wait for him. (See Scott's Tactics, Vol. III., pp. 24.) I have but few words to say, and these are them : Should any of you happen to be killed in the coming battle, let me implore you to *Die without a groan.* It sounds better in history, as well as in the great, heart-stirring romances of the weekly palladiums of freedom. How well it reads, that ' Private Muggins received a shot in the neck and *died without a groan.*' Soldats ! bullets have been known to pass clean through the thickest trees, and so I may be shot myself. Should such a calamity befall our distracted country, I shall *die without a groan,* even though I am a grown person. Therefore, fear nothing. The eyes of the whole civilized world are upon you, and History and Domestic Romance expect to write that you *died without a groan."*

At the conclusion of this touching and appropriate speech, my boy, all the men exclaimed : " We will !" except a young person from New York, who said that he'd rather " Groan without a die ;" for which he was sentenced to read Seward's next letter.

The Army being formed into a Great Quadrilateral (See Raymond's Tactics), moved forward at a double-quick, and reached Accomac just as the impatient sun was rushing down. With the exception of a mule, the only Virginian to be seen was a solitary Chivalry, who had strained himself trying to raise some interest from a Confederate Treasury Note, and couldn't get away.

Observing that only one man was in sight, Captain

Villiam Brown, who had stopped to tie his shoe behind a large tree on the left, made a flank movement on the Chivalry.

"Is these the borders of Accomac?" says he, pleasantly.

"Why!" says the Chivalry, giving a start, "you must be Lord Lyons."

"What makes you think that?" asked Villiam.

"Oh, nothing—only your grammar," says Chivalry.

This made Villiam very mad, my boy, and he ordered the bombardment to be commenced immediately; but as all the powder had been placed on board a vessel which could not arrive under two weeks, it was determined to take possession without combustion. Finding himself master of the situation, Captain Villiam Brown called the solitary Chivalry to him, and issued the following

PROCLAMATION.

CITIZEN OF ACCOMAC! I come among you not as a incendiary and assassin, but to heal your wounds and be your long-lost father. Several of the happiest months in my life were not spent in Accomac, and your affecting hospitality will make me more than jealously-watchful of your liberties and the pursuit of happiness. (See the Constitution.)

Citizen of Accomac! These brave men, of whom I am a spectator, are not your enemies; they are your brothers, and desire to embrace you in fraternal bonds. They wish to be considered your guests, and respectfully invite you to observe the banner of our common forefathers. In proof whereof I establish the following orders :

I.—If any nigger come within the lines of the United States Army to give information, whatsomever, of the movements of the enemy, the aforesaid shall have his head knocked off, and be returned to his lawful owner, according to the groceries and provisions of the Fugitive Slave Ack. (See the Constitution.)

II.—If any chicken or other defenceless object belonging to the South, be brought within the lines of the United States Army, by any nigger, his heirs, administrators, and assigns, the aforesaid shall have his tail cut off, and be sent back to his rightful owner at the expense of the Treasury Department.

III.—Any soldier found guilty of shooting the Southern Confederacy, or bothering him in any manner whatsomever, the same shall be deemed guilty of disorderly conduct, and be pronounced an accursed abolitionist.

VILLIAM BROWN, Eskevire,
Captain Conic Section Mackerel Brigade,
Commanding Accomac.

The citizen of Accomac, my boy, received this proclamation favorably, and said he wouldn't go hunting Union pickets until the weather was warmer. Whereupon Villiam Brown fell upon his neck and wept copiously.

The Union Army, my boy, now holds undisputed possession of over six inches of the sacred soil of Accomac, and this unnatural rebellion has received a blow which shakes the rotten fabric to its shivering centre. The strong arm of the Government has at last reached the stronghold of treason, and in a few years this decisive movement on Accomac will be followed by the advance of our army on the Potomac.

Yours, with expedition,

ORPHEUS C. KERR.

LETTER XXII.

TREATING OF VILLIAM'S OCCUPATION OF ACCOMAC, AND HIS WISE
DECISION IN A CONTRABAND CASE.

WASHINGTON, D. C., December 16th, 1861.

AFTER sleeping with Congress for two days, my
boy, and observing four statesmen and a small page
driven to the verge of apoplexy by the exciting tale
called the President's Message, I thought it was about
time to mingle with the world again, and sent my
servant, Percy de Mortimer, to bring me my gothic
steed Pegasus. After a long search in the fields after
that chaste architectural animal, my boy, he met a
Missouri picket chap, and says he :

"Hev you seen a horse hereabout, my whisky-
doodle ?"

"Hoss !" says Missouri, spitting with exquisite
precision on one of De Mortimer's new boots. "No,
I aint seen no hoss, my Fejee bruiser ; but there's an
all-fired big crow-roost down in that corner, I reckon ;
and it must be alive, for I heard the bones rattle when
the wind blew."

My *valet*, Mr. De Mortimer, paid no heed to his
satirical lowness, my boy, but proceeded majestically

to where my gothic beast was eating the remains of a straw mattress. Brushing a few crows from the backbone of the fond charger, upon which they were innocently roosting, he placed the saddle amidships, and conducted the fiery stallion to my hotel.

Mounting in hot haste, I was about to start for Accomac, when the General of the Mackerel Brigade came down the steps in hot haste, and says he :

" Is the Army of the Potomac about to advance ?"

" Why do you ask ?" says I.

" Thunder !" says he, " I've been so long in one spot that I was going to get out my naturalization papers as a citizen of Arlington Heights. Ah !" says he, with a groan, " when the advance takes place I shall be too old to enjoy it."

I asked him why he didn't make arrangements to have his grandson take his place, if he should become superanuated before the advance took place ; and he said that he be dam.

On reaching Accomac, my boy, I found the Conic Section of the Mackerel Brigade reconnoitering in force after a pullet they had seen the night before. Which they couldn't catch it.

Captain Villiam Brown, my boy, has his head quarters in a house with the attic and cellar on the same floor. I found two fat pickets playing poker on the roof, six first class pickets doing up Old Sledge on the rail-fence in front of the door, and eight consumptive pickets eating a rooster belonging to the Southern Confederacy on the roof of a pig-pen.

As I entered the airy and commodious apartment of the commander-in chief, I beheld a sight to make the muses stare like the behemoth of the Scriptures, and cause genius to take another nip of old rye. There was the cantankerous captain, my boy, seated on a keg of gunpowder, with his head laid sideways on a table ; one hand grasping a bottle half full of the Oath, and the other writing something on a piece of paper laid at right angles with his nose.

" Hallo, my interesting infant," says I, " are you drawing a map of Pensacola for an enlightened press ?"

" Ha !" says Villiam, starting up, and eyeing me closely through the bottom of a bottle, " you behold me in the agonies of composition. Read this poickry," says he, " and if it aint double X with the foam off, where's your Milton ?"

I took the paper, my boy, which resembled a specimen-card of dead flies, and read this poem :

> " The God of Bottles be our aid,
>   When rebels crack us ;
>   We'll bend the bottle-neck to him,
>   And he will Bacchus.
>   " By Capt. VILLIAM BROWN, Eskevire."

I told Villiam that everything but the words of his poem reminded me of Longfellow, and says he :

"Don't mention my undoubted genius in public; because if Seward knew that I wrote poickry, he'd think I wanted to be President in 1865, and he'd get the Honest Old Abe to remove me. I think," says Villiam, abstractedly, "that the Honest Old Abe is like a big bumble bee with his tail cut off, when his Cabinet comes humming around him."

Villiam once stirred up the monkeys in a menagerie, my boy, and his metaphors from Natural History are chaste.

At this moment a file of the Mackerel Brigade came in, bringing a son of Africa, who looked like a bottle of black ink wrapt up in a dirty towel, and a citizen of Accomac, who claimed him as his slave.

"Captain," says the citizen of Accomac, "this nigger belongs to me, and I want him back. Besides, he stole a looking-glass from me, and has got it hid somewheres."

Villiam smiled like a pleased clam, and says he : "You say he stole a looking-glass ?"

"I reckon," says Accomac.

"Prisonier !" says Villiam, to the Ethiop, "did you ever see the devil ?"

"Nebber, sar, since missus died."

"Citizen of Accomac," says Villiam, sternly, "you have told a whopper ; and I shall keep this child of oppression to black the boots of the United States of America. You say he stole a looking-glass. He says he has never seen the devil. Observe now," says Villiam, argumentatively, "how plain it is, that if he *had* even *looked* at your looking-glass, he *must* have seen the devil about the same time."

The citizen of Accomac saw that his falsehood was discovered, my boy, and returned to the bosom of his family cursing like a rifled parson. Villiam then adjourned the court for a week, and sent the contraband out to enjoy the blessings of freedom, digging trenches.

It is pleasing, my boy, to see our commanders dispensing justice in this manner ; and I don't wonder at the President's wanting to abolish the Supreme Court.   Yours, judicially,

ORPHEUS C. KERR.

LETTER XXIII.

CONCERNING BRITISH NEUTRALITY AND ITS COSMOPOLITAN EFFECTS, WITH SOME ACCOUNT OF HOW CAPTAIN BOB SHORTY LOST HIS COMPANY.

WASHINGTON, D. C., December 20th, 1861.

WHEN Britain first, at Napoleon's command, my boy, arose from out the azure main, this was her charter, her charter of the land, that Britains never, never, never shall be slaves as long as they have a chance to treat everybody else like niggers. Suffer me also to remark, that, Britannia needs no bulwarks, no towers along the steep; her march is o'er the mountain wave, her home is on the deep—where she keeps up her neutrality by smuggling contraband Southern confederacies, and swearing like a hardshell chaplain when Uncle Sam's ocean pickets overhaul her.

Albion's neutrality is waking up a savage spirit in the United States of America, as you will understand from the following Irish Idle which was written

PRO PAT-RIA.

Two Irishmen out of employ,
    And out at the elbows as aisily,
Adrift in a grocery-store
    Were smoking and taking it lazily.
The one was a broth of a boy,
    Whose cheek-bones turned out and turned in again,
His name it was Paddy O'Toole—
    The other was Misther McFinnigan.

" I think of enlistin'," says Pat,
    " Because do you see what o'clock it is;
There's nothin' adoin' at all
    But drinkin' at Mrs. O'Docharty's.
It's not until after the war
    That business times will begin again,
And fightin's the duty of all "—
    " You're right, sir," says Misther McFinnigan.

" Bad luck to the rebels, I say,
    For kickin' up all of this bobbery,
They call themselves gintlemen, too,
    While practin' murder and robbery;
Now if it's gintale for to steal,
    And take all your creditors in again,
I'm glad I'm no gintleman born "—
    " You're right, sir," says Misther McFinnigan.

" The spalpeens make bould to remark
    Their chivalry couldn't be ruled by us;
And by the same token I think
    They're never too smart to be fooled by us.
Now if it's the nagurs they mane
    Be chivalry, then it's a sin again
To fight for a cause that is black "—
    " You're right, sir," says Misther McFinnigan.

"A nagur's a man, ye may say,
    And aiqual to all other Southerners;
But chivalry's made him a brute,
    And so he's a monkey to Northerners;
Sure, look at the poor cratur's heels,
    And look at his singular shin again;
It's not for such gintlemen fight "—
    "You're right, sir," says Misther McFinnigan.

"The nagur States wanted a row,
    And now, be me sowl, but they've got in it!
They've chosen a bed that is hard,
    However they shtrive for to cotton it.
I'm thinkin', when winter comes on
    They'll all be inclined to come in again;
But then we must bate them at first "—
    "You're right, sir," says Misther McFinnigan.

"Och hone! but it's hard that a swate
    Good-lookin' young chap like myself indade,
Should loose his ten shillins a day
    Because of the throuble the South has made:
But that's just the raison, ye see,
    Why I should help Union to win again ·
It's that will bring wages once more "—
    "You're right, sir," says Misther McFinnigan.

"Joost mind what ould England's about,
    A sendin' her throops into Canaday;
And all her ould ships on the coast
    Are ripe for some treachery any day.
Now if she should mix in the war—
    Be jabers! it makes me head spin again!
Ould Ireland would have such a chance !"—
    "You're right, sir," says Misther McFinnigan.

"You talk about Irishmen, now,
    Enlistin' by thousands from loyalty;
But *wait till the Phœnix Brigade*
    Is called to put down British Royalty !

It's then with the Stars and the Stripes
 All Irishmen here would go in again,
To strike for the Shamrock and Harp!"—
  "You're right, sir," says Misther McFinnigan.

"Och, murther! me blood's in a blaze,
 To think of bould Corcoran leading us
Right into the camp of the bastes
 Whose leeches so long have been bleeding us!
The Stars and the Stripes here at home
 To Canada's walls we would pin again,
And wouldn't we raise them in Cork?"—
  "You're right, sir," says Misther McFinnigan.

"And down at the South, do ye mind,
 There's plinty of Irishmen mustering,
Deluded to fight for the wrong
 By rebel mis-statements and blustering;
But once let ould England, their foe,
 To fight with the Union begin again,
And sure, they'd desert to a man!"—
  "You're right, sir," says Misther McFinnigan.

"There's niver an Irishmen born,
 From Maine to the end of Secessiondom,
But longs for a time and a chance
 To fight for this country in Hessian-dom;
And so, if ould England should try
 With treacherous friendship to sin again,
They'll all be on one side at once"—
  "You're right, sir," says Misther McFinnigan.

"We've brothers in Canada, too—
 (And didn't the Prince have a taste of them?)—
To say that to Ireland they're true ·
 Is certainly saying the laste of them.
If, bearing our flag at our head,
 We rose Ireland's freedom to win again,
They'd murther John Bull in the rear!"—
  "You're right, sir," says Misther McFinnigan.

" Hurroo ! for the Union, me boys,
  And divil take all who would bother it,
Secession's a nagur so black
  The divil himself ought to father it ;
Hurroo ! for the bould 69th,
  That's prisintly bound to go in again ;
It's Corcoran's rescue they're at "—
  " You're right, sir," says Misther McFinnigan.

" I'm off right away to enlist,
  And sure won't the bounty be handy-O !
 To kape me respectably dressed
  And furnish me dudheens and brandy-O !
I'm thinkin', me excellent friend,
  Ye're eyeing that bottle of gin again ;
You wouldn't mind thryin' a drop "—
  " You're *right,* sir," says Misther McFinnigan.

British neutrality, my boy, reminds me of a chap
I once knew in the Sixth Ward. Two solid men,
who didn't get drunk more than once a day, were
running for alderman, and they both made a dead set
on this chap ; but they hadn't any money, and he
couldn't see it.

" See here, old tops," says he, " I'll be a neutral
this time ; so go in porgies !"

Well, my boy, the election came off, and neither
of the old tops was elected. No, sir ! Now, who do
you suppose *was* elected ?

The *Neutral Chap,* my boy !

Mad as hornets with the hydrophobia, the two old
tops went to see him, and says they :

"Confound your picture, didn't you promise to be neutral?"

The chap dipped his nose into a cocktail, and then says he, blandly:

"I *was* neutral, old Persimmonses. I only went to fifty Democrats, and got 'em to vote for me. Then to be neutral, I had to get fifty of the other feller's Black Republicans to do the same thing. Then I voted twelve times for myself, *and went in.*"

It was a very beautiful case, my boy, and the old tops were only heard to utter—they were only known to exclaim—they were barely able to articulate—that neutrality didn't pay.

Early yesterday morning, my boy, Company B, Regiment 3, Mackerel Brigade, went down toward Centreville on a reconnoissance in force under Captain Bob Shorty. The Captain is a highly intellectual patriot, and don't get his sword twisted between his legs when he carries it in his hand. He led the company through the mud like a Christmas duck, until they came to a thicket in which something was seen to move.

"Halt, you tarriers!" says Captain Bob Shorty, in a voice trembling with bravery. "Form yourselves into a square according to Hardee, while I stir up this here bush. There's something in that bush," says he, "and it's either the Southern Confederacy, or some other cow."

The captain then leaned up to a tree to make him steady on his pins, my boy, and rammed his sword into the bushes like a poker into a fire—thus :

Nobody hurt on our side.

What followed, my boy, can be easily told. At an early hour on the evening of the same day, a solitary horseman might have been seen approaching Washington. It was Captain Bob Shorty, with his hat caved in, and a rainbow spouting under his left eye. He went straight to the head-quarters of the General of the Mackerel Brigade, and says he :

"General, I've reconnoitered in force, and found the enemy both numerious and cantankerous."

"Beautiful !" says the general ; "but where is your company ?"

"Well, now," says Captain Bob Shorty, "you'd hardly believe it ; but the last I see of that ere company, it was engaged in the pursuit of happiness at the rate of six miles an hour, with the rebels at the wrong end of the track. Dang my rations !" says

Captain Bob Shorty, "if I don't think that ere bob-tailed company has got to Richmond by this time."

"Thunder !" says the general, "didn't they kill any of the rebels ?"

"Nary a Confederacy," says Captain Bob Shorty. "The bullets all rolled out of them ere muskets of theirs before the powder got fairly on fire. Them muskets," continued Captain Bob Shorty, "would be good for a bombardment. You might possibly hit a city with them at two yards' range ; but in personal encounters they are inferior to the putty-blowers of our innocent childhood."

As the captain made this observation, my boy, he stepped hurriedly to the table, lifted a tumbler containing the Oath to his pallid lips, took a seat in the coal-scuttle, and burst into a flood of tears.

Deeply affected by this touching display of a beautiful trait in our common nature, the general placed a small piece of ice on the captain's slanting brow, and hid his own emotions in a bottle holding about a quart.

In reference to the beautiful battle-piece, accompanying this epistle, my boy, allow me to observe that it was taken on the spot by the *Chiar' oscuro* artist, Patrick de la Roach, well-known in his native Italy as "Roachy." He studied in Rome (New York), and has a style peculiar for its width of tone and length of breath. The dark complexion of the figures in this fine picture represents the effects of the Virginia sun. Our troops are much tanned. The work was painted in oil colors with a bit of charcoal, my boy, and a copy of it will probably be ordered for the Capitol.   Yours, for high old art,

ORPHEUS C. KERR.

LETTER XXIV.

NARRATING THE MACKEREL BRIGADE'S MANNER OF CELEBRATING
CHRISTMAS, AND NOTING A DEADLY AFFAIR OF HONOR BETWEEN
TWO WELL-KNOWN OFFICERS.

WASHINGTON, D. C., December 26th, 1861.

A MERRY Christmas and Happy New Year, my
boy, and the same to yourself. The recurrence of
these gay old annuals makes me feel as ancient as the
First Families of Virginia, and as grave as a churchyard. How well I remember my first Christmas !
Early in the morning, my dignified paternal presented me with a beautiful spanking, and then my
maternal touched me up with her slipper to stop my
crying. Sensible people are the women of America,
my boy ; they slap a boy on his upper end, which
makes him howl, and then hit him on the other end
to stop his noise. There's good logic in the idea, my
boy. That first Christmas of mine was memorable
from the fact that my present was a drum, on which
I executed a new opera of my own composition with
such good effect, that in the evening, a deputation of
superannuated neighbors and old maids waited on my

father with a petition that he would send me to sea immediately.

But to return to the present, suffer me to observe that last Wednesday was celebrated by the Mackerel Brigade in a manner worthy of the occasion. Two hundred turkeys belonging to the Southern Confederacy were served up for dinner, and from what I tasted, I am satisfied that they belonged to the First Families. They were very tough, my boy.

In the evening, there was a ball, to which a number of the women of America were invited. Captain Villiam Brown came up from Accomac on purpose to attend, and looked, as the General of the Mackerel Brigade genteelly expressed it, like a bag of indigo that had been out without an umbrella in a hard shower of brass buttons. The general has an acute perception of the Beautiful, my boy.

Villiam took the Oath six times, and then took a survey of the festive scene through the bottom of a tumbler. The first person he recognized was the youngest Miss Muggins, waltzing like a deranged balloon with Captain Bob Shorty: Captain Bob was spinning around like a dislocated pair of tongs, and smirked like a happy fiend. Villiam gave one stare, put the tumbler in his pocket, and then made a beeline for the pair.

" Miss Muggins," says he, " you'll obleege me by

dropping that air mass of brass buttons and moustaches, and dancing with me."

" I beg your parding, sir," says Miss Muggins, with dignity, " but I chooses my own company."

" Villiam," says Captain Bob Shorty, " if you don't take that big nose of yours away, it will be my painful duty to set it a little further back in your repulsive countenance."

Then Villiam *was* mad. He hastily buttoned his coat up to the neck, took a bite of tobacco, and says he :

" Captain Shorty, we have lived like br-r-others ; I have borrowed many a quarter of you ; and you promised that when I died, you would wrap me up in the American flag. But now you are mine enemy, and—ha ! ha !—I am yours. Wilt fight ?"

'Twas enough !

" I wilt," responded Captain Bob Shorty. And in ten minutes' time these desperate men stood face to face on the banks of the Potomac, the ghastly moon looking solemnly down upon them through a rift of floating shrouds ; and one of the First Families of Virginia pickets squinting at them from a neighboring bush. Villiam's second was Colonel Wobert Wobinson of the Western Cavalry, Captain Bob Shorty's was Samyule Sa-mith. The fifth of the party was a fat surgeon from St. Louis, who stood with his sleeves rolled up and a big jack-knife in his hand. The surgeon also had a stomach pump with him, my boy, and twelve boxes of anti-bilious pills. The weapons were pistols, and the distance seventy paces.

Captain Villiam Brown was observed to shiver, as he took his place, and was so cold, that he took aim at the surgeon instead of his antagonist. The surgeon called his attention to this little error ; and he immediately rectified his mistake by pointing his weapon point-blank at Samyule Sa-mith.

" You blood-thirsty cuss !" shouted Samyule, with great emotion, " what are you pointing at me for ?"

" I was thinking of my poor grandmother," said Villiam, feelingly ; and immediately fired at the moon.

Simultaneously, Captain Bob Shorty sent his bullet skimming along the ground, in the direction of Washington, and said that he wanted to go home.

The surgeon decided that nobody was hurt ; and the two infuriated principals commenced to reload their pistols, with horrible calmness.

Now it came to pass, that while Captain Villiam Brown was stooping down fixing his weapon, his hand became unsteady, and he pulled the trigger, without meaning to. Bang ! went the concern, and whiz ! went the ball right between the legs of Colonel Wobert Wobinson, causing that noble officer to skip four times, and swear awfully.

" Treachery !" says Captain Bob Shorty, spinning around in great excitement, and letting drive at Samyule Sa-mith who happened to be nearest.

" Gaul darn ye !" screamed Samyule, turning purple in the face, " you've gone and shot all the rim of my cap off."

" I couldn't help it," says Bob, looking into the barrel of his pistol with great intensity of gaze.

At this moment, Villiam, who had loaded up again, tried to put the hammer of his weapon down on the cap ; but his hand slipped, and the charge exploded, barking the shins of the fat surgeon, and sending a bullet clean through his stomach-pump.

The surgeon just took a seat, my boy, rubbed his shins half a second, took four boxes of pills, and then began to cuss! Marshal Rynders can cuss *some*, my boy, but that fat surgeon could beat him and all the Custom-House together.

But suddenly a strange sound reduced all else to silence. It came first like the rumbling of a barrel of potatoes, and then grew into a fiendish chuckle. It was found to proceed from a neighboring bush, and on proceeding thither the party beheld a sight to make the pious weep. Rolling about in the brush was one of the First Families of Virginia pickets, kicking his heels in the air, and laughing himself right straight into apoplexy.

" O Lord !" says he, going into a fresh convulsion,

"take me prisoner and hang me for a rebel, but I never *did* see such a good one as that air gay old duel. If you'd kept on," says the picket, turning purple in the face, "I really reckon I should a busted myself."

Captain Villiam Brown was greatly scandalized at this unseemly mirth, my boy, and requested the surgeon to cut the picket's head off; but Colonel Wobert Wobinson interposed, and the laughing chap was only made prisoner.

"And now, Villiam," says Captain Bob Shorty, "we've had the satisfaction of gentlemen, and can be friends again. I spurns Miss Muggins. The American flag is my only bride, and as for you!—well, I think rather more of you than I do of my own father."

"Come to my arms!" exclaimed Villiam, falling upon his neck, and improving the opportunity to take the Oath from his canteen.

It was an affecting sight, my boy; and as those two noble youths walked amicably back to the camp together, the fat surgeon remarked to Samyule Sa-mith that they reminded him of Damon and Pythias just returned from the Syracuse Convention.

Yours, for the Code,
ORPHEUS C. KERR.

LETTER XXV.

PRESENTING THE CHAPLAIN'S NEW YEAR POEM, AND REPORTING THE
SINGULAR CONDUCT OF THE GENERAL OF THE MACKEREL BRIGADE
ON THE DAY HE CELEBRATED.

WASHINGTON, D. C., January 2d, 1862.

ANOTHER year, my boy, has dawned upon a struggle
in which the hopes of freedom and integrity all over
the world are breathlessly involved ; and if the day-
star of Liberty is destined to go down into the ocean
wave, what is to become of the unoffending negroes ?
I extract this beautiful passage, my boy, from the
forthcoming speech of a fat Congressman, who is a
friend to the human race, and charges the Administration with imbecility and with mileage. I conversed
with him the other evening, and, after discussing various topics, asked him what he thought of the Washington statue as it stood ? He winked three times,
and then says he :

"The only Washington statue I know anything
about, is *statu quo.*"

The chaplain of the Mackerel Brigade joined seriously in our staff festivities on New Year's eve, my
boy ; but as midnight approached he grew very silent,

and at a quarter of twelve he arose from his seat by the fire and asked permission to read something which he had written.

"I would not retard your inevitable inebriation," says he to us, as he drew a manuscript from one of his pockets, "but it is only fitting that we should pay some regard to

"THE DYING YEAR.

"Dying at last, Old Year!
Another stroke of yonder clock, and thou
    Wilt pass the threshold of the world we see
Into the world where Yesterday and Now
    Blend with the hours of the No More To Be.

"I saw the moon last night
Rise like a crown from the dim mountain's head,
    And to the Council of the Stars take way;
For thou, the king, though kinsman of the dead,
    Swayed still the sceptre of Another Day.

"I see the moon to-night,
Sightless and misty as a mourner's eye,
    Behind a vail; or, like a coin to seal
The lids of Time's last-born to majesty,
    Touched with the darkness of a hidden Leal.

"Mark where yon shadow crawls
By slow degrees beneath the window-sill,
    Timed by the death-watch, ticking slow and dull;
The tide of night is rising, black and still—
    Old Year, thou diest when 'tis at its full!

"Ay! moan and moan again,
And shake all Nature in thine agony,
    And tear the ermine robes that mock thee now
Like gilded fruit upon a blasted tree;
    To-morrow comes! To-morrow, where are Thou?

" Wouldst thou be shrived, Old Year?
Thou subtle sentence of delusive Time,
   Framed but to deepen all the mystery
Of Life's great purpose ! Come, confess the crime,
   And man's Divinity shall date from thee !

" Speak to my soul, Old Year;
Let but a star leave its bright eminence
   In thy death-struggle, if this deathless Soul
Holds its own destiny and recompense
   In the grand mast'ry of a GOD'S control !

" No sound, no sign from thee ?
And must I live, not knowing why I live,
   Whilst Thou and years to come pass by me here
With faces hid, refusing still to give
   The one poor word that bids me cease to fear ?

" That word, I charge thee, speak !
Quick ! for the moments tremble on the verge
   Of the black chasm where lurks the midnight spell,
And solemn winds already chant thy dirge—
   Give Earth its Heaven, or Hell a deeper Hell !

" Speak ! or I curse thee here !
I'll call it YEA if but a withered twig,
   Tossed by the wind, falls rattling on the roof;
I'll call it YEA, if e'en a shutter creak,
   Breathe but on me, and it shall stand for proof !

" Too late ! The midnight bell—
The crawling shadow at its witching flood,
   With the deep gloom of the Beyond is wed,
And I, unanswered, sit within and brood,
   And thou, Old Year, art silent—Thou art DEAD !"

When the chaplain finished his reading, my boy, I
told him that he must excuse the party for going to
sleep, as they were really very tired.

On New Year's day, my boy, the General of the Mackerel Brigade desired me to make a few calls with him ; and appeared at my lodgings in a confirmed state of kid gloves, which he bought for the express purpose of making a joke.

"A happy New Year to you, my Duke of Wellington," says I. " You look as frisky as a spring lamb."

Immediately a look of intense meaning came over his Corinthian face, and he remarked, with awful solemnity :

" Thunder ! you might better call me a goat, my Prushian blue, seeing that I've got a couple of kids on hand just now."

The joke was a good article in the glove line, my boy, and I don't think that the general had been studying over it more than four hours before we met.

We made our first call at a house where the ladies were covered with smiles as with a garment ; and remarked that the day was fine. The general smiled in return, until his profile reminded me of a cracked tea-pot ; and says he : " Ladies, allow me to tender the compliments of the season. In this wine," says he, " which I hold in my hand, I behold the roses of your cheeks when you blush, and the sparkle of your eyes when you laugh. Let us hope that another New Year will find our unhappy country free from her enemies, and the curse of African slavery blotted out of the map."

I whispered to the general that slavery wasn't on the map at all ; and he confidentially informed me, that I be dam.

We then repaired to a house where the ladies had a very happy expression of countenance, and told us that it was a pleasant day. The general accidentally filled a wine glass with the deuce of the grape, and says he : " Ladies, suffer me to articulate the compliments of the season. This aromatic beverage," says he, " is but a liquid presentment of your blushes and glances. Let us trust that within a year our country will resume the blessings of peace, and the unhappy bondman will be obliterated from the map."

One of the ladies said, " te-he."

Another said that she felt " he ! he ! he !"

" I believe her, my boy !"

As we returned to the street, I told the general that he'd better leave out the map at the next place, and he said that he'd do it if he was'nt afraid that Congress would'nt confirm his appointment, if he did.

We then visited a family where the ladies had faces beaming with happiness, and observed that it was really a beautiful day. The general happened to be placed near a cut-glass goblet, and says he : "Ladies, in compliance with the day we celebrate, I offer the compliments of the season. This mantling nectar," says he, "blushes like women and glitters like her orbs. Let us pray that in the coming twelve months, the stars and stripes will be re-established, and the negro removed from the map."

He also said hic, my boy ; and one of the ladies wanted to know what that meant ?"

I told her that *Hic* was a Latin term from Cicero de Officiis, and meant *Hic jacet*—hear lies.

" O !" says she, " te-he-he !"

On reaching the sidewalk this time, my boy, the general clasped my hand warmly, and said he'd never forget me. He said I was his dear friend, and must never leave him ; and I said I wouldn't.

We then called at a house where the ladies all smiled upon us, and remarked that we were having charming weather. The general raised a glass, and says he :

" Ge-yurls, I am an old man ; but you are the complimens of season. You are blushing like the wine-glass, and also your sparkles. On another New Year's day let our banner—certainly let us all do it. And the negro slavery blot out the map."

As he uttered these feeling words, my boy, he bowed to me and kissed my hand. After which he looked severely at his pocket-handkerchief, and tried to leave the room by way of the fire-place.

I asked him if he hadn't better take some soda ;
and he said, that if I would come and live with him
he would tell me how he came to get married. He
said he loved me.

Shortly after this we called at a residence where
the ladies all looked very happy and said that it was
a fine day. The general threw all the strength of his
face into one eye, and says he :

"Ladles, we are compl'm'ns, and you are the negroes on the map. This year—pardon me, I should
intro-interror-oduce my two friends who is drunk—
this year I say, our country may be hap—"

Here the general turned suddenly to me with tears
in his eyes, and asked me to promise that I would
never, never leave him. He said that I was a
gen'l'm'n, and ought to give up drinking. I conducted him tenderly to the hall, where he em-
braced me passionately, and invited me to call and
see him.

As soon as he had made a few remarks to a lamp-
post, requesting it to call at Willard's as it went
home, and tell his wife that he was well, I took his
arm, and we moved on at right angles.

It is worthy of remark that at our next calling-
place the ladies all beamed with joy, and told us that
it was a delightful day. The general took a looking-
glass for a window, and stood still before it, until I
tapped him on the shoulder.

"D'you zee that drunken fool standing there in the street?" says he, pointing at the mirror. "It's Lord Lyons, s'drunk as a fool."

I told him that he saw only his own figure in the glass, and he said he would see me safe home if I would go right away. Chancing at the moment to catch sight of a wine-glass, my boy, he walked toward it in a circle, and hastily filled the outside of it from an empty decanter. Then balancing himself on one foot, and placing his disengaged hand on a pyramid of *blanc mange* to support himself, he said impressively :

"Ladles, and gentle-lemons, the army will move on the first of May, and—"

Here the general went down under the table like a stately ship foundering at sea, and was heard to ask the wine-cooler to tell his family that he died for his country.

Owing to the very hilly nature of the street, my boy, I was obliged to accompany the general home in a hack ; and as we rolled along towards the hotel, he disclosed to me an agitated history of his mother's family.

When last I saw him he was trying to make out why the chambermaid had put four pillows on his bed, and endeavoring to lift off the two extra ones without disturbing the others.

Candidly speaking, my boy, this New-Year's-calls business is not a sensible calling, and simply amounts to a caravan of monkeys attending a menagerie of trained crinoline.

Yours, philosophically,

ORPHEUS C. KERR.

LETTER XXVI.

GIVING THE PARTICULARS OF A FALSE ALARM, AND A BIOGRAPHICAL
SKETCH OF THE OFFICER COMMANDING.

WASHINGTON, D. C., January 11th, 1862.

SCARCE had the glorious sun shot up the dappled
orient on Monday morn, my boy, when the Com-
mander-in-Chief of the Mackerel Brigade received
a telegraphic dispatch which reads as follows :

"General Frost has appeared near Centreville, and
is now covering the wood and road in our rear."

It bore no signature, my boy ; but the general believed the danger to be imminent, and ordered Captain
Bob Shorty to take ten thousand men, and make a
reconnoissance towards Centreville.

"Bob, my cherub," says he, "if you can get behind
the rebel Frost, and take the whole Confederacy prisoners, don't administer the Oath until the Eagle of
America is avenged."

Bob smiled like a happy oyster, and says he :

"Domino !"

'Twas nigh upon the hour of noon when Captain

Bob Shorty and his veterans approached the beautiful village of Centreville. Cross-trees had been placed under the horses of the cavalry to keep them from falling down, and the infantry were arranging themselves so that the bayonets of the front rank shouldn't stick into the rear rank's eyes every time they turned a corner, when a solitary contraband might have been seen eating hoe-cake by the solemn road-side.

"Confederate," said Captain Bob Shorty, approaching him with his sword very much between his legs, "hast seen the rebel Frost and his myrmidions? I come to give him battle, having heard that he was hereabouts."

The Ethiopian took a pentagonal bite of hoecake, and says he :

"Tell Massa Lincon that the frost war werry thick last night, but hab gone by this time."

Captain Bob Shorty took off his cap, my boy, looked carefully into it, put it on again, and frowned awfully.

"Comrades," says he, addressing the troops, "you have all heard of a big thing on Snyder. You now behold it before you. This here reconnoissance," says he, "is what the French would call a *few-paw*. We must turn it into a foraging expedition. Charge on yonder hay-stack, and remember me in your prayers !"

'Twas early eve, my boy, when that splendid army returned to Potomac's shore, with two haystacks for the horses, and ten Confederate chickens for supper.

Nobody hurt on our side.

I inclose the following brief sketch of the gallant soldier who commanded in this brilliant affair.

CAPTAIN ROBERT SHORTY.

This brave young officer was born in the Sixth Ward of New York, and was twenty-one years old upon arriving of age. When but a lad, he studied tobacco and the girls, and ran to fires for his health. When eligible to the right of franchise, he voted seven times in one day, and attracted so much attention from the authorities that his parents resolved to make a lawyer of him. On the breaking out of the war with Mexico, he offered his services to the Government as a major-general, but, for some reason, was not accepted. He will probably be sent to supersede General Halleck, in Missouri, as soon as any one of St. Louis writes to ask the President for another change.

The general was so pleased when he heard of this spirited action, my boy, that he offered to review the Mackerel Brigade the next morning, and privately informed me that he considered the Southern Confederacy doomed to expire in less than three months. He said that it was already tottering to its fall, which must take place in the Spring.

Perhaps so, my boy—perhaps so !

Yours, for the flag,

ORPHEUS C. KERR.

LETTER XXVII.

TOUCHING INCIDENTALLY UPON THE CHARACTER OF ARMY FOOD, AND
CELEBRATING THE GREAT DIPLOMATIC EXPLOIT OF CAPTAIN VILLIAM
BROWN AT ACCOMAC.

WASHINGTON, D. C., January 19th, 1862.

IN the early part of the week I resolved to go
down to Accomac, on a flying visit to Captain Villiam
Brown and the Conic Section of the Mackerel Brigade.
Accordingly, I went to the shoemaker's after my
gothic steed Pegasus. The shoemaker, had said, my
boy, that there was enough loose leather hanging
about the architectural animal to make me a nice
pair of slippers, and I gave him permission to cut
them out. The operation only made the Morgan's
back look a little more like the roof of a barn ; but
I like him all the better for that, because he sheds
the rain easier.

The General of the Mackerel Brigade at first intended to accompany me to Accomac ; and says he
to Samyule Sa-mith, the orderly, says he : "Samyule !
just step down to the anatomical museum of the
Western chaps, and buy me the best horse you can
find in the collection. Here's a dollar and half—

fifty cents for the horse and a dollar for yc
trouble."

Samyule came back in about forty minutes, a]
says he :.

" Colonel Wobert Wobinson, of the Western Ca·
alry, says I must come again this afternoon, as l
don't know whether there'll be any horses left (
not."

" Thunder !" says the General. " How left ?"

" Vy," says Samyule, " he can't tell whether an'
horses will be left until the boys have had their din·
ner, can he !"

" Ah !" says the General, contemplatively, " I forgot the beef-soup recommended by the doctors. It
will be a pleasant change for the boys," says he,
" from the mutton that was so plenty just after them
mules died."

Speaking of dinner, my boy ; let me tell you about
a curious occurrence in our camp lately. Just after
a load of rations had come in, a New York chap says
to me, says he :

" I'm glad they're going to put down the Russ
pavement here pretty soon ; for it's getting damp as
thunder."

" Id-jut !" said I, sarcastically, " where have you
seen any Russ pavement ?"

He just took me softly by the arm, my boy, and
led me a little way, and pointed, and says he :

" If you'll just look there, you'll see some of the blocks."

" Why," says I, " those are army biscuit for the men."

" Biscuit !" says he, rubbing his stomach, and turning up his eyes like a cat with the apoplexy—" if them's biscuit, Bunker Hill Monument must be built of flour—that's all."

And he went out and took the Oath.

On arriving at Accomac, my boy, I asked a blue-and-gold picket where Villiam Brown was, and he said that he was in the library.

The library was used by the former occupants of the residence as a hen-house, and contains two volumes—Hardee abridged, and " Every Man His Own Letter-Writer," Seward's edition.

I found Captain Villiam Brown seated on what was formerly a Shanghai's nest, my boy, with his feet out of the window, and his head against a roost. He was studying the last-named book, and sipping Old Bourbon the Oath, in the intervals. The intervals were numerous.

" Son of the Eagle," says I, " you remind me of Sir Walter Scott, at Abbotsford."

Villiam looked abstractedly at me, at the same time moving the tumbler a little further from my hand, and says he :

" I've been in the agonies of diplomacy, but feel

much better. "Ha !" says Villiam, beaming like a
new comet, "I've preserved our foreign relations
peaceful, without humbling the United States of
America."

I asked an explanation, and he informed me that
on the evening before, one of his men had boarded an
Accomac scow in Goose Creek, and captured two oppressed negroes, named Johnson and Peyton, who
were carrying news to the enemy. "At first," says
Villiam, sternly, "I thought of letting them off with
hanging, but I soon felt that they deserved something
worse, and so—" says Villiam, with a malignant
scowl that made my blood run cold—"and so, I sentenced them to read Sumner's speech on the Trent
affair."

On the following morning there came the following
letter from the righteously-exasperated citizens of
Accomac, which Villiam labeled as

DOCKYMENT I.

Sweet Villiam—Sir:—I am instructed by the
neutral Government of Accomac to assure the United
States of America, that the feeling at present existing between the two Governments is of such a cordial
nature, that love itself never inspired more heaving
emotions in the buzzums of conglomerated youth.

Therefore, the outrage committed by the United
States of America on the flag of Accomac, in removing from its protection two gentlemen named John-

son and Peyton, is something for demons to rejoice over. The daughter of the latter gentleman has already slapped her mother in the face, and bared her buzzum to the breeze.

I am instructed by the government of Accomac to demand the instant return of the two gentlemen, together with an ample apology for the base deed, and the amount of that little bill for forage.

Again assuring you of the cordial feeling existing between the two countries, and the passionate affection I feel for yourself, I am, dear sir, most truly, dear sir, as ever, respected sir, your attached

WILLIAM GOAT.

On receiving this communication from Mr. Goat, my boy, Captain Villiam Brown removed Lieutenant Thomas Jenks from the command of the artillery, and ordered six reviews of the troops without umbrellas. He then had a small keg of the Oath rolled into the library, rumpled up his hair, shut one eye, and replied to Mr. Goat with

DOCKYMENT II.

LORD GOAT—SIR :—I take much felicity in receiving your lordship's note, which shows that the neutral Government of Accomac and the United States of America still cherish the feelings that do credit to Anglo-Saxon hearts of the same parentage.

The two black beings, at present stopping in the barn attached to the present head-quarters, were contraband of war ; but were, nevertheless, engaged in the peaceful occupation of asking the protection of your lordship's government.

Were I to decide this question in favor of the United States of America, I should forever forfeit the right of every American citizen to treat niggers as sailable articles, since I would thereby deny their right to sail. The Congress of the United States of America has been fighting for this right for more than a quarter of a century, and I cannot find it in me heart to debar it of that divine privilege for the future.

I might cite Wheaton, Story, Bulwer, Kent, Marryat, Sheridan, and Busteed, to sustain my position, were I familiar with those international righters.

Therefore I am compelled to humble your lordship's government by returning the two black beings aforesaid, and beg leave to assure your lordship that I am your lordship's only darling,

VILLIAM BROWN, Eskevire,

Captain Conic Section, Mackerel Brigade.

After reading this able and brilliant document, my boy, I told Villiam that I thought he had made a very good point about negroes always being "sailable articles," and he said that was diplomacy.

"Ah!" says he, sadly, "my father always said that if you could not get over a rail fence by high-jump-acy, there was nothing like dip-low-macy. My dad was a natural statesman. Ah!" says Villiam, in a fine burst of filial emotion, " I wonder where the durned old fool is now."

This idea plunged him into such a depth of reverie, that I left him without another word, mounted Pegasus, and ambled reflectively back to the Capitol.

Diplomacy brings out the intellect of a nation, my boy, and is a splendid thing to use until we get our navy finished.

Yours, in memory of Metternich,
ORPHEUS C. KERR.

LETTER XXVIII.

CONCERNING THE CONTINUED INACTIVITY OF THE POTOMAC ARMY, AND
SHOWING HOW IT WAS POETICALLY CONSTRUED BY A THOUGHTFUL
RADICAL.

WASHINGTON, D. C., January 30th, 1862.

NOTWITHSTANDING the hideous howlings of the
Black Republicans, my boy, and the death of six
Confederate pickets from old age, the Army of the
Potomac will not commence the forward movement
until the mud subsides sufficiently to show where
some of the camps are. The Mackerel Brigade dug
out a regiment yesterday, near Alexandria ; but
there's no use of continuing the business without a
dredging-machine.

I was talking to Captain Bob Shorty, on Tuesday,
respecting the inactivity of the army, and says he :

" It's all very well to talk about making an advance,
my beauty ; but I've known one of the smartest men
in the country to fail in it."

" What mean you, fellow ?" says I.

" Why," says he, " you know Simpson, your
uncle ?"

" I believe you, my boy !" says I.

"Well!" says Captain Bob Shorty, "that air Simpson is one of the smartest old cusses in the country—yet there ain't no 'On to Richmond' about *him*. I asked him once, myself, to make an advance. I asked him to make an advance on my repeater, and he said he couldn't."

This argument, my boy, exposes thoroughly the base disloyalty and fiendish designs of the newspaper brigadiers who are constantly urging McClellan to advance—advance! Let them all be sent to Fort Lafayette, and the moral effect on this cursed rebellion will be such that it will utterly collapse in two hours and forty-three minutes.

The serious New Haven chap, of whom I spoke to you some time ago, takes a "radical" view of our long halt, and gives his ideas in

THE MIDNIGHT WATCH.

Soldier, soldier, wan and gray,
  Standing there so very still,
On the outpost looking South,
  What is there to-night to kill?

Through the mist that rises thick
  From the noisome marsh around,
I can see thee like a shade
  Cast from something underground.

And I know that thou art old,
  For thy features, sharp, and thin,
Cut their lines upon the shroud
  Damply folding thee within.

Fit art thou to watch and guard
　O'er the brake and o'er the bog;
By the glitter of thine eyes
　Thou canst pierce a thicker fog.

Tell me, soldier, grim and old,
　If thy tongue is free to say,
What thou seest looking South,
　In that still and staring way?

Yonderward the fires may glow
　Of a score of rebel camps;
But thou canst not see their lights,
　Through the chilling dews and damps.

Silent still, and motionless?
　Get thee to the tents behind,
Where the flag for which we fight
　Plays a foot-ball to the wind.

Get thee to the bankments high,
　Where a thousand cannon sleep,
While the call that bids them wake
　Bids a score of millions weep.

Thou shalt find an army there,
　Working out the statesman's plots,
While a poison banes the land,
　And a noble nation rots.

Thou shalt find a soldier-host
　Tied and rooted to its place,
Like a woman cowed and dumb,
　Staring Treason in the face.

Dost thou hear me? Speak, or move!
　And if thou wouldst pass the line,
Give the password of the night—
　Halt! and give the countersign.

God of Heaven! what is this
   Sounding through the frosty air,
In a cadence stern and slow,
   From the figure looming there!

"Sentry, thou hast spoken well"—
   Through the mist the answer came—
"I am wrinkled, grim, and old,
   May'st thou live to be the same!

"Thou art here to keep a watch
   Over prowlers coming nigh;
I can show thee, looking South,
   What is hidden from thine eye.

"Here, the loyal armies sleep;
   There, the foe awaits them all;
Who can tell before the time
   Which shall triumph, which shall fall?

"O, but war's a royal game,
   Here a move and there a pause;
Little recks the dazzled world
   What may be the winner's cause.

"In the roar of sweating guns,
   In the crash of sabres crossed,
Wisdom dwindles to a fife,
   Justice in the smoke is lost.

"But there is a mightier blow
   Than the rain of lead and steel,
Falling from a heavier hand
   Than the one the vanquished feel.

"Let the armies of the North
   Rest them thus for many a night;
Not with them the issue lies,
   'Twixt the powers of Wrong and Right.

"Through the fog that wraps us round
   I can see, as with a glass,
Far beyond the rebel hosts
   Fires that cluster, pause, and pass.

"From the wayside and the wood,
   From the cabin and the swamp,
Crawl the harbingers of blood,
   Black as night, with torch and lamp.

"Now they blend in one dense throng;
   Hark! they whisper, as in ire—
Catch the word before it dies—
   Hear the horrid murmur—' Fire!'

"Mothers, with your babes at rest,
   Maidens in your dreaming-land—
Brothers, children—wake ye all!
   The Avenger is at hand.

"Born by thousands in a flash,
   Angry flames bescourge the air,
And the howlings of the blacks
   Fan them to a fiercer glare.

"Crash the windows, burst the doors,
   Let the helpless call for aid;
From the hell within they rush
   On the negro's reeking blade.

"Through the flaming doorway arch,
   Half-dressed women frantic dart;
Demon! spare that kneeling girl—
   God! the knife is in her heart.

"By his hair so thin and gray
   Forth they drag the agéd sire;
First, a stab to stop his pray'r—
   Hurl him back into the fire.

"What! a child, a mother's pride,
　　Crying shrilly with affright!
Dash the axe upon her skull,
　　Show no mercy—she is white.

"Louder, louder roars the flame,
　　Blotting out the Southern home,
Fainter grow the dying shrieks,
　　Fiercer cries of vengeance come.

"Turn, ye armies, where ye stand,
　　Glaring in each others' eyes;
While ye halt, a cause is won;
　　While ye wait, a despot dies.

"Greater victory has been gained
　　Than the longest sword secures,
And the Wrong has been washed out
　　With a purer blood than yours."

Soldier, by my mother's pray'r!
　　Thou dost act a demon's part;
Tell me, ere I strike thee dead,
　　Whence thou comest, who thou art.

Back! I will not let thee pass—
　　Why, that dress is Putnam's own!
Soldier, soldier, where art thou?
　　Vanished—like a shadow gone!

The Southern Confederacy may come to that yet,
my boy, if it don't take warning in time from its
patron Saint. I refer to Saint Domingo, my boy,—
I refer to Saint Domingo.

　　　　　　　　　Yours, musingly,
　　　　　　　　　ORPHEUS C. KERR.

LETTER XXIX.

INTRODUCING A VERITABLE "MUDSILL," ILLUSTRATING YANKEE BUSI-
NESS TACT, NOTING THE DETENTION OF A NEWSPAPER CHARTO-
GRAPHIST, AND SO ON.

WASHINGTON, D. C., February 2d, 1862.

I NEVER really knew what the term "mudsill"
meant, my boy, until I saw Captain Bob Shorty on
Tuesday. I was out in a field, just this side of Fort
Corcoran, trimming down the ears of my gothic steed
Pegasus, that he might look less like a Titanic rabbit,
when I saw approaching me an object resembling a
brown-stone monument. As it came nearer, I discovered an eruption of brass buttons at intervals in
front, and presently I observed the lineaments of a
Federal face.

"Strange being!" says I, taking down a pistol
from the natural rack on the side of my steed, and at
the same time motioning toward my sword, which I
had hung on one of his hip bones, "Art thou the
shade of Metamora, or the disembodied spirit of a
sand-bank ?"

"My ducky darling," responded the æolian voice
of Captain Bob Shorty, " you behold a mudsill just

emerged from a liquified portion of the sacred soil. The mud at present inclosing the Mackerel Brigade is unpleasant to the personal feelings of the corps, but the effect at a distance is unique. As you survey that expanse of mud from Arlington Heights," continued Captain Bob Shorty, " with the veterans of the Mackerel Brigade wading about in it up to their chins, you are forcibly reminded of a limitless plum-pudding, well stocked with animated raisins."

" My friend," says I, " the comparison is apt, and reminds me of Shakspeare's happier efforts. But tell me, my Pylades, has the dredging for those missing regiments near Alexandria proved successful ?"

Captain Bob Shorty shook the mire from his ears, and then, says he :

" Two brigades were excavated this morning, and are at present building a raft to go down to Washington after some soap. Let us not utter complaints against the mud," continued Captain Bob Shorty, reflectively, " for it has served to develop the genius of New England. We dug out a Yankee regiment from Boston first, and the moment those wooden-nutmeg chaps got their breath, they went to work at the mud that had almost suffocated them, mixed up some spoiled flour with it, and are now making their eternal fortunes by peddling it out for patent cement."

This remark of the captain's, my boy, shows that

the spirit of New England still retains its natural
elasticity, and is capable of greater efforts than lignum
vitæ hams and clocks made of barrel hoops and old
coffee-pots. I have heard my ancient grandfather
relate an example of this spirit during the war of
1812. He was with a select assortment of Pequog
chaps at Bladensburg, just before the attack on
Washington, and word came secretly to them that
the Britishers down in the Chesapeake were out of
flour, and would pay something handsome for a supply. Now, these Pequog chaps had no flour, my
boy ; but that didn't keep them out of the speculation. They went into the nearest graveyard, dug up
all the tombstones, and put them into an old quartz-
crushing machine, pounded them to powder, sent the
powder to the coast, and *and sold it to the Britishers
for the very best flour, at twelve dollars and a half
a barrel!*

And can such a people as this be conquered by a
horde of godless rebels ? Never ! I repeat it, sir—
never ! Should the Jeff. Davis mob ever get possession of Washington, the Yankees would build a wall
around the place, and invite the public to come and
see the menagerie, at two shillings a head.

On Wednesday, some of our dryest pickets caught
a shabby, long-haired chap loafing around the camps
with a big block and sheet of paper under his arm,

and brought him before the general of the Mackerel Brigade.

" Well, Samyule," says the general to one of the pickets, " what is your charge against the prisonier ?"

" He is a young man which is a spy," replied Sam-yule, holding up the sheet of paper ; " and I take this here picture of his to be the Great Seal of the Southern Confederacy."

" Why thinkest thou so, my cherub ? and what does the work of art represent ?" inquired the general.

" The drawing is not of the best," responded Sam-yule, closing one eye, and viewing the picture criti-cally ; " but I should say that it represented a ham, with a fiddle laid across it, and beefsteaks in the cor-ners."

" Miserable vandal !" shouted the long-haired chap, excitedly, " you know not what you say. I am a Federal artist ; and that picture is a map of the coast of North Carolina, for a New York daily paper."

" Thunder !" says the general—" if that's a map, a patent gridiron must be a whole atlas."

I believe him, my boy !.

As a person of erudition, it pleased me greatly, my boy, to observe that our more moral New York regi-ments cultivate a taste for reading, and are even so literary that they can't so much as light their pipes without a leaf out of a hymn-book. I was talking

to an angular-shaped chap from Montgomery county
the other day about this, and says he :

"Talk about reading ! Why, there's fifty newspapers sent in a wrapper to our officers alone, every
day. There's ten each of the *Tribune* and *Times*,
ten each of the *Boston Post* and *Gazette*, ten of the
Montgomery Democrat, and one *New York Herald*."

"Look here ! my second Washington," says I,
"your story don't hang together. You say you have
fifty papers daily ; but according to my account that
copy of the *Herald* makes fifty-one."

" Did I not tell you that they came in a wrapper ?'
says the chap, with great dignity.

" You did," says I.

" Well," says he, " the *Herald* is the wrapper."

This morning, my boy, I went with Colonel Wobert
Wobinson to look at some new horses he had just
imported from the Erie Canal stables for the Western
cavalry, and was much pleased with the display of
bone-work. One animal, in particular, interested me
greatly ; he was born in 1776, had both of his hind-
legs broken on the frontier, in one of the battles of
1812, and lost both his eyes and his tail at the taking
of Mexico. The colonel stated that he had selected
this splendid animal for his own use in the field.

Another fine calico animal of the stud was attached
to the suite of Washington at the famous crossing of
the Delaware, and is said to have surprised the Hes-

sians at Trenton as much as the army did. Previous to losing his teeth he was sold to a Western dealer in hides for three dollars ; and the dealer, being an enthusiastic Union man, has let the Government have the animal for one hundred and ten dollars.

A mousseline-de-laine mare also attracted my notice. She was sired by the favorite racer of the Marquis de Lafayette, and has been damned by everybody attempting to drive her. The pretty beast comes from the celebrated Bone Mill belonging to the Erie Canal, and only cost the Government two hundred dollars.

Believing that the public funds are being judiciously expended, my boy, I remain,

Fondly thine own, ORPHEUS C. KERR.

LETTER XXX.

DESCRIPTION OF THE GORGEOUS FÊTE AT THE WHITE HOUSE, INCLUD-
ING THE OBSERVATIONS OF CAPTAIN VILLIAM BROWN : WITH SOME
NOTE OF THE TOILETTES, CONFECTIONS, AND PUNCH.

WASHINGTON, D. C., February 7th, 1862.

NOTWITHSTANDING your general ignorance of Natural History, my boy, you may be aware that when
the eagle is wounded by the huntsman, instead of
seeking some thick-set tree or dismal swamp, there to
die like a common bird, he soars straight upward in
the full eye of the sun, and bathes in all the glories
of noonday, while his eyes grow dull with agony, and
his talons are stiffening in death ; nor does he fall
from the dazzling empyrean until the last stroke of
fate hurls him downward like a thunderbolt.

Our Union, my boy—our Land of the Eagle—is
stricken sorely, and perhaps to death ; but like the
proud bird of Jove, it disdains to grow morbid in its
agonies ; and the occasional sighs of its patient
struggling millions, are lost in sounds of death-defy-
ing revelry at the dauntless capital.

·All the best-looking uniforms in the army were invited to Mrs. Lincoln's ball at the White House on

Wednesday, and of course I was favored, together
with the general of the Mackerel Brigade, and Captain Villiam Brown, of Accomac. My ticket, my
boy, was as aristocractic as a rooster's tail at sunrise :

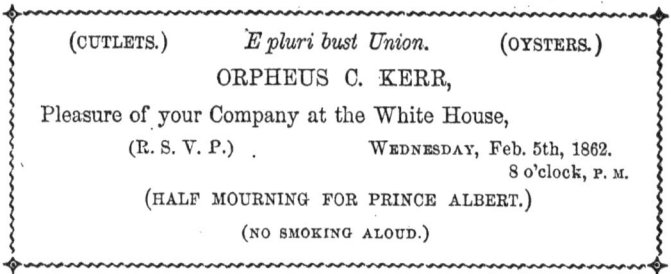

(CUTLETS.)   *E pluri bust Union.*   (OYSTERS.)

ORPHEUS C. KERR,

Pleasure of your Company at the White House,

(R. S. V. P.)   WEDNESDAY, Feb. 5th, 1862.

8 o'clock, P. M.

(HALF MOURNING FOR PRINCE ALBERT.)

(NO SMOKING ALOUD.)

At an early hour on the evening of the *fête*, the
general of the Mackerel Brigade came to my room in
a perfect perspiration of brass buttons and white
kids, and I asked him what "no smoking aloud"
meant.

"Why," says he, putting his wig straight and
licking a stray drop of brandy from one of his gloves,
"it means that if you try to 'smoke' any of the generals at the ball as to the plan of the campaign, you
mustn't do it 'aloud.' Thunder !" says the general,
in a fine glow of enthusinsm, "the only plan of the
campaign that I know anything about, is the rata-
plan."

Satisfied with the general's explanation, I proceeded
with my toilet, and presently beamed upon him in such
a resplendent conglomeration of ruffles, brass buttons,

epaulettes and Hungarian pomade, that he said I reminded him of a comet just come out of a feather-bed,
with its tail done up in papers.

"My Magnus Apollo," says he, "the way you bear
that white cravat shows you to be of rich but genteel
parentage. Any man," says he, "who can wear a
white cravat without looking like a coachman, may
pass for a gentleman-born. Two-thirds of the clergy-
men who wear it look like footmen in their grave-
clothes."

We then took a hack to the White House, my
boy, and on arriving there were delighted to find that
the rooms were already filling with statesmen, miss-
statesmen, mrs-statesmen, and officers, who had so
much lace and epaulettes about them that they
looked like walking brass-founderies with the front-
door open.

The first object that attracted my special attention,
however, was a thing that I took for a large and ornamental pair of tongs leaning against a mantel,
figured in blue enamel, with a life-like imitation of a
window-brush on top. I directed the general's attention to it, and asked him if that was one of the unique
gifts presented to the Government by the late Japa-
nese embassy ?

"Thunder !" says the general, "that's no tongs.
It's the young man which is Captain Villiam Brown,
of Accomac. Now that I look at him," says the gen-

eral, thoughtfully, "he reminds me of an old-fashioned straddle-bug."

Stepping from one lady's dress to another, until I reached the side of the Commander of the Accomac, I slapped him on the back, and says I :

" How are you, my blue-bird ; and what do you think of this brilliant assemblage ?"

" Ha !" says Villiam, starting out of a brown study, and putting some cloves in his mouth, to disguise the water he'd drank on his way from Accomac—" I was just thinking what my poor old mother would say if she could see me and the other snobs here to-night. When I look on the women of America around me to-night," says Villiam, feelingly, "and see how much they've cut off from the tops of their dresses, to make bandages for our wounded soldiers, I can't help feeling that their ' neck-or-nothing ' appearance—so far from being indelicate, is a very delicate proof of their devoted love of Union."

" I agree with you, my azure humanitarian," says I. " There's precious little *waist* about such dresses."

Villiam closed one eye, turned his head one-side like a facetious canary, and says he :

Now lovely woman scants her dress, with bandages the sick to bless ; and stoops so far to war's alarms, her very frock is under arms !"

I believe him, my boy !

Returning to the General, we took a turn in the East Room, and enjoyed the panorama of youth, beauty, and whiskers, that wound its variegated length before us.

The charming Mrs. L——, of Illinois, was richly attired in a frock and gloves, and wore a wreath of flowers from amaranthine bowers. She was affable as an angel with a new pair of wings, and was universally allowed to be the most beautiful woman present.

The enthralling Miss C——, from Ohio, was elegantly clad in a dress, and wore number-four gaiters. So brilliant was her smile, that when she laughed at one of Lord Lyons' witicisms, all one corner of the room was wrapped in a glare of light, and several nervous dowagers cried " Fire !" Her beauty was certainly the most beautiful present.

The fascinating Miss L——, of Pennsylvania, was superbly robed in an attire of costly material, with expensive flounces. She wore two gloves and a complete pair of ear-rings, and spoke so musically that the leader of the Marine Band thought there was an æolian harp in the window. She was certainly the most beautiful woman present.

The bewitching Mrs. G——, from Missouri, was splendidly dressed in a breastpin and lace flounces, and wore her hair brushed back from a forehead like Mount Athos. Her eyes reminded one of diamond springs sparkling in the shade of whispering willows. She was decidedly the finest type of beauty present.

The President wore his coat and whiskers, and bowed to all salutations like a graceful door-hinge.

There was a tall Western Senator present, who smiled so much above his stomach, that I was reminded of the beautiful lines :

> " As some tall cliff that lifts its awful form,
> Swells from the vale, and midway leaves the storm;
> Though round its base a country's ruin spread,
> Eternal moonshine settles on its head."

Upon going into the supper-room, my boy, I beheld a paradise of eatables that made me wish myself a knife and pork, with nothing but a bottle of mustard to keep me company. There were oysters *à la fundum;* turkeys *à la ruffles;* chickens *à la Methusaleh;* beef *à la Bull Run;* fruit *à la stumikake;* jellies *à la Kallararmorbus;* and ices *à la aguefitz.*

The ornamental confectionary was beautifully symbolical of the times. At one end of the table, there was a large lump of white candy, with six carpet-tacks lying upon it. This represented the " Tax on Sugar." At the other end was a large platter, containing imitation mud, in which two candy brigadiers were swimming towards each other, with their swords between their teeth. This symbolized " War."

These being very hard times, my boy, and the Executive not being inclined to be too expensive in its marketing, a most ingenious expedient was adopted to make it appear that there was just twice as much of certain costly delicacies on the table as there really was. About the centre of the table lay a large mirror, and on this were placed a few expensive dishes. Of course, the looking-glass gave them a double effect. For instance, if there was a pound of beefsteak on the plate, it produced another pound in the glass, and the effect was two pounds.

When economy can be thus artistically blended with plentitude, my boy, money ceases to be king, and butcher-bills dwindle. Hereafter, when I receive for my rations a pint of transparent coffee and two granite biscuit, I shall use a looking-glass for a plate.

It was the very which-ing hour of the night when the general and myself left the glittering scene, and we had to ask several patrols " which" way to go.

On parting with my comrade-in-arms, says I :

" General, the ball is a success."

He looked at me in three winks, and says he :

" It *was* a success — particularly the bowl of punch !"   Yours, for soda-water,

ORPHEUS C. KERR.

LETTER XXXI.

WASHINGTON, D. C., February 16th, 1862.

THERE is still much lingual gymnastics, my boy,
concerning the recent *fête* sham-pate at the White
House ; but Colonel Wobert Wobinson, of the Western Cavalry, has extinguished the grumblers by proving that the entertainment was strictly Constitutional.
He profoundly observes, my boy, that it comes under
the head of that clause of the Constitution which
secures to the people of America the "pursuit of happiness ;" and, as he justly remarks, if you stop the
"pursuit of happiness," where's the Instrument of
our Liberties ?

It pleases me greatly to announce, my boy, that
the General of the Mackerel Brigade believes in
McClellan, and gorgeously defends him against the
attacks of that portion of the depraved press which
has friends dying of old age in the Army of the
Potomac.

"Thunder !" says he to Captain Bob Shorty, stirring the Oath in his tumbler with a tooth-brush—

"the way Little Mac is devoting himself to the military squelching of this here unnatural rebellion, is actually outraging his physical nature. He reviews his staff twice a day, goes over the river every five minutes, studies international law six hours before dinner, takes soundings of the mud every time the dew falls, and takes so little sleep, that there's two inches of dust on one of his eye-balls. Would you believe it," says the General, placing the tumbler over his nose to keep off a fly, "his devotion is such that his hair is turning gray and will probably dye !"

Captain Bob Shorty whistled. I do not mean to say that he intended to be musically satirical, my boy ; but if I should hear such a canary-bird remark after *I'd* told a story, somebody would go home with his eyes done up in rainbows.

"Permit *me*," says Captain Bob Shorty, hurling what remained of the Oath into the aperture under his moustache. "You convince me that Little Mac's devotion is extraordinary," continued Captain Bob Shorty, dreamily ; "but he don't come up to a chap I once knew, which was a editor. Talk about devotion ! and outraging nature !" says Captain Bob Shorty, spitting with exquisite accuracy into the eyes of the regimental cat; "why, that ere editor threw body, soul, and breeches into his work ; and so completely identified himself with a free and enlightened press, that his first child was a *newsboy.*"

The General of the Mackerel Brigade arose from his seat, my boy, wound up his watch, brushed off his boots, threw the cat out of the window, and then says he :

"Robert, name of Shorty, did you ever read in the Bible about Ananias, who was struck dead for telling a telegraph ?"

"I heard about him," says Captain Bob Shorty, "when I was but a innocent lamb, and wore my mother's slipper on my back about as often as she wore it on her foot."

"Well," says the general, with the air of a thoughtful parent, "it's my opinion that if you'd been Ananias, the same streak of lightning would have buried you and paid the sexton."

From this logical and vivid conversation, my boy, you will understand that our leading military men have perfect faith in the genius of McClellan, and believe that he is equal to fifty yards of the Star-Spangled Banner. His great anaconda has gathered itself in a circle around the doomed rabbit of rebellion, and if the rabbit swells he's a goner.

This great anaconda, my boy, may remind hellish readers of the anaconda once seen by a chap of my acquaintance living in the Sixth Ward. This chap, my boy, came tearing into a place where they kept the Oath on tap, and says he :

"I've just seen an anaconda down Broadway."

"Anna who ?" says a red-nosed Alderman, dipping his finger into the water on the stove to see if it was warm enough to melt some brandy-refined sugar.

"I said Anaconda, you ignorant cuss," says the chap.

"Was it the real insect ?" says the Alderman.

"It was a real, original, genuine Anaconda," says the chap.

"Ah !" says the Alderman, "somebody's been stuffin' you."

"No, sir !" says the chap, but somebody's been stuffin' the Anaconda, though."

He'd been to the Museum.

If there should be among your unfortunate readers, my boy, any persons of such depraved minds as to perceive a likeness between this Anaconda and that Anaconda, may they be sent to Fort Lafayette, and compelled to read Tupper's poems until the rabbit of rebellion is reduced to his last quarter !

Early this morning a couple of snuff-colored pickets brought a female Southern Confederacy into camp, stating that she had called them nasty things and spit all over their guns. She said that she wanted to see the loathsome creature that commanded them, and her eyes flashed so when they took her by the arm, that her vail took fire twice, and her eyebrows smoked repeatedly.

The General of the Mackerel Brigade received her

courteously, only poking her in the ribs to see if she had any Armstrong guns concealed about her. Says he:

"Have I the honor of addressing the wife of the Southern Confederacy ?"

The female confederacy drew herself up as proudly as the First Family of Virginia when the butcher's bill comes to be paid, and replied, in soprano of great compass :—

"I am that injured woman, you ugly swine."

The General bowed until his lips touched a pewter mug on the table, and then says he :

" My dear madam, your words touch a tender chord in my heart, and it will give me pleasure to serve you. Your words, madam," continued the general, with visible emotion, "are precisely those which my beloved wife not unfrequently addresses to me. Ah ! my wife ! my wifey !" says the general, hysterically, "how often have you patted me on my head, and told me that my face looked like a chunk of beeswax with three cracks in it."

The wife of the Southern Confederacy sneered audibly, and called for a fan. There being no fan nearer than the office of Secretary Welles, she used a small whisk-broom. Says she :

" Miserable hireling of a diabolical Lincoln, your wife is nothing to me. She is a creature ! I do not come here to hear her wrongs, but to express the undying wish that you and all your horde may be welcomed with muddy hands to hospitable graves. All I want is to be let alone."

" My dear Mrs. S. C.," says the general, with a touch of brass and irony, " it is a matter of the utmost indifference to me whether you are ' to be let alone,' or with the next house and lot."

" I insist upon being let alone," screamed the female Confederacy, spitting angrily.

" I am not touching you," says the general.

" All I want is to be let alone," shrieked the exasperated lady ; " and I *will* be let alone !"

The General of the Mackerel Brigade hastily wiped his mouth with a bottle, and then says he :

" Madam, if sandwiches are not plenty where you come from, it ain't for the want of tongue."

On hearing this gastronomic remark, my boy, the injured wife of the Southern Confederacy swept from the room like an insulted Minerva, and departed for Secessia. It was observed that she frowned like a thunder-cloud at every Federal she passed, excepting one picket. Him she smiled on. She had detected him the act of admiring her ankles as she picked her way through the mud.

Woman, my boy, has really many sweet qualities ; and if her head is sometimes in the wrong, she has always a reserve of genuine goodness of heart in the neighborhood of her gaiters. ·

Yours, for the Sex, ORPHEUS C. KERR.

LETTER XXXII.

COMMENCING WITH A BURST OF EXULTATION OVER NATIONAL VICTO-
RIES, REFERRING TO A SENATORIAL MISTAKE, DEPICTING A WELL-
KNOWN CHARACTER, AND REPORTING THE RECONNOISSANCE OF THE
WESTERN CENTAURS.

WASHINGTON, D. C., February 21st, 1862.

Now swells Columbia's bosom with a pride, that
sets her eyes ablaze with living fire ; and, with
her arms upreaching to the skies, she draws in air
new crowns with stars adorned, to ring the temples
of her conquering chiefs. Far in the West, she sees
the livid sparks struck by Achilles from the hostile
sword, and in the South beholds how Ajax bold de-
fies the lightning of the rebel guns. Then clasping
to her breast the flag we love, and donning swift
Minerva's gleaming helm, she stands where Morn's
first glories kiss the hills, and breathes the pæan of a
fame redeemed !

Three cheers for the chaps who pocketed Fort
Donelson & Co., my boy, and may the rebels never
have an easier boat to row than Roanoke. The other
day I was talking with a New England Senator about
the taking of the fort, and says I :

"It was a gay victory, my learned Theban ; but it makes me mad when I think how that slippery rascal, Floyd, found an egress down the river."

The Senator pulled up his collar, my boy, observed to the tumbler-sergeant that he would take the same with a little more sugar in it, and then says he :

"In that observation you sum up the whole cause of this unnatural strife. It is, indeed, the negro, whose wrongs are now being revenged upon us by an inscrutable Whig Providence ; and if the Government does not speedily strike the fetters from the slave, that slave may yet be used to fight horribly against us. I shall cite the significant fact you mention in my next exciting speech."

I opened my eyes at this outburst until they looked like the bottoms of two quart bottles beaming in the sunshine, and then says I :

"You talk as fluently as a Patent Office Report, my worthy Nestor ; but I don't exactly perceive what my remark has to do with the colored negro."

"Why," says he, "didn't you say that the traitor Floyd found a *negress* down the river ?"

For an instant, my boy, I felt very dizzy, and was obliged to lean my head against a tumbler for a moment.

"Your ears, my friend," says I, "are certainly long enough to hear correctly what is said to you ;

but this time you've made a slight mistake. I said that Floyd had found *an egress* down the river."

The Senator looked at me for a moment, and says he :

" Sold by a soldier ! Good morning."

I wonder how those nice, pleasant, gentlemanly chaps down in South Carolina enjoy Uncle Samuel's latest hit ? I can fancy their damaging effects, my boy, upon the constitution of

THE SOUTH CAROLINA GENTLEMAN.

Down in the small Palmetto State, the curious ones may find
A ripping, tearing gentleman, of an uncommon kind—
A staggering, swaggering sort of chap, who takes his whiskey straight,
And frequently condemns his eyes to that ultimate vengeance which
     a clergyman of high standing has assured us must be the sin-
     ner's fate ;
               A South Carolina gentleman,
               One of the present time.

You trace his genealogy, and not far back you'll see
A most undoubted octoroon, or mayhap a mustee ;
And if you note the shaggy locks that cluster on his brow,
You'll find that every other hair is varied with a kink, that seldom
     denotes pure Caucasian blood ; but, on the contrary, betrays an
     admixture with a race not particularly popular now—
               This South Carolina gentleman,
               One of the present time.

He always wears a full-dress coat—pre-Adamite in cut—
With waistcoat of the loudest style, through which his ruffles jut.
Six breastpins deck his horrid front : and on his fingers shine
Whole invoices of diamond rings, which would hardly pass muster
     with the Original Jacobs in Chatham street, for jewels gen-u-ine—
               This South Carolina gentleman,
               One of the present time.

He chews tobacco by the pound, and spits upon the floor,
If there is not a box of sand behind the nearest door ;
And when he takes his weekly spree, he clears a mighty track
Of everything that bears the shape of whisky-skin, gin-and-sugar,
       brandy-sour, peach-and-honey, irrepressible cocktail, rum-and-
       gum, and luscious apple-jack—
               This South Carolina gentleman,
               One of the present time.

He looks on grammar as a thing beneath the notice quite
Of any Southern gentleman whose grandfather was white ;
And as for education—why, he'll plainly set it forth,
That such d—d nonsense never troubles the heads of the Chivalry;
       though it may be sufficiently degrading to merit the per-
       sonal attention of the poor wretches unfortunate enough to
       make their living at the North—
               This South Carolina gentleman,
               One of the present time.

He licks his niggers daily, like a true American ;
And "takes the devil out of them " by this sagacious plan.
He tries his bowie knives upon the fattest he can find ;
And if the darkey winces, why—he is immediately arrested at the
       instance of the First Families in the neighborhood, on a charge
       of conversing with a fiendish abolitionist, and conspiring to
       poison all the wells in the State with strychnine, and arm the
       slaves of the adjoining plantations with knives and pistols ; for
       all of which he is very properly sentenced to five hundred
       ·lashes—after which to prison he's consigned (by)
               This South Carolina gentleman,
               One of the present time.

If for amusement he's inclined, he coolly looks about
For a parson of the Methodists, or some poor peddler lout ;
And having found him, has him hung from some majestic tree—
Then calls his numerous family to enjoy with him the instructive and
       entertaining spectacle of a "suspected abolitionist" receiving
       his just reward at the hands of an incensed com-mu-ni-ty—
               This South Carolina gentleman,
               One of the present time.

He takes to euchre kindly, too; and plays an awful hand,
Especially when those he tricks his style don't understand;
And if he wins, why then he stoops to pocket all the stakes;
But if he loses, then he says unto the unfortunate stranger, who has
     chanced to win: "It's my opinion that you are a cursed aboli-
     tionist; and if you don't leave South Carolina in one hour, you
     will be hung like a dog." But no offer to pay his loss he
     makes—
             This South Carolina gentleman,
             One of the present time.

Of course he's all the time in debt to those who credit give—
Yet manages upon the best the market yields to live;
But if a Northern creditor asks him his bill to heed,
This honorable gentleman instantly draws two bowie-knives and a
     pistol, dons a blue cockade, and declares, that in consequence
     of the repeated aggressions of the North, and its gross viola-
     tions of the Constitution, he feels that it would utterly degrade
     him to pay any·debt whatever; and that, in fact, he has at last
     determined to SECEDE!—
             This South Carolina gentleman,
             One of the present time.

And when, at length, to Charleston of the other world he goes,
He leaves his children mortgages, with all their other woes.
As slowly fades the vital spark, he doubles up his fists,
And softly murmurs through his teeth: "I die under a full conviction
     of my errors in life, and freely forgive all men; but still I only
     hope that somewhere on the other side of Jordan I may just
     come across some ab-o-li-tion-ists ! !"—
             This South Carolina gentleman,
             One of the present time.

Yesterday afternoon, my boy, Colonel Wobert
Wobinson, of the Western Centaurs, ordered Captain Samyule Sa-mith to make a reconnoissance
toward Flint Hill with a company of skeleton

cavalry, having learned that several bushels of oats were stored there.

Samyule drew up his company in line against a fence, and then says he :

" Comrades, we go upon a mission that is highly dangurious, and America expects every hoss to do his duty. If we meet the rebels," continued Samyule, impressively, " they will try hard to capture some of our hosses ; for they're badly off for gridirons down there, and three or four of our spirited animals would supply them for the season. If any of you see them coming after the hardware, just put your gridirons on a gallop and fall back."

At the conclusion of this speech, Private Peter Jenkins observed that he'd been falling back ever since he got his horse ; for which he was sentenced to laugh at all the colonel's jokes for a week.

Would that I possessed the fiery pen of bully Homer, to describe the gallant advance of that splendid *corps*, as it trotted fiercely on to victory or death. At its head was Captain Samyule Sa-mith, mounted on a horse of some degree of merit, his coat-tails flapping behind him like banners at half-mast, and his form bouncing about in the saddle like an inspired jumping-jack. There was Lieutenant Tummis Kagcht, recently of the German navy, riding an animal with prows as sharp as a yacht and that was broadside to to the road at least half the time. There was private

Peter Jenkins, seated directly over the tail of a yellow-enameled charger, that walked at right-angles with the fences, and never stopped to take breath until it had gone three yards.

There was Sergeant O'Pake, late of Italy, who bestrode a sorrel, whose side was full of symmetrical gutters to carry the rain off, and who kept his octagon head directly under the right arm of the horseman ahead of him. There was private Nick O'Demus, with his sabre tucked neatly into the eyes of his neighbor, managing an anatomical curiosity that walked half of the time on his hind-legs, and creaked when it came to ruts in the road.

Onward, right onward, went this glittering cavalcade, my boy, until they came to an outskirt of Flint Hill, where a solitary remnant of a First Family might have been seen sitting on a fence, eating a sandwich.

" Tr-r-aitor !" shouted Captain Samyule Sa-mith, in tones of milk-souring thunder, " where is the rest of the Confederacy, and what do you think of the news from Fort Donelson ?"

The Confederacy hiccupped gloomily, my boy, as he took an impression of its front teeth on the sandwich, and says he :

" The melancholy days are come—the saddest of the year."

" That's very true," said Samyule, pleasantly, " and

proves you to be a person of some eddication. But tell me, sweet hermit of the dale," pursued Samyule, " where are the oats we have heard about ?"

The solitary Confederacy checked a rising cough with another bite at his ration, and says he :

" You have the oats already ; for they were eaten last night by six Confederate chickens, and my slave, Mr. Johnson, sold them chickens to a prospecting detachment of the Mackerel Brigade this morning. Don't talk to me any more," continued the Confederacy, sadly, " for I am very miserable, and haven't seen a quarter in six months."

Samyule seemed touched, and put his hand halfway into his pocket, but remembered his probable children, and refrained from romantic generosity.

".Let me see Mr. Johnson," says he, reflectively, " and I will question him concerning the South."

The Confederacy indulged in a plaintive cat-call, whereupon there emerged from an adjacent clump of bushes a beautiful black being, richly attired in a heavy seal-ring and a red neck-tie. It was Mr. Johnson.

" You have sent for me," says Mr. Johnson, with much dignity, " and I have come. If you do not want me, I will return."

" You have seen the tragic Forrest ?" said Samyule.

" The forest is my home," replied Mr. Johnson,

"and in its equal shade my humble hut stands sa-
credly embowered. As the gifted Whittier might
say :

> "There lofty trees uprear in pillared state,
> And crystal streams the thirsty deer elate ;
> While through the halls that base the dome of leaves
> Fall sunshine-harvests spread in golden sheaves.

> "There toy the birds in sweet seclusion blest,
> To leap the branches or to build the nest,
> While from their throats the grateful song outpoured
> Wakes woodland orchestras to praise the Lord.

> "There walks the wolf, no longer driven wild
> By panting hounds and huntsman blood-defiled;
> But tamed to kindness, seeketh peacefully
> The soothing shelter of a hollow tree.

> "Who would be free, and tow'r above his race,
> In the full freedom spurning man and place,
> Deep in the forest let him rear his clan
> Where God himself stands face to face with man."

Just as the oppressed African finished this rhythm-
ical statement of his platform, my boy, a huge horse-
fly, alighting on the nose of Captain Samyule Sa-mith,
awoke that hero from the refreshing slumber into
which he had fallen.

"Tell me, Johnson," says he, "how you got your
eddication, for I thought that persons from Afric's
sunny mountain went to school about as often as a
cat goes to sea."

Mr. Johnson placed his hand upon his breast with
much stateliness, and says he : "I entered Yale Col-

lege as a Spaniard, and having graduated with all honors, returned to my master, and was at once employed in cotton culture. I am contented and happy, and have never seen an uncomfortable day since my wife was sold. Go, stranger, and tell your people that the South may be overwhelmed, but she can never be conquered while Johnson has a seal ring to his back."

On hearing this speech, my boy, Samyule said :

"About face ! skeletons ;" and the gridiron cavalry returned to camp in a brown study.

The intelligence of the southern slaves is really wonderful, my boy, and if it should ever come to a head, look out for a rise in wool.

Yours, contemplatively,

ORPHEUS C. KERR.

LETTER XXXIII.

EXEMPLIFYING THE TERRIBLE DOMESTIC EFFECTS OF MILITARY IN-
ACTIVITY ON THE POTOMAC, AND DESCRIBING THE METAPHYSICAL
CAPTURE OF FORT MUGGINS.

WASHINGTON, D. C., March 3d, 1862.

I KNOW a man, my boy, who was driven to lunacy
by reliable war news. He was in the prime of life
when the war broke out, and took such an interest in
the struggle that it soon became nearly equal to the
interest on his debts. With all the enthusiasm of
vegetable youth he subscribed for all the papers, and
commenced to read the reliable war news. In this
way he learned that all was quiet on the Potomac,
and immediately went to congratulate his friends,
and purchase six American flags. On the following
morning he wrapt himself in the banner of his country
and learned from all the papers that all was quiet on
the Potomac. His joy at once became intense ; he
hoisted a flag on the lightning-rod of his domicil,
purchased a national pocket-handkerchief, bought six
hand-organs that played the Star-Spangled Banner,
and drank nothing but gunpowder tea. In the next
six months, however, there was a great change in our

military affairs ; the backbone of the rebellion was
broken, the sound of the thunder came from all parts
of the sky, and fifty-three excellent family journals
informed the enthusiast that all was quiet on the Potomac. He now became fairly mad with bliss, and
volunteered to sit up with a young lady whose brother
was a soldier. On the following morning he commenced to read Bancroft's History of the United
States, with Hardee's Tactics appended, only pausing long enough to learn from the daily papers that
all was quiet on the Potomac. Thus, in a fairy
dream of delicious joy, passed the greater part of this
devoted patriot's life ; and even as his hair turned
gray, and his form began to bend with old age, his
eye flashed in eternal youth over the still reliable war
news. At length there came a great change in the
military career of the Republic ; the rebellion received
its death-wound, and Washington's Birthday boomed
upon the United States of America. It was the
morning of that glorious day, and the venerable patriot was tottering about the room with his cane,
when his great-grandchild, a lad of twenty-five, came
thundering into the room with forty-three daily papers
under his arm.

"Old man !" says he, in a transport, "there's great
news."

"Boy, boy !" says the aged patriot, "do not trifle
with me. Can it be that—"

"Bet your life—"

"Is it then a fact that—"

"Yes—"

"Am I to believe that—"

"ALL IS QUIET ON THE POTOMAC!"

It was too much for the venerable Brutus; he clutched at the air, spun once on his left heel, sang a stave of John Brown's body, and stood transfixed with ecstacy.

"Thank Heving," says he, "for sparing me to see this day!"

After which he became hopelessly insane, my boy, and raved so awfully about all our great generals turning into mud-larks that his afflicted family had to send him to the asylum.

This veracious and touching biography will show you how dangerous to public health is reliable war news, and convince you that the Secretary's order to the press is only a proper insanitary measure.

I am all the more resigned to it, my boy, because it affects me so little that I am even able to give you a strictly reliable account of a great movement that lately took place.

I went down to Accomac early in the week, my boy, having heard that Captain Villiam Brown and the Conic Section of the Mackerel Brigade were about to march upon Fort Muggins, where Jeff Davis, Beauregard, Mason, Slidell, Yancey, and the whole rebel

Congress were believed to be intrenched. Mounted on my gothic steed Pegasus, who only blew down once in the whole journey, I repaired to Villiam's department, and was taking notes of the advance, upon a sheet of paper spread on the ground, when the commander of Accomac approached me, and says he :

" What are you doing, my bantam ?"

" I'm taking notes," says I, " for a journal which has such an immense circulation among our gallant troops that when they begin to read it in the camps, it looks, from a distance, as though there had just been a heavy snow-storm.'

"Ah !" says Villiam, thoughtfully, " newspapers and snow-storms are somewhat alike ; for both make black appear white. But," said Villiam philosophically, " the snow is the more moral ; for you can't lie in that with safety, as you can in a newspaper. In the language of General Grant at Donelson," says Villiam, sternly : " I propose to move upon your works immediately."

And with that he planted one of his boots right in the middle of my paper.

" Read that ere Napoleonic dockyment," says Villiam, handing me a scroll. It was as follows :

EDICK.

Having noticed that the press of the United States of America is making a ass of itself, by giving information to the enemy concerning the best methods of carrying on the strategy of war, I do hereby assume control of all special correspondents, forbidding them to transact anything but private business ; neither they, nor their wives, nor their children, to the third and fourth generation.

I. It is ordered, that all advice from editors to the War Department, to the general commanding, or the generals commanding the armies in the field, be absolutely forbidden ; as such advice is calculated to make the United States of America a idiot.

II. Any newspaper publishing any news whatever, however obtained, shall be excluded from all railroads and steamboats, in order that country journals, which receive the same news during the following year, may not be injured in cirkylation.

III. This control of special correspondents does not include the correspondent of the London Times, who wouldn't be believed if he published all the news of the next Christian era. By order of

VILLIAM BROWN, Eskevire,
Captain Conic Section Mackerel Brigade.

I had remounted Pegasus while reading this able State paper, my boy, and had just finished it, when a nervous member of the advance-guard accidentally touched off a cannon, whose report was almost immediately answered by one from the dense fog before us.

"Ha !" says Captain Villiam Brown, suddenly leaping from his steed, and creeping under it—to examine if the saddle-girth was all right—" the fort is right before us in the fog, and the rebels are awake. Let the Orange County Company advance with their howitzers, and fire to the north-east."

The Orange County Company, my boy, instantly wheeled their howitzers into position, and sent some pounds of grape toward the meridian, the roar of their weapons of death being instantaneously answered by a thundering crash in the fog.

Company 3, Regiment 5, Mackerel Brigade, now went forward six yards at double-quick, and poured in a rattling volley of musketry, dodging fearlessly when exactly the same kind of a volley was heard in the fog, and wishing that they might have a few rebels for supper.

"Ha !" says Captain Villiam Brown, when he noticed that nobody seemed to be killed yet ; " Providence is on our side, and this here unnatural rebellion is squelched. Let the Anatomical Cavalry charge into the fog, and demand the surrender of Fort Muggins," continued Villiam, compressing his lips with mad valor, " while I repair to that tree back there, and see if there is not a fiendish secessionist lurking behind it."

The Anatomical Cavalry immediately dismounted from their horses, which were too old to be used in a charge, and gallantly entered the fog, with their sabres between their teeth, and their hands in their pockets —it being a part of their tactics to catch a rebel before cutting his head off.

In the meantime, my boy, the Orange County howitzers and the Mackerel muskets were hurling a continuous fire into the clouds, stirring up the angels, and loosening the smaller planets. Sturdily answered the rebels from the fog-begirt fort ; but not one of our men had yet fallen.

Captain Villiam Brown was just coming down from the top of a very tall tree, whither he had gone to search for masked batteries, when the fog commenced lifting, and disclosed the Anatomical Cavalry returning at double-quick.

Instantly our fire ceased, and so did that of the rebels.

" Does the fort surrender to the United States of America ?" says Villiam, to the captain of the Anatomicals.

The gallant dragoon, sighed, and says he :

" I used my magnifying glass, but could find no fort."

At this moment, my boy, a sharp sunbeam cleft the fog as a sword does a vail, and the mist rolled away from the scene in two volumes, disclosing to our view a fine cabbage-patch, with a dense wood beyond.

Villiam deliberately raised a bottle to his face, and gazed through it upon the unexpected prospect.

"Ha!" says he sadly, "the garrison has cut its way through the fog and escaped, but Fort Muggins is ours! Let the flag of our Union be planted on the ramparts," says Villiam, with much perspiration, "and I will immediately issue a proclamation to the people of the United States of America."

Believing that Villiam was somewhat too hasty in his conclusions, my boy, I ventured to insinuate that what he had taken for a fort in the fog, was really nothing but a cabbage inclosure, and that the escaped rebels were purely imaginary.

"Imaginary!" says Villiam, hastily placing his canteen in his pocket. "Why, didn't you hear the roar of their artillery?"

"Do you see that thick wood yonder?" says I.

Says he, "It is visible to the undressed eye."

"Well," says I, "what you took for the sound of rebel firing, was only the echo of your own firing in that wood."

Villiam pondered for a few moments, my boy, like one who was considering the propriety of saying nothing in as few words as possible, and then looked angularly at me, and says he:

"My proclamation to the press will cover all this, and the news of this here engagement will keep until the war is over. Ah!" says Villiam, "I wouldn't

have the news of this affair published on any account ;
for if the Government thought I was trying to cabbage in my Department, it would make me Minister
to Russia immediately."

As the Conic Section of the Mackerel Brigade returned slowly to head-quarters, my boy, I thought
to myself : How often does man, after making something his particular forte, discover at last that it is
only a cabbage-patch, and hardly large enough at
that for a big hog like himself !

Yours, philanthropically,
ORPHEUS C. KERR.

LETTER XXXIV.

BEGINNING WITH A LAMENTATION, BUT CHANGING MATERIALLY IN
TONE AT THE DICTUM OF JED SMITH.

WASHINGTON, D. C., March 8th, 1862.

Two days ago, my boy, a letter from the West
informed me that an old friend of mine had fallen in
battle at the very moment of victory. One by one,
my boy, I have lost many friends since the war began,
and know how to bear the stroke ; but what will they
say in that home to which the young soldier wafted a
nightly prayer ?   Thither, alas ! he goes

NO MORE.

Hushed be the song and the love-notes of gladness
    That broke with the morn from the cottager's door—
Muffle the tread in the soft stealth of sadness,
    For one who returneth, whose chamber-lamp burneth
                        No more.

Silent he lies on the broad path of glory,
    Where withers ungarnered the red crop of war.
Grand is his couch, though the pillows are gory,
    'Mid forms that shall battle, 'mid guns that shall rattle
                        No more.

Soldier of Freedom, thy marches are ended—
    The dreams that were prophets of triumph are o'er—
Death with the night of thy manhood is blended—
    The bugle shall call thee, the fight shall enthrall thee
            No more.

Far to the Northward the banners are dimming,
    And faint comes the tap of the drummers before;
Low in the tree-tops the swallow is skimming;
    Thy comrades shall cheer thee, the weakest shall fear thee
            No more.

Far to the Westward the day is at vespers,
    And bows down its head, like a priest, to adore;
Soldier, the twilight for thee has no whispers,
    The night shall forsake thee, the morn shall awake thee
            No more.

Wide o'er the plain, where the white tents are gleaming,
    In spectral array, like the graves they're before—
One there is empty, where once thou wert dreaming
    Of deeds that are boasted, of One that is toasted
            No more.

When the Commander to-morrow proclaimeth
    A list of the brave for the nation to store,
Thou shalt be known with the heroes he nameth,
    Who wake from their slumbers, who answer their numbers
            No more.

Hushed be the song and the love-notes of gladness
    That broke with the morn from the cottager's door—
Muffle the tread in the soft stealth of sadness,
    For one who returneth, whose chamber-lamp burneth
            No more.

To escape my own thoughts, I went over into a camp of New England chaps, yesterday, my boy, and one of the first high-privates my eyes rested on was

Jed Smith, of Salsbury. He winked to the chaps
lounging near him, when he noted my doleful look,
and says he :

"You're mopish, comrade. Hez caliker proved
deceitful ?"

"No," says I, indifferently. "Calico rather shuns
me, as a general thing, my Down-easter, on account
of my plain speaking."

This startled him, my boy, as I expected it would,
and says he :

"That's jest like the mock-modesty of the wimmin
folks all the world over, and a body might think they
had the hull supply and nothin' shorter ; but I tell ye
it's the heartiest sow that makes the least noise, and
half this here modesty is all sham.   Onct in a while
these here awful modest critters git shook down a bit,
I guess ; and gheewhillikins ! ef it don't do me good
to see it.   I recollect I was goin' down from Augusty
some two years ago, in the old stage that Sammy
Tompkins druv, and we had one of the she-critters
aboard—and she *was* a scrouger, I tell ye ! Bonnet
red as a blaze, and stuck all over with stiff geeranium
blows, a hump like a Hottentot gal, and sich ankles !
but hold your horses, I'm gettin' ahead of time.   We
was awful crowded, and no mistake—piled right on
top of each other, like so many layers of cabbage ;
and the way that gal squealed when we struck a rut,
was a caution to screech owls.   And she was takin'

up her sheer of the coach, too, I guess ; and kind of stretched her walkin' geer way under the seat in front of her, and out t'other side, just to brace herself agin the diffikilties of travel. It being pretty bad goin' down in them parts, she had on a pair of her brother's butes, and they was what she wouldn't have had seen if she'd knowed it. One of the fellers on the middle seat was Zeb Green—gone to glory some time ago— and when he spied them butes, he winked to me, and sung out :

" Gheewhillikins ! who owns these ere big trotters ?"

" Now, ye see, the she-critter was one of yer modest ones, and she wouldn't have owned up for the world, after that. Says she :

" ' I guess they ain't mine.'

" Zeb see her game in a twinklin', and he was a tall one for a lark ; so says he :

" ' I rayther guess there's petticuts goes with them mud mashers.'

" The gal she flamed up at that, and says she :

" ' I guess you're barkin' up the wrong saplin', Major, and yer must have a most audacious turkey on, not to know yer own butes.'

" Sich lyin' tuk Zeb all aback for a minute ; but he combed up his bristles again, and tried her on another trail.

" ' Now, you don't mean to come for to insinuate

that them ere's *my* butes, and I not know it ?' says
he :

" She was in for it then, and wouldn't back down ;
so says she :

" ' In course I do, Major, and you'd better look out
fur your own leather.'

" Zeb took a chaw of his terbacky, and says he :

" ' Well, if you says it's so, I'm bound to swaller
the oyster ; but I'll be dod-rotted if my bute-maker
won't hev to shave my last next winter.'

" I seen right off that Zeb was up to the biggest
kind of a spree, and I knew them butes was the gist
of it ; cause ye see the she-critter couldn't hull 'em
in nohow, after what she'd said.

" We went wrigglin' along for a while as still as
cats in a milk-house, and the butes stayed where they
was.   But pretty soon Zeb began to grow uneasy like,
and screwed up his ugly nose, like as if he was took
with the pangs, and the doctor gone a courtin'.

" ' Gheewhillikins !' says he, at last, ' I shan't stand
this here much longer, if there *is* company in the
parlor !'

" We all looked at him, and says one feller :

" ' I guess, Major, you're took putty bad.'

" Zeb gave his phizog another twist, an' says he :

" ' You'd better believe it, squire.   I've got corns
on them ere feet of mine that'd make a preacher
swear, and them butes pinch like all tarnation.'

"I see right off how the smoke was blowin', and says I :

"'Off with 'em, Zeb! We're all in the family, and won't mind you.'

"That was all the old he-one was waitin' fur ; and as quick as I said it, he had one of that modest gal's feet in his hand, and twisted off the bute in a twinklin' ! ! We all see a perfect Wenus of a foot, and a golfired ankle, and then it was jerked away quicker'n a flash, and the critter screamed like a rantankerous tom-cat with his tail under a cheese-knife !

"'Murder !—you nasty thing,' says she, 'give me my bute.'

"With that, me, and Zeb, and the hull bilin' of us roared right out ; and says Zeb, says he, as he handed her the bute with a killin' bow—says he :

"'Young woman, I guess I've taken your modesty, as the wimmen call it, down a peg. You sed them was *my* butes, and in course I had a right to shed 'em ; but ef they're your'n now, why keep 'em to yourself, for massy's sake !'

"That settled the gal down some, I tell ye ; and it give her such a turn that her putty face was like a rose when we stopt at the Red Tavern."

We were so much pleased with this story, my boy, that we entreated the opponent of mock modesty to spin us another.

"Well, feller citizens," says he, "I don't mind if I do tell ye about

A JOFIRED WAGON-TRADE

I onct made down in Texas. You see I was doin' a right smart chance of trade down in that deestrict with clocks, fur caps, Ingin meal, and other necessaries of life ; and onct in a while I went it blind on a spekullation, when there was a chance to get a bargain, and pay fifty per cent. on a stiff swindle. They was an old chap of a half breed they called Uncle Johnny, down there, and somehow he got wind of my pertikler cuteness, and he guessed he could run a pretty sharp saw on me, if he only got a sight.

"I heerd he was after me, and thinks I 'you'll get a roastin', my boy, ef you pick up this hot-chestnut ;' but I was consated beyond my powers then, and he was jist one huckleberry above my tallest persimmon. We cum together one night at Bill Crown's tavern, and the fust thing the old cuss said was :

"'Jerewsalem crickets! I'm like a fellow jist out of a feather bed and no mistake. I tell ye that 'ere wagging uv mine rides jist about as slick as a railroad of grease, and if it warn't so allfired big, I wouldn't sell it for its weight in Orleans bank notes.'

"I kinder thought I smelt a putty big bed-bug ; but I glimpsed outer the door, and there stood the wagon under the shed, and lookin' orful temptin'. It war a big four wheel consarn, with a canvas top, and about as putty a consarn for family use as ever I sot my winkers on. Thinks I :

" 'You don't fetch me this time, hoss ; for I'll be jist a neck ahead of you !'

" So I stood a minit, and then says I :

" ' Without lookin' nor nuthin', Uncle Johnny, I'll jest give you $50 for that 'ere hearse.'

" He kinder blinked around, and says he :

" ' I'd rather sell my grandmother ; but the con-sarn's yourn, cunnel. Show yer hand.'

" He was too willin' to suit me ; but the game was outer cover, and I wouldn't back down. So I give him the rags, and went out to look at my bargain. Would you 'bleave it, the old varmint had jist fetched that ere wagon down to the shed, and sot it un end on, so that I didn't see how the fore-wheels wasn't thar ! Fact ! They had marvelled, and the fore-axles was restin' on two hitchin' stakes : Jist as I got through cussin',' I heerd a jofired larfin, and thar was the robber and his friends standin' in the door, splittin' their sides at me. Thinks I, ' I went cheap, then, my beauty ; but look out for a hail-storm when the wind's up next time.' I borreyed a horse, and took that ar bargain to my shanty ; and then I sot down and went to thinkin'. Fur two days I war as melancholy as a chicken in gooseberry time, tryin' to

hit some plan to get even with the cuss. All to onct
somethin' struck me, and I felt better. Ye see there
was great talk down thar jist then, about the doctor's
gig what they heard tell on, but not a one was there
in the hull deestrict. I'd seen one up in York, and
thinks I, ' Ef I don't make a doctor's two-wheeler
outer that ere wagon, then bleed me to death
with a oyster-knife !' So I jist got a big saw, and
went to work quiet like, and cut that ere wagon right
in two in the middle—cover and all. Then I took
the shafts and fastened them onto the hind part, and
rigged up a dash-board. And then I took part of the
cut-off piece for a seat, and painted the hull thing
with black paint ; and dod-rot me if ef I didn't hev
a doctor's gig as rantankerous as you please ! I knew
it would fetch a thunderin' price fur its novelty to
any one ; but I was after Uncle Johnny, and nobody
else. One night I druv down to the tavern at a
tearin' rate, and the fust feller I see was hisself, a
standin' in the door, and sippin' kill-me-quick. He
was kinder took down when he see me comin' it so
piert in my new two-wheeler, and some of his friends
inside axed him what was the matter. He kept as
still as a mouse in a pantry until I come up, and then
says he :

" ' What's that ere concern of yourn, hoss ?'

" Says I :

" ' It's one of them doctor's flyers as I'd rather ride

in it than in Queen Victory's bang-up, A, No. 1, stage-coach. It's a scrouger."

" He kinder stuck a minute, and then says he :

" ' What'll ye take for it, hoss ?'

" I made out as though I didn't keer, and says I :

" ' It was sent to me by a cousin up in York, and I don't keer to sell ; but yer may take it for $250.'

" He turned green about the gills at that, and says he :

" ' Say $100, and I'll take it with my eyes shut.'

" 'It's yourn,' says I. ' Give us the rags.'

" He smelt a bug that time ; but it was too late ; so he forked out the rale stuff, and then went to look at the two-wheeler.

" ' Thunder !' says he, blinkin' at the seat. ' I've seen that afore, or my name isn't what my father's wus !'

" ' Better 'blieve it,' says I ; ' that's your four-wheeler shaved down to the very latest York-fashion.'

" Then he *did* cuss ; but twarn't no use. The trade was a trade, and all the boys larfed till their tongues hung out. I treated all round, and as I left 'em, says I :

" Uncle Johnny, when ye want to trade agin, jist pick out a grindstun that isn't too hard for yer blade.' "

At the conclusion of this tale of real life I returned

to the city, my boy ; impressed with the conviction
that the purpose of the sun's rising in the East is to
give the New Englanders the first chance to monopolize the supply, should daylight ever be a sailable
article.

Yours. admiringly,

ORPHEUS C. KERR.

LETTER XXXV

WASHINGTON, D. C., March 14th, 1862.

PATRIOTISM, my boy, is a very beautiful thing. The surgeon of a Western regiment has analyzed a very nice case of it, and says that it is peculiar to this hemisphere. He says that it first breaks out in the mouth, and from thence extends to the heart causing the latter to swell. He says that it goes on raging until it reaches the pocket, when it suddenly disappears, leaving the patient very Constitutional and conservative. "Bless me!" says the surgeon, intently regarding a spoon with a tumbler round it, "if a genuine American ever dies of patriotism it will be because the Tax Bill hasn't been applied soon enough."

I believe him, my boy !

On Monday morning, just as the sun was rising, like a big gold watch "put up" at some celestial Simpson's, the sentinels of Fort Corcoran were seized with horrible tremblings at a sight calculated to make perpendicular hair fashionable. As far as the eye could reach on every side of the Capital, the ground was black with an approaching multitude, each man of which wore large spectacles, and carried a serious carpet-bag and a bottle-green umbrella.

" Be jabers !" says one of the sentinels, whose imperfect English frequently causes him to be taken for the Duc de Chartres, " it's the whole Southern Confederacy coming to boord with us."

" Aisey, me boy," says the other sentinel, straightening the barrel of his musket and holding it very straight to keep the fatal ball from rolling out, " it's the sperits of all our pravious descindants coming to ax us, was our grandmother the Saycretary of the Navy."

Right onward came the multitude, their spectacles glistening in the sun like so many exasperated young planets, and their umbrellas and carpet-bags swinging like the pendulums of so many infuriated clocks.

Pretty soon the advance guard, who was a chap in a white neck-tie and a hat resembling a stove-pipe in reduced circumstances, poked a sentinel in the ribs with his umbrella, and says he :

" Where's Congress ?"

" Is it Congress ye want ?" says the sentinel.

" Yessir !" says the chap. " Yessir. These are friends of mine—ten thousand six hundred and forty-two free American citizens. We must see Congress.

Yessir !—dammit. How about that tax-bill ? We come to protest against certain features *in* that bill."

" Murther an turf !" says the sentinel, " is it the taxes all of them ould chaps is afther blaming ?"

" Yessir !" says the chap, hysterically jamming his hat down over his forehead and stabbing himself madly under the arm with his umbrella. " Taxes is a outrage. Not *all* taxes," says the chap with sudden benignity, " but the taxes which fall upon us. Why don't they tax them as is able to pay, without oppressing us ministers, editors, merchants, lawyers, grocers, peddlers, and professors of religion ?" Here the chap turned very purple in the face, his eyes bulged greenly out, and says he : " Congress is a ass."

" That's thrue for you," says the sentinel : " they ought to eximpt the whole naytion and tax the rest of it."

The multitude then swarmed into Washington, my boy, and if they don't smother the Tax Bill, it will be because Congress is case-hardened.

The remainder of the Mackerel Brigade being ordered to join the Conic Section at Accomac for an irresistible advance on Manassas, I mounted my gothic steed Pegasus on Tuesday morning.

Pegasus, my boy, has greatly improved since I rubbed him down with Snobb's Patent Hair Invigorator, and his tail looks much less like a whisk-broom than it did at first. It is now fully able to maintain itself against all flies whatsoever. The general of the Mackerel Brigade rode beside me on a spirited black frame, and says he :

"That funereal beast of yours is a monument of the home affections. Thunder !" says the general, shedding a small tear of the color of Scheidam Schnapps, "I never look at that air horse without thinking of the time I buried my first baby ; its head is shaped so much like a small coffin."

On reaching Accomac, my boy, we found Captain Villiam Brown at the head of the Conic Section of the Mackerel Brigade, dressed principally in a large sword and brass buttons, and taking the altitude of the sun with a glass instrument operated by means of a bottle.

"Ah !" says Villiam, "You are just in time to hear my speech to the sons of Mars, previous to the capture of Manassas by the United States of America."

Hereupon Villiam mounted a demijohn laid length-wise, and says he :

"FELLOW-ANACONDAS :—Having been informed by a gentleman who has spent two weeks at Manassas, that the Southern Confederacy has gone South for its health, I have concluded that it is time to be offensive. The great Anaconda, having eluded Barnum, is about to move on the enemy's rear :

" 'Rear aloft your peaks, ye mountings,
   Rear aloft your waves, O sea !,
   Rear your sparkling crests, ye fountings,
   For my love's come back to me.'

The day of inaction is past, and now the United States of America is about to swoop down like a exasperated Eagle, on the chickens left by the hawk. Are you ready, my sagacious reptiles, to spill a drop or so for your soaking country ? Are you ready to rose up as one man—

" 'The rose is red,
   The wi'lets blue,
   Sugar is sweet, and
   Bully for you.'

" Ages to come will look down on this day and say : 'They died young.' The Present will reply : ' I don't see it ;' but the present is just the last thing for us to think about. Richmond is before us, and there let it remain. We shall take it in a few years :

" 'It may be for years and it may bo for ever,
   Then why art thou silent, O pride of mo heart.'

which is poickry. I hereby divide this here splendid army into one *corpse dammee*, and take command of it."

At the conclusion of this thrilling oration, my boy, the *corpse dammee* formed itself into a hollow square, in the centre of which appeared a mail-clad ambulance.

I looked at this carefully, and then says I to Villiam :

" Tell me, my gay Achilles, what you carry in
that ?"

" Ha !" says Villiam, balancing himself on one
leg, " them's my Repeaters. This morning," says
Villiam, sagaciously, " I discovered six Repeaters
among my men. Each of them voted six times last
election day, and I've put them where they can't be
killed. Ah !" says Villiam, softly, " the Democratic
party can't afford to lose them Repeaters."

Here a rather rusty-looking chap stepped out of the
ranks, and says he :

" Captain, I'm a Repeater too. I voted four times
last election."

" It takes six to make a reliable Repeater," says
Villiam.

" Yes," says the chap : " but I voted for different
coves—twice for the Republican candidate and twice
for the Democrat."

" Ha !" says Villiam, " you're a man of intelleck.
Here, sargent," says Villiam, imperiously, " put this
cherubim into the ambulance."

" And, sargent," says Villiam, thoughtfully, "give
him the front seat."

And now, my boy, the march for Manassas commenced, being timed by the soft music of the band.
This band, my boy, is *sui generis*. Its chief artist is

an ardent admirer of Rossini, who performs with great accuracy upon a night-key pressed closely against the lower lip, the strains being much like those emitted by a cart-wheel in want of grease. Then comes a gifted musican from Germany, whose instrument is a fine-tooth comb wrapped in paper, and blown upon through its vibratory covering. The remainder of the band is composed chiefly of drums, though the second-base achieves some fine effects with a superannuated accordeon.

Onward moved the magnificent pageant toward the plains of Manassas, the Anatomical Cavalry being in advance, and the Mackerel Brigade following closely after.

Arriving on the noted battle-field, we found nothing but a scene of desolation ; the rebels gone ; the masked batteries gone ; and nothing left but a solitary daughter of the sunny South, who cursed us for invading the peaceful homes of Virginia, and then tried to sell us stale milk at six shillings a quart.

When Captain Villiam Brown, surveyed this spectacle, my boy, his brows knit with portentous anger, and says he :

" So much for wasting so much time. Ah !" says Villiam, clutching convulsively at his canteen, " we have met the enemy, and they are hours—ahead of us."

The only thing noticeable we found, my boy, upon

searching the late stamping ground of the Southern Confederacy, was a beautiful "romaunt," evidently written by an oppressed Southern Union man, who had gone from bad to verse, and descriptive of

THE SOUTHERN VOLUNTEER'S FAREWELL TO HIS WIFE.

Fresh from snuff-dipping to his arms she went,
    And he, a quid removing from his mouth,
Pressed her in anguish to his manly breast
    And spat twice, longingly, toward the South.

"Zara," he said, and hiccup'd as he spoke,
    "Indeed I find it most (hic) 'stremely hard
To leave my wife, my niggers, and my debts,
    And march to glory with the 'Davis Guard;'

"But all to arms the South has called her sons,
    And while there's something Southern hands can steal,
You can't (hic) 'spect me to stay here at home
    With heartless duns for ever at my heel.

"To-night a hen-coop falls; and in a week
    We'll take the Yankee capital, I think;
But should it prove (hic) 'pedient not to do't,
    Why, then, we'll take—in short, we'll take a drink.

"I reckon I may perish in the strife—
    Some bullet in the back might lay me low—
And as my business needs attendin' to,
    I'll give you some directions ere I go.

"That cotton-gin I haven't paid for yet—
    The Yankee trusted for it, dear, you know,
And it's a most (hic) 'stremely doubtful thing,
    Whether it's ever used again, or no.

"If Yankee's agent calls while I am gone,
  It's my (hic) 'spress command and wish, that you
Denounce him for an abolition spy,
  And have him hung before his note is due.

"That octoroon—who made you jealous, love—
  Who sews so well and is so pale a thing;
She keeps her husband, Sambo, from his work—
  You'd better sell her—well, for what she'll bring.

"In case your purse runs low while I'm away—
  There's Dinah's children—two (hic) 'spensive whelps;
They won't bring much the way the markets are,
  But then you know how every little helps.

"And there's that Yankee schoolmistress, you know,
  Who taught our darlings how to read and spell;
Now don't (hic) 'spend a cent to pay *her* bill;
  If she aren't tarred and feathered, she'll do well!

"And now, my dear, I go where booty calls,
  I leave my whisky, cotton-crop, and thee;
Pray, that in battle I may not (hic) 'spire,
  And when you lick the niggers think of me.

"If on some mournful summer afternoon
  They should bring home to you your warrior dead,
Inter me with a toothpick in my hand,
  And write a last (hic) *jacet* o'er my head."

We found this in the shed lately used by the chiv-
alric Constarveracy as a guard-house, my boy, and
read it with deep emotion.

                    Yours, Manassastonished,
                        ORPHEUS C. KERR.

LETTER XXXVI.

CONCERNING THE WEAKNESSES OF GREAT MEN, THE CURIOUS MISTAKE
OF A FRATERNAL MACKEREL, AND THE REMARKABLE ALLITERATIVE
PERFORMANCE OF CAPTAIN VILLIAM BROWN.

WASHINGTON, D. C., March 20th, 1862.

WHEN a wise, benign, but not altogether Rhode-
Island Providence saw fit to deal out a few mountains to Eastern Tennessee and Western Virginia,
my boy, it is barely possible that Providence had an
eye to the present crisis of our subtracted country,
and intended to furnish the coming Abe with a fit
place for the lofty accommodation of such great men
as were not in immediate demand among the poli-
ticians. I am not topographical by nature, my boy;
I never went up to the top of the White Mountains
to see the sun rise, and didn't see; nor did I ever
scale Mount Blanc for the purpose of allowing a fog
to settle on my lungs; but it's my private opinion,
my boy, my private opinion, that, were it not for the
perpendicular elevations of the earth's surface in the
States named, it would be necessary for the honest
Old Abe either to turn General Fremont into a reduced
Consul, and commission him to furnish proofs of the

nation's reverence for the name of Lafayette, or coop him up somewhere in solitary grandeur, like a rabbit in a Warren.

"Great men," says the General of the Mackerel Brigade, as he and I were looking at some sugar together, the other night, through concave glasses— "great men," says he, "are like the ears of black-and-tan terriers; they are good for ornaments, but you must cut off some of them when you would give them rats.   Thunder!" says the general, taking a perpendicular view of the sugar—"if we didn't cut off great men occasionally, there'd be more presidential nominations to ratify next election than ever before struck terrier to the heart of an old-line whig."

But you have yet to learn, my boy, what was *the* great reason for sending Fremont to the everlasting hills.   On Tuesday I asked a knowing veteran at Willard's what it really was. He looked at me for a moment in immovable silence; then he softly placed his spoon-gymnasium on a table, looked cautiously in all directions, crept up to my ear on tiptoe, and says he:

"*Kerridges!*"

"Son of a bottle!" says I, "your information is about as intelligible as the ordinary remarks of Ralph Waldo Emerson."

The knowing veteran suffered his nose to take a steam-bath for a moment, and then says he:

"Kerridges! Kerridges with six horses and the American flag flying out of the back window. Fremont's great mistake at the West was kerridges—*and* six horses. Did he wish to buy some shoe-strings for his babes—'Captain Poneyowiski,' says he to his chamberlain, 'order the second steward to tell the scarlet-and-grey groom to send the kerridge and six horses round to the door, with a full band on the box.' Did he wish to make a call on the next block and obtain some Bath note-paper—'General Nockmynoseoff,' says he to his first esquire in waiting, 'issue a proclamation to my Master in Chancery to instantly command the Master of the Horse to get ready the kerridge with six horses, and send the Life-Guard to clear the way.' In fact," says the knowing veteran, frowning mysteriously, "it is rumored that when he came home from Debar's theatre one night, and found the front door of his head-quarters accidentally locked, he instantly ordered up the kerridge *and* six horses, to take him round to the back entrance. Now," says the knowing veteran, suddenly striking the table a glass blow that splashed, and assuming an air of embittered argument—"they've sent him to the mountains to suppress his kerridge."

This explanation, my boy, may be all a fiction, but certain it is that General Fremont has not the carriage he had six months ago."

On Wednesday the gothic steed Pegasus bore me

once more to Manassas, where I found the Mackerel Brigade vowing vengeance for the recent rebel atrocities, of which I found many outrageous evidences.

Just as I arrived on the ground, my boy, a Mackerel chap came running out of a deserted rebel tent with a round object in his hand, and immediately commenced to tear his hair and speak the language of the Sixth Ward.

"My brother! my brother!" says he, eyeing his horrible trophy with tearful emotion. "O! that I should live to see your beloved skull turned into a cheese-box by rebels! You was a Boston alderman, a moral man, and a candidate for the Legislature, before you came to this here horrid war to be killed by rebels, and have your skull aggravated into a secession utensil."

Here the General of the Mackerel Brigade glanced at the heart-sickening trophy, and says he to the Mackerel chap:

"Why, you poor ignorant cuss! that there is nothing but a cocoanut-shell hollowed out." ·

"Is it?" says the inferior Mackerel, brightening up, "is it? Well," says he, feelingly, "I took it for the skull of my brother, the Boston Alderman—it's so hard and thick."

These beautiful displays of fraternal emotion are quite frequent, my boy, and are calculated to shed a lustre of sanctity over the discoveries of our troops.

The capture of Richmond being deferred until the younger drummers of the brigade are old enough to vote in that city, I found Captain Villiam Brown and Captain Bob Shorty seated at a table in a tent—the former being engaged with a pen and a decanter, while the latter drew a map of the campaign with a piece of lemon-peel dipped in something fragrant.

It was beautiful to look at these two slashing heroes, as they sat there in the genial glare of canvas-strained noon-day, with a quart vessel between them.

" Comrade," says Captain Bob Shorty to me, cordially, " this here is what we call intellectual relaxation, with a few liquid vowels to make it consonant with our tastes."

" Yes !" says Captain Villiam Brown, with a fascinating and elaborate wink at the decanter, " the physical man having taken Manassas, the human intelleck is now in airy play. Ah !" says Villiam, majestically passing me the disentangled curl-paper on which he had been writing, " read what I have penned for the perusal of the United States of America."

I grasped the document, my boy, and found on it inscribed the following efficacious effusion :

FLOYD.

Felonious Floyd, far-famed for falsifying,
Forever first from Federal forces flying,
From fabrications fanning Fortune's flame,
Finds foul Fugacity factitious Fame.

Fool! facile Fabler! Fugitive flagitious!
Fear for Futurity, Filcher fictitious!
Fame forced from Folly, finding fawners fled,
Feeds final Failure—failure fungus-fed.
                By CAPTAIN VILLIAM BROWN, Eskevire.

"Well, my juvenile Union-blue," says. Villiam, smiling like a successful cherubim, "what do you think of that piece of American intelleck?"

"I think," says I, "that it is worthy of an F. F. V."

What followed, my boy, is none of your business, though a sentry near by subsequently observed that he heard the sound of soft, mellifluous gurgles come from the interior of the tent.

Poetry, my boy, is man's best gift; and that, I suppose, is the reason why it is so popular in young women's boarding-schools.

Yours, in particular metre,

ORPHEUS C. KERR.

LETTER XXXVII.

WASHINGTON, D. C., March 28th, 1862.

THE most interesting natural curiosity here, next
to Secretary Welles' beard, is the office of the Secretary of the Interior. Covered with spider-webs, and
clothed in the dust of ages, my- boy, sit the Secretary
and his clerks, like so many respectable mummies in
a neglected pyramid. The Department of the Interior, my boy, is in a humorous condition ; the sales
of public lands for the past year amount to about ten
shillings, the only buyer being a conservative Dutchman from New Jersey, who hasn't heard about the
war yet.

These things weigh upon my spirit, and I was glad
to order up my Gothic stallion, Pegasus, the other
day, and rattle down to Manassas once more.

Upon reaching that celebrated field of Mars, my
boy, I found the General of the Mackerel Brigade in
his tent, surrounded by telegraphic instruments and
railroad maps, while the Conic Section was drawn up
in line outside.

"You appear to be much absorbed, my venerable Spartan," says I to the General, as I handled the diaphanous vessel he was using as an act-drop in the theatre of war.

The General frowned like an obdurate parent refusing to let his only daughter marry a coal-heaver, and says he :

"I'm absorbed in strategy.   Eighteen months ago, I was informed by a contraband that sixty thousand unnatural rebels were intrenched somewhere near here, and having returned the contraband to his master, to be immediately shot, I resolved to overwhelm the rebels by strategy.   Thunder !" says the General, perspiring like a pitcher of ice-water in June, "if there's anything equal to diplomacy it's strategy.   And now," says the General, sternly, "it's my duty to order you to write nothing about this to the papers.   You write about my movements ; the papers publish it, and are sent here ; my adjutant takes the papers to the rebels ; and so, you see, my plans are all known.   I have no choice but to suppress you."

"But," says I, "you might more surely keep the news from the rebels by arresting the adjutant."

"Thunder !" says the general, "I never thought of that before."

Great men, my boy, are never so great but that they can profit occasionally by a suggestion from the humblest of the species.   I once knew a very great man

who went home one night in a shower, and was horri-
fied at discovering that he could not get his umbrella
through the front door. He was a very great man,
understood Sanscrit, made speeches that nobody could
comprehend, and had relatives in Beacon-street, Boston. There he stood in the rain, my boy, pushing his
umbrella this way and that way, turning it endways
and sideways, holding it at acute angles and obtuse
angles ; but still it wouldn't go through the door, nor
anything like it. By-and-by there came along a chap
of humble attainments, who sung out :

" What's the matter, old three-and-sixpence ?"

The great man turned pantingly round, and says
he :

" Ah, my friend, I cannot get my umbrella into the
house. I've been trying for half an hour to wedge it
through the door, but I can't get it through and know
not how to act."

The humble chap stood under a gas-light, my boy,
and by the gleams thereof his mouth was observed to
pucker loaferishly.

" Hev you tried the experiment of *shutting up* that
air umbrella ?" says he.

The great man gave a start, and says he :

" Per Jovem !   I didn't think to do that."

And he shut his umbrella and went in peacefully.

The Conic Section was to make its great strategic
movement, my boy, under Captain Bob Shorty ; and,

led by that fearless warrior, it set out at twilight. Onward tramped the heroes according to Hardee, for about an hour, and then they reached a queer-looking little house with a great deal of piazza and a very little ground-floor. With his cap cocked very much over one eye, Captain Bob Shorty knocked at the door, and was answered by a young maiden of about forty-two.

" Hast seen any troops pass here of late ?" asked Captain Bob Shorty, with much dignity.

The Southern maiden, who was a First Family, sniffed indignantly, and says she :

" I reckon not, poor hireling Hessian."

" Forward—double-quick—march !" says Captain Bob Shorty, with much vehemence ; " that ere young woman has been eating onions."

" Onward, right onward through the darkness, went the Conic Section of the Mackerel Brigade, eager to engage the rebel foe and work out the genius of strategy. Half an hour, and another house was reached. In response to the captain's knock a son of chivalry stuck his head out of a window, and says he :

" There's nobody at home."

Peace, ignoramius !" says Captain Bob Shorty, majestically ; " the United States of America wishes to know if you have seen any troops go by to-night."

" Yes," says the chivalry, " my sister saw a com-. pany go by just now, I reckon."

" Forward—double quick—march !" says Captain Bob Shorty, " we can catch the Confederacy alive if we're quick enough."

And now, my boy, the march was resumed with new vigor, for it was certain that the enemy was right in front, and might be strategically annihilated. A long time passed, however, without the discovery of a soul, and it was after midnight when the next house was gained.

A small black contraband came to the door, and says he :

" By gorry, mars'r sogerum, what you hab ?"

" Tell me, young Christy's minstrel," says Captain Bob Shorty, " have any troops passed here to-night ?"

The contraband turned a summerset, and says he :

" Mars' and misses hab seen two companies dis berry night, so helpum God."

" Forward—double quick—march !" says Captain Bob Shorty. " Two companies is rather heavy for this here band of Spartans, but it is sweet to die for one's country."

The march went on, my boy, until we got to the next house, where the inmates refused to appear, but shouted that they had seen *three* companies go past.

At this Captain Bob Shorty was heard to scratch his head in the darkness, and says he :

" This here strategy is a good thing at decent odds : but when it's three to one, it's more respectable to have all quiet on the Potomac. Halt, fellow wictims, and let us wait here until the daily sun is issued by the divine editor."

The orb of light was calmly stealing up the east, my boy, when Captain Bob Shorty sprang from his blanket and observed the house, before which the Conic Section was encamped, with protruding eyes.

" By all that's blue !" says Captain Bob Shorty, " if that ain't the werry identical house where we saw the vinegar maiden last night !"

And so it was, my boy ! The Conic Section of the Mackerel Brigade had been going round and round on a private race-course all night, stopping four times at the same judge's stand, and going after their own tails, like so many humorous cats.

Strategy, my boy, is a profound science, and don't cost more than two millions a day, while the money lasts.   Yours, in deep cogitation,

ORPHEUS C. KERR.

LETTER XXXVIII.

INTRODUCING THE VERITABLE "HYMN OF THE CONTRABANDS," WITH
EMANCIPATION MUSIC, AND DESCRIBING THE TERRIFIC COMBAT A LA
MAIN BETWEEN CAPTAIN VILLIAM BROWN, OF THE UNITED STATES
OF AMERICA, AND CAPTAIN MUNCHAUSEN, OF THE SOUTHERN CON-
FEDERACY.

WASHINGTON, D. C., April 4th, 1862.

KNOWING you to be a connoisseur in horse-flesh,
my boy, it is but proper I should tell you that I have
leased my steed, the gothic Pegasus, for a few days to
an army carpenter, that gentleman having expressed
a wish to use my architectural animal as a model for
some new barracks. Pegasus, my boy, when viewed
lengthwise, presents a perspective not unlike a
Hoboken cottage, and eminent builders tell me that
his back is the very beau ideal of a combination roof.
I sent a side-view photograph of the fiery stallion to
a venerable grandmother not long since, and she
wrote back that she was glad to see I had my quarters elevated on piles to avoid dampness, but should
think the hut would smoke with such a crooked
chimney ! The old lady is rather hard of hearing,
my boy, and makes trifling mistakes without her
spectacles.

In the absence of my war-horse I hired a respectable hack to take me to Manassas, the driver saying
that he would not charge me more than ten dollars
an hour, as he had seen better days himself. What
his seeing better days had to do with me I didn't exactly see, my boy ; but I hired the chariot, and we
went down the river at a pace sometimes achieved by
that carriage in a funeral which contains the parents
of the deceased.

Wet towels, soda-water, and a few wholesome
kicks in the rear having rendered Company 3, Regiment 5, Mackerel Brigade, sufficiently certain of their
legs to march a polka in the space of an ordinary
corn field, Captain Villiam Brown placed himself at
their head, and, flanked by a canteen and an adjutant, the combined pageant was just about to move
on a reconnoitering expedition as I came up.

" Ha !" said Villiam, hastily placing his shirt-frill
over the neck of a bottle that accidentally peeped
from his bosom—"I am about to lead these noble
beings on the path of glory, and you shall participate
in the beams."

Without a word, I turned his left wing ; and as
the band, which consisted of a fat Dutchman and a
night-key bugle, struck up " Drops of Brandy," we
moved onward, like the celestial vision of childhood's
dream.

Like the radiance of a higher heaven streaming

through the golden-tinted windows of some grand old cathedral, fell the softened light of that April afternoon, on budding Nature, as we halted before a piece of woods just this side of Strasburg. On the new leaves of the trees in front of us the sunshine coined a thousand phantom cataracts of specie, and in the vale below us a delicate purple shadow wrestled with the hill-reflected fire of the sun. Deep silence fell on Company 3, Regiment 5, Mackerel Brigade ; the band put his instrument on the ring with the key of his trunk, and Villiam softly reconnoitred through a spy-glass furnished with a cork. Suddenly the tones of a rich, manly voice swelled up from the bosom of the valley.

"Hush !" says Villiam, sternly eyeing the band, who had just hiccupped—"'tis the song of the Contrabands."

We all listened, and could distinctly hear the following words of the singer :

"They're holding camp-meeting in Hickory Swamp,
    O, let my people go ;
De preacher's so dark dat he carry um lamp,
    O, let my people go.
De brudders am singing dis jubilee tune,
    O, let my people go ;
Two dollars a year for de Weekly Tribune,
    O, let my people go !"

As the strain died away in the distance, the adjutant slapped his left leg.

"Why," said he, dreamily, "that must be Greeley down there."

"No !" says Villiam, solemnly, "it is one of the wronged children of tyranny warbling the suppressed hymn of his injured people. It is a sign," says Villiam, trembling with bravery, "that the Southern Confederacy is somewhere around ; for when you hear the squeak of the agonized rat," said Villiam, philosophically, "you may be sure that the sanguinary terrier is on the war-path."

Scarcely had he spoken, my boy, when there emerged from the edge of the wood before us a rebel company, headed by an officer of hairy countenance and much shirt collar. This officer's face was a whisker plantation, through which his eyes peeped forth like two snakes coiled up in a window-brush. His dress was shoddy, his air was toddy, and a yard of valuable stair-carpet enveloped his manly shoulders.

"Halt !" said he to his file of reptiles, whose general effect was that of a congress of rag-merchants just come in from a happy speculation in George-Law muskets.

"Sir," said the officer, bowing in a graceful semicircle, "I am somewhat in the First Family way, own a plantation, drink but little water at home, and have the honor to be Captain Munchausen, of the Southern Confederacy."

" Dost fence ?" says Villiam, grimly drawing his sword.

" Fence !" says Captain Munchausen, also drawing his disguised crowbar. " Didst ever hear, boy, or read, of that great fencer of the olden time, ·the Chevalier St. George ?"

" Often," says Villiam, in a tone that was as plainly the echo of a lie as is that of the delicate female eater of slate-pencils, when she says that she never could bear pork and beans.

" Well," says Captain Munchausen, haughtily, " the chevalier was so extremely jealous of my superior skill, that he actually went and died nearly a hundred years before I was born."

"Soap," says Villiam, like one talking in his sleep, " is sometimes made with powerful lie."

" By Chivalry !" says Captain Munchausen, cholerically ; " I swear, I never told a single lie in all my life."

" A *single* lie !" says Villiam, abstractedly ; " ah, no ! for the lies of the Southern Confederacy are all married, and have large families."

This domestic speech, my boy, was too much for Munchausen. Asking one of the rag merchants to hold his three-ply overcoat, and carefully removing his fragmentary cap, that none of the cold potatoes should spill out of it, he planted the remains of his right boot slightly in advance of the skeleton of his left, and thundered :

" 'Sblood !"

Quick as the lightning leaps along the cloud did Captain Villiam Brown send the great toe of his dexter foot to meet that of his foe ; his Damascus blade lay across the opposing brand, and he whispered :

" 'Sdeath !"

It was a beautiful sight—by Minerva it was !

" Stop !" says Villiam, suddenly hauling in his weapon again ; " it shall never be said that I took advantage of a foeman."

As he uttered these memorable words, my boy, this ornament of the service plucked an infant demijohn from his fearless bosom and magnanimously passed it to his antagonist.

A soft commotion was visible in the whiskers of Captain Munchausen—the suburb of a smile as it were ; a cavern opened in their midst, the vessel ascended curvilinearly thereto, and the sound was as the trickling of water down a mountain gulch.

The adjutant took his seat on the sleeping body of the band, and with pencil and paper prepared to record the combat. The opposing champions faced each other, and as Villiam once more raised his blade he smiled horribly.

Then, my boy, was witnessed a scene to make old Charlemagne's paladins dance High-jinks in their graves, and call all the Arturian knights to life again. *Carte et tierce!* but it was a spectacle for Hector and Achilles.   With swords pointed straight at each other's noses did the valorous heroes skip wildly back, and then as wildly forward.   Slam ! bang ! crack ! smack ! right and left ! over and under ! parry, feint, and *première force!*   Now did they hop fierily along on opposite sides of the road, eyeing each other like demoniac Thomas Cats upon the moonlit fence. Ever and anon did they dart furiously to the centre, cutting the blessed atmosphere to invisible splinters, and slaying imaginary legions.

But a crisis was at hand !   In one of his terrible chops, the cool and collected Villiam brought his deadly weapon down full upon the knuckles of the enemy.   But for the fact that Villiam's sword was not quite as sharp as the side of an ordinary three-story house, Munchausen's hand would never more have wielded trenchant blade.   As it was, he hastily dashed his brand to the ground, crammed his knuckles into his mouth, struck up an impassioned dance, and mumbled, in extreme agitation :

" Golfire your cursed abolition soul !"

It was beautiful, my boy, to see how the calm Villiam leaned upon his sword and smiled.

" Ah !" says Villiam, " so perish the foes of the

Union, the Constitution, and the Enforcement of the Laws. I have bruised the Confederacy.—Adjutant!" says Villiam, in a sudden burst of pardonable exultation, "score one for the United States of America!"

Now it happened, my boy, that, as Villiam said this, he turned to where the adjutant was sitting, and bent down to give particular directions. His body was thus made to assume somewhat of the shape of the letter U, the curve being sharply toward the enemy. In an instant Captain Munchausen regained his sword, grasped it after the manner of a flail, and, with a prodigious spank, applied it to the unguarded portion of my hero's anatomy.

High sprang the almost assassinated Villiam into the air, with sparks pouring from his eyes, and Union oaths hissing from his working jaws.

"Adjutant!" roared Captain Munchausen, "score one for the Southern Confederacy!"

No sooner had Villiam reached the ground and picked up the cork that had fallen from his bosom as he ascended, than he plunged rampagiously at his adversary, and aimed a blow at his head that must have taken it off had Captain Munchausen been about a yard taller. As it was, the stroke mercilessly split the air, and caused my hero to spin like a mighty top.

In vain did the shameless Confederate swordsman endeavor to get in a hit as Villiam went round; the sword of the Union met him at every turn, and right quickly was the avenging blade humming around his head again. Inspired with the strength of Hercules, the endurance of Prometheus, and the fire of Pluto, the gorgeous Villiam Brown went at his work once more, like a feller of great trees, and in another moment his awful blade twanged upon the foeman's head.

Down went Captain Munchausen singing inverted psalms, with a whole nest of rockets exploding in his brain. Pale turned his rag merchants at the sight, and one of them immediately deserted to our side and swore that he had always been a Union man.

Villiam leaned upon his blade, and kindly remarked :

" His head is broken ; I heard it crack."

" 'Tis false !" says Captain Munchausen, gloomily ; " that is an old crack—I've had it ever since I was a boy."

" Ah !" says Villiam, airily, " I'm afraid my blow has caused more than one funeral in the inseck kingdom, for the cut went right through the hair. Have a comb ?" says Villiam, pleasantly.

Captain Munchausen made no reply, my boy, but motioned for his men to bear him from the field. It was noticed however, that, as he was being carried into the wood, he asked a gentleman in remarkable tatters, to take him to the last ditch.

As the Southern Confederacy disappeared, Captain Villiam Brown hammered his sword straight with a bit of stone, forced it into its scabbard, and turned majestically to Company 3, Regiment 5, Mackerel Brigade, several members of which were engaged in the athletic game of pitch-penny.

"Let the band be awakened," says Villiam.

A Mackerel at once proceeded to break the slumbers of the orchestra, by shaking a bottle near his ear —that experiment having never been known to fail in the case of a pronounced musical character.

"Ha!" says Villiam, with much spirit, "we will march to the national airs of our distracted country !"

After sounding several cat-calls on his night-key bugle, in the manner of all great instrumentalists who wish to know about their instruments being in tune, the band struck up "Ale to the Chief," and we marched to quarters like so many heroes of ancient Rum.

Shall treason triumph in our land, my boy, while there's a sword to wave ? I think not, my boy, I think not. Though Columbia did not rule the wave, her champions would see to it that she never waived the rule.   Yours, for the Star-Spangled,

ORPHEUS C. KERR.

LETTER XXXIX.

SHOWING HOW A REBEL WAS REDUCED, AND CONVERTED TO "RECON-
STRUCTION," BY THE VALOROUS ORANGE COUNTY HOWITZERS.

WASHINGTON, D. C., April 13th, 1862.

THE stirring times are come again, the maddest of
the year, and I am beginning to believe, my boy, that
what is to be will be as what has been has. Though
still without my Gothic charger, Pegasus, that symmetrical racer having been borrowed for a writing-
desk by a Secretary of the Fronterior, I am enabled to
keep up communications with the Mackerel *corpse
dammee* down the river, and ten thousand star-spangled banners flash through my veins as I relate the
recent great artillery expedition of the Orange County
Howitzers.

It seems, my boy, that an intellectual member of
the Mackerel Brigade got tired of investing Yorktown,
and wandered away in pursuit of adventure. As he
peregrinated in the neighborhood of a rebel domicil,
he beheld what he took for the bird of our country,
stalking out of the barnyard, and was taking measures
to confiscate it, when the proprietor made his appearance, and says he :

"Hessian, spare that goose!"

The Mackerel chap gave a tragic start, and says he :

" 'Tis the Eagle I would rescue, Horatio ; the bird celebrated by my brother, the Congressman, in all his speeches."

" Well," says the foul traitor, "it is undoubtedly what the Congressman takes for an Eagle, as I am aware that Congressmen generally treat the American Eagle as if he were a goose ; but as that gander happens to belong to one of the very First Families of Virginia, and cost me four shillings, it becomes my painful duty to resist your habeas corpus act." · And with that he drove the beautiful bird into the barnyard, and locked the gate.

Fired to fury by this insult from one of those whom our army had come to protect, the Mackerel chap went immediately back to quarters, and appealed to his comrades for vengeance.

That gifted officer Samyule Sa-mith, heard his burning words, and says he :

" The cannon of the Union shall speak in this matter. Let the Orange County Howitzers get ready for action, and I will lead them against the Philistine."

Instantly arose the notes of dreadful preparation ; the guns were mobilized, six English gentlemen in the hosiery business were invited to view the coming battle, and just as the moon rose above the trees, the artillery started for the rebel stronghold.

Arriving before the offending house, the howitzers were placed in line, and all got ready for the bombardment. It was just possible, my boy, that two men might have marched into that house, and captured the misguided Confederacy without slaughter. You may be unable to see what use there was in bringing artillery and forming in line of battle ; but you are very ignorant, my boy ; you know nothing about strategy and war.

"Soldiers," says Samyule, "remember that the eyes of the whole world are upon you at this moment, and endeavor to hit the house as often as possible. We will fire one round without ball," says Samyule, "to see if the powder is first-class."

Now it chanced that while the loading-up was going on, the gallant Lieutenant Lemons got his legs wonderfully entangled in the lanyard of his piece, and kept turning the howitzer around in a manner strongly expressive of nervous agitation. Suddenly he stepped across to where Samyule was standing, and whispered in his ear.

"O, I see," says Samyule, kindly, "you were educated at West Point, and want to know which end of the cannon ought to be pointed at the enemy. Well," says Samyule, instructively, "you'd better point the end with a hole in it."

Everything being in readiness, my boy, the combined battery launched its thunders on the air, creating a great sensation in the neigboring hen-roosts, and causing a large rooster to fall from a branch in the midst of his refreshing slumbers.

"Now, that the powder has sustained its reputation," says Samyule, impressively, "let the two-inch balls be hurled at the enemy's works."

As the house was full ten yards off, this second discharge failed to hit it ; but it brought the Southern Confederacy to the window in his night-cap, and says he :

"There's no use of my trying to sleep, if you chaps keep making such a noise down there."

"Unhappy man," says Samyule, solemnly; "we come here to reduce you, and will listen to nothing but unconditional surrender."

The Confederacy gaped, and says he :

"I'm very sleepy, and can't talk to you now ; but I'll call over in the morning."

And he shut the window, and went back to bed. A frown was observed to steal over the face of Samyule. He has a peculiar countenance, my boy, and a frown affects it strangely. Take his mouth and moustache together, and they remind you of a mouse sunning himself on the edge of his hole ; and when the frown comes on, the mouse acts as though he had a stomach-ache.

"Comrades," says Samyule, "the enemy requires

another round, and we must do it on the square.
Fire !"

Like four-and-twenty thunder-storms the howitzers
roared together, and had not the Orange County veterans forgotten to put in any balls, there is reason to
believe that some windows would have been broken.
Another discharge, however, was more successful, as
it knocked the top off the chimney.

The Southern Confederacy appeared at the window
again, and says he :

" If you fellows don't quit that racket down there,
you'll irritate me pretty soon."

This significant remark caused a sudden cessation
of the bombardment, and Samyule hastily called a
council of war.

" Gentlemen," says Samyule, " a new issue has
arisen. If we irritate the Southern Confederacy, all
hopes of future Union and reconstruction may be
destroyed."

A chap who was a conservative democrat suddenly
flamed up at this, and says he :

" The abolitionists caused this terrible war, and it
is our business, as no-party men, to finish it Constitutionally. If we irritate this man, no power on
earth will ever make him submit to reconstruction.
Ask him."

Here the democratic chap took a large taste of tobacco, and sighed for his country.

"Mr. Davis," says Samyule to the Confederacy at the window, "if we do not irritate you, will you consent to be reconstructed?"

"Reconstructed!" says the Confederacy, thoughtfully; "reconstructed! Ah!" says he, "you mean, will I consent to be born again?"

"Yes," says Samyule, metaphysically; "will you consent to be borne again, as we have borne with you heretofore?"

The Confederacy thought awhile, and then says he: "Consider me reconstructed."

As that was all the Constitution asked, of course there was no more to be done, and the Orange County Howitzers returned to their original position in the mire, the English gentlemen remarking that the appearance and discipline of our troops were satisfactory to Albion.

Fighting according to the Constitution, my boy, is such an admirable way of preventing carnage, that some doctor ought to take out a patent for it as a cheap medicine.

Yours to come, and
ORPHEUS C. KERR,

LETTER XL.

RENDERING TRIBUTE OF ADMIRATION TO THE WOMEN OF AMERICA,
WITH A REMINISCENCE OF HOBBS & DOBBS, ETC.

WASHINGTON, D. C., April 18th, 1862.

HAVING a leisure hour at my disposal, my boy, and being reminded of infatuating crinoline by the reception of certain bird-like notes in chirography strongly resembling the exquisite edging on delicious pantalettes, I turn my attention to that beautiful creation which is fearfully and wonderfully maid, and wears distracting gaiters.

Woman, my boy, at her worst, is a source of real happiness to the sterner sex. There's a chap in the Mackerel Brigade who got very melancholy one day after receiving a letter from home, wherein he was affectionately called " a unnatural and wicious creetur" for not sending his better-half a new dress and some hair-pins. Seeing his affliction, and divining its cause, another Mackerel stepped up to him, and says he :

" Is it the old woman which is on a tare ?"

The married chap groaned, and says he :

" She's mad as a hornet. I do believe," says the married chap, turning very pale, " that she'll take away my night-key, and teach my babes to call me the Old File."

" Well," says the comforting Mackerel, " then why did you get married ? Why didn't you stay a single bachelor like me, and enjoy the pursuit of happiness in the Fire Department ?"

" Happiness !" says the married chap, " why it was expressly to enjoy happiness that I wedded. Step this way," says the married chap, with a horrible smile, leading his consoler aside, " ain't the women of America mortal ?"

" Yes," says the Mackerel thoughtfully.

" And don't they die ?"

" Yes," says the Mackerel. " That is to say," added the Mackerel, contemplatively, " they some-times die when there's new and expensive tombstones in fashion."

" Peter Perkins !" says the married chap, with a smile of wild bliss, " I wouldn't miss the happiness I shall feel when my angel returns to her native hev-ings, for the sake of being twenty bachelors. No !" says the married chap, clutching his bosom, " I've lived on the thought of that air bliss ever since the morning my female pardner threw my box of long-sixes out of the window, and called in the police be-cause I brought a waluable terrier home with me."

Here the married chap uncorked his canteen and eyed it with speechless fury.

Tears came to the eyes of the unwomantic Mackerel ; he extended his hand, and says he :

" Say no more, Bobby—say no more. If you ain't got the correck idea of Heaven there's no such place on the map."

I give you this touching conversation between two of nature's noblemen, my boy, that you may appreciate that beautiful dispensation of Providence which endows woman with the slighter failings of humanity, yet gives her the power to brighten the mind of inferior man with glorious visions of joy beyond the grave.

My arm has been strengthened in this war, my boy, by the inspiration of woman's courage, and aided by her almost miraculous foresight. Only yesterday, a fair girl of forty-three summers, thoughtfully sent me a box, containing two gross of assorted fish-hooks, three cook-books, one dozen of Tubbscs best spool-cotton, three door-plates, a package of patent geranium-roots, two yards of Brussels carpet, Rumford's illustrated work on Perpetual Intoxication, ten bottles of furniture-polish, and some wall-paper. Accompanying these articles, so valuable to a soldier on the march, was a note, in which the kind-hearted girl said that the things were intended for our sick and wounded troops, and were the voluntary tributes of a

loyal and dreamy-souled woman. I tried a dose of
the furniture-polish, my boy, on a chap that had the
measles, and he has felt so much like a sofa ever since,
that a coroner's jury will sit on him to-morrow.

The remainder of this susceptible young creature's
note, my boy, was calculated to move a heart of stone.
She asked if it hurt much to be killed, and said she
should think the President might sue Jeff Davis, or
commit habeas corpus or some other ridiculous thing,
to stop this dreadful, spirit-agonizing war. She said
that her deepest heart-throbs and dream-yearnings
were for the crimson-consecrated Union, and that she
had lavished her most harrowing hope-sobs for its
heaven-triumph. She said that she had a friend,
named Smith, in the army, and wished I could find
him out, and tell him that the human heart, though
repining at the absence of the beloved object, may be
coldly proud as a scornful statute to the stranger's
eye, but pines like a soul-murdered water-lily on
the lovely stream of its twilight-brooding contem-
plations.

Anxious to oblige her, my boy, I asked the General
of the Mackerel Brigade if he knew a soldier "of the
name of Smith ?"

The General thought awhile, and says he :

" Not one. There are many of the name of
Sa-mith," says the general, screening his eye from the
sun with a bottle, " and the Smythes are numerous ;

but the Smiths all died as soon as the Prince of Wales came to this country."

This is an age of great aristocracy, my boy, and the name of Smith is confined to tombstones. I once knew a chap named Hobbs, who made knobs, and had a partner named Dobbs ; and he never could get married until he changed his title ; for what sensitive and delicately-nerved female would marry a man whose business-card read, " Try Hobbs & Dobbs' Knobs ?" Finally, he called himself De Hobbs, and wedded a Miss Podger—pronounced Po-gshay. After that, he cut his partner, ordered his friends to cease calling him Jack, and in compliance with the wishes of his wife's family, got out a business-card like this :

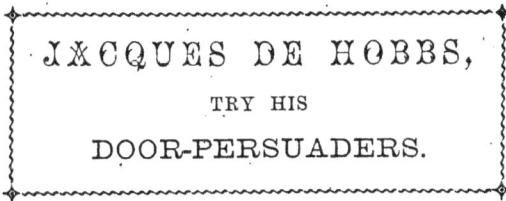

```
┌──────────────────────────────────┐
│   JACQUES DE HOBBS,               │
│            TRY HIS                │
│       DOOR-PERSUADERS.            │
└──────────────────────────────────┘
```

But, to return to the women of America, there was one of them came out to our camp not long ago, my boy, with six Saratoga trunks full of moral reading for our troops. She was distributing the cheerful works among the veterans, when she happened to to come across Private Jinks, who had just got his rations, and was swearing audibly at the collection of wild beasts he had found in one of his biscuits.

" Young man," says she, in a vinegar manner, " do you want to be damned ?"

Private Jinks reflected a moment, and says he :

" Really, mem, I don't know enough about horses to say."

The literary agent was greatly shocked, but recovered in time to hand the warrior a small book, and told him to read it and be saved.

It was a small and enlivening volume, my boy, written by a missionary lately served up for breakfast by the Emperor of Glorygoolia, and entitled " The Fire that Never is Quenched."

Jinks looked at the book, and says he :

" What district is that fire in ?"

The daughter of the Republic bit off a small piece of cough candy, and says she :

" It's down below, young man, where you bid fair to go."

" And will it never be put out ?" says Private Jinks.

The deeply-affected crinoline shook her head until all her combs rattled, and says she :

" No, young man ; it will burn, and burn, young man."

" Then I'm safe enough !" says Private 'Jinks, slapping his knee ; " for I'm a member of Forty

Hose, and if that air fire is to keep burning, they'll have to have a paid Fire Department down there, and shut us fellows out."

The daughter of the Republic instantly left him, my boy ; and when next I saw her, she was arguing with one of the chaplains, who pretended to believe that firemen sometimes went to Heaven.

Woman, my boy, is an angel in disguise ; and if she had wings what a rise there would be in bonnets !

Yours, for the next Philharmonic,

ORPHEUS C. KERR.

LETTER XLI.

CITING A NOTABLE CASE OF VOLUNTEER SURGERY, AND GIVING AN
OUTLINE SKETCH OF "COTTON SEMINARY."

WASHINGTON, D. C., April 25th, 1862.

THERE is a certain something about a sick-room,
my boy, that makes me think seriously of my latter
end, and recognize physicians as true heroes of the
bottle-field. The subdued swearing of the sufferer
on his bed, the muffled tread of the venerable nurse,
as she comes into the room to make sure that the
brandy recommended by the doctor is not too mild
for the patient, the sepulchral shout of the regimental
cat as she recognizes the tread of Jacob Barker, the
sergeant's bull-terrier, outside ; all these are things
to make the spectator remember that we are but dust,
and that to return to dust is our dustiny.

Early in the week, my boy, a noble member of the
Pennsylvania Mud-larks was made sick in a strange
manner. A draft of picked men from certain regiments was ordered for a perilous expedition down the
river. You may be aware, my boy, that a draft is
always dangerous to delicate constitutions ; and, as
the Mud-lark happened to burst into a profuse per-

spiration about the time he found himself standing in this draft, he, of course, took such a violent cold that he had to be put to bed directly. I went to see him, my boy; and whilst he was relating to me some affecting anecdotes of the time when he used to keep a bar, a member of the Medical Staff of the United States of America came in to see the patient.

This venerable surgeon first deposited a large saw, a hatchet, and two pick-axes on the table, and then says he :

"How do you find yourself, boy ?"

The mud-lark took a small chew of tobacco with a melancholy air, and says he :

"I think I've got the guitar in my head, Mr. Sawbones, and am about to join the angel choir."

"I see how it is," says the surgeon, thoughtfully ; "you think you've got the guitar, when it's only the drum of your ear that is affected. Well," says the surgeon, with sudden pleasantness, as he reached after his saw and one of the pick-axes, "I must amputate your left leg at once."

The mud-lark curled himself up in bed like a wounded anaconda, and says he :

"I don't see it in that light."

"Well," says the surgeon, in a sprightly manner, "then suppose I put a fly-blister on your stomick, and only amputate your right arm ?"

The surgeon was formerly a blacksmith, my boy,

and got his diploma by inventing some pills with iron
in them.   He proved that the blood of six healthy
men contained enough iron to make six horse-shoes,
and then invented the pills to cure hoarseness.

The sick chap reflected on what his medical adviser
had said, and then says he :

" Your words convince me that my situation must
be dangerous.   I must see some relative before I permit myself to be dissected."

" Whom would you wish me to send for ?" says the
surgeon.

" My grandmother, my dear old grandmother," said
the Mud-lark, with much feeling.

The surgeon took me cautiously aside, and says
he :

" My poor patient has a cold in his head, and his
life depends, perhaps, on the gratification of his
wishes.   You have heard him ask for his grandmother," says the surgeon, softly, " and as his grandmother lives too far away to be sent for, we must
practice a little harmless deception.   We must send
for Secretary Welles of the Navy Department, and
introduce him as the grandmother.   My patient will
never know the difference."

I took the hint, my boy, and went after the Secretary ; but the latter was so busy examining a model
of Noah's Ark that he could not be seen.   Happily,
however, the patient recovered while the surgeon was

getting his saw filed, and was well enough last night to reconnoitre in force.

The Mackerel Brigade being still in quarters before Yorktown, I am at leisure to stroll about the Southern Confederacy, my boy ; and on Thursday I paid a visit to Cotton Seminary, just beyond Alexandria, where the Southern intellect is taught to fructify and expand. This celebrated institution of learning is all on one floor, with a large chimney and heavy mortgage upon it, and a number of windows supplied with ground glass—or, rather, supplied with a certain openness as regards the ground.

Upon entering this majestic edifice, the master, Prex Peyton, descended at once from the barrel on which he was seated, and gave me a true Virginian welcome :

" Though you may be a Lincoln horde," says he, in a manorial manner, " the republic of intellect recognizes you only as a man. The Southern mind knows how to recognize a soul apart from its outer circumstances ; for what say the logicians ? *Deus est anima brutorem!* Take a seat on yonder barrel, friend Hessian, and you shall hear the wisdom of the youthful minds. First class in computation stand up."

As I took a seat, my boy, the first class in computation came to the front ; and it is my private impression, my boy—my private impression—that each child's father was the owner of a rag plantation at some period of his life.

"Boys," says the master, "how is the table of Confederate money divided ?"

"Into pounds, shillings, and pence."

"Right. Now, Master Mason, repeat the table."

Master Mason, who was a germ of a first family, took his fingers out of his mouth, and says he :

"Twenty pounds of Confederate bonds make one shilling, twenty shillings make one penny, six pennies one drink."

"That's right, my pretty little cherubs," says the master. "Now go and take your seats, and study your bowie-knife exercises. Class in Geography, stand up."

The class in geography consisted of one small Southern Confederacy, my boy, with a taste for tobacco.

"Master Wise," says the master, confidently, "can you tell us where Africa is ?"

Master Wise sniffed intelligently, and says he :

"Africa is situated at the corner of Spruce and Nassau streets, and is bounded on the north by Greeley, on the south by Slavery, on the east by Sumner, and on the west by Lovejoy."

"Very true, my bright little fellow," says the master ; "now go back to your chawing."

"You see, friend Hessian," says the master, turning to me, "how much superior Southerners are, even as children, to the depraved Yankees. In my teaching experience, I have known scholars only six years old to play poker like old members of the church, and a pupil of mine euchred me once in ten minutes."

I thanked him for his courtesy, and was proceeding to the door, when I observed four boys in one corner, with their mouths so distorted that they seemed to have subsisted upon a diet of persimmons all their lives.

"Venerable pundit," says I, in astonishment, "how came the faces of those offspring so deformed?"

"O !" says the master, complacently, "that class has been studying Carlyle's works."

I retired from Cotton Seminary, my boy, with a firm conviction of the utility of popular education, and a hope that the day might come when a Professorship of Old Sledge would be created in the New York University.

Yours, for a higher civilization,

ORPHEUS C. KERR.

LETTER XLII.

REVEALING A NEW BLOCKADING IDEA, INTRODUCING A GEOMETRICAL
STEED, AND NARRATING THE WONDERFUL EXPLOITS OF THE MACK-
EREL SHARPSHOOTER AT YORKTOWN.

WASHINGTON, D. C., May 2d, 1862.

SPEAKING of the patriarch of the Navy Department, my boy, they say that the respected Ancient
has under consideration a new and admirable plan for
making the blockade efficient. The idea is, to furnish
all the naval captains with spectacles made of looking-glass, so that when they are asleep, on the quarter-
deck, their glasses will reflect the figure of any rebel
craft that may be trying to slip by. These spectacles could all be ready in twenty years ; and when
the Secretary told a Congressman of the plan, the
latter thought carefully over the suggestion, "as
dripping with coolness it rose from the Welles," and
says he :

"My dear madam, the idea lacks but one thing—
the looking-glass spectacles ought to be supplied with
a comb and brush, so that the captain could fix himself up after capturing the pirate. Ah, madam," says
the Congressman, hastily picking up the Jack of

Clubs, which he had accidentally pulled out with his
pocket-handkerchief, " you will rank next to Mary,
the mother of Washington, in the affections of future
generations."

The *mother* of Washington, my boy !—the MOTHER
of Washington !—why, the Secretary is already celebrated as the grandmother of Washington—city.

On the occasion of my last visit to Yorktown, my
boy, I found the Mackerel Brigade so well up in animal spirits that each chap was equal to a pony of
brandy, and capable of capturing any amount of glass
artillery.   At the present time, my boy, the brigade
is formed in the shape of a clam-shell, with the right
resting on a beer wagon, and the left on a traveling
free-lunch saloon.   I was examining the new battery
of the Orange County Howitzers—whose guns have
such large touch-holes that the chaps keep their
crackers and cheese in them when not in action—and
was also overhearing the remarks of a melancholy
Mackerel concerning what he wished to be done with
his effects in case he should perish with old age before the battle commenced—when I beheld Captain
Villiam Brown, approaching me on the most geometrical beast I ever saw—an animal even richer in
sharp corners, my boy, than my own gothic steed,
Pegasus.

" Ha !" says Villiam, hastily swallowing something
that brought tears to his eyes, and taking a bit of

lemon-peel to clear his voice, " you are admiring my Arabian courser, and wondering whether it is one of the three presented to Secretary Seward by the Emperor of Egypt."

" You speak truly, my Bayard," says I ; " that superb piece of horseflesh looks like the original plan of the city of Boston—there's so many bisecting angles about him."

" Ah !" says Villiam, with an agreeable smile, " in the words of the anthem of childhood—

" ' The angles told me so.' "

Villiam's idea of angels, my boy, constitutes a theory of theology in itself.

" What call you the charger ?" says I.

" Euclid," says Villiam, pausing for a moment, to catch the gurgle of a canteen just reversed.   " Ah !" says Villiam, recovering his presence of mind, " this here marvel of natural history is a guaranteed 2.40."

" No !" says I.

" Yes," says Villiam, calculatingly, " this superb animal is a sure 2.40—he cost me just Two dollars and Forty cents.   But come with me," said Villiam, proudly, " and see the sharp-shooter contingent I have just organized to aid in the suppression of this here unnatural rebellion."

I followed the splendidly-mounted warrior, my boy, to a spot not far from the nearest point of the enemy's

lines, where I found a lengthy Western chap polish-
ing a rifle with a powerful telescope on the end of it.
He had just been organized, and was preparing to
make some carnage.

"Now then, Ajack," said Villiam, classically, "let
us see you pick off that Confederacy over there,
which looks like a mere fly at this distance."

The sinewy sharpshooter sprang to his feet, called
a drummer-boy to hold his chew of tobacco, looked
at the rebel gunner through his telescope, shut up the
telescope, took aim with both eyes shut, turned away
his head, and *fired!*

I must say, my boy, that I at first thought the
Confederacy was not hit at all, inasmuch as he only
scratched one of his legs and squinted along his gun ;
but Villiam soon showed me how exquisitely accu-
rate the sharpshooter's aim had been.

"The bullet struck him," says Villiam, confidently, "and would have reached his heart, but for the
Bible given him by his mother when he left home,
which arrested its fatal progress. Let us hope," says
Villiam, seriously, "that he will henceforth search
the Scriptures, and be a dutiful son."

I felt the tears spring to my eyes, for I once had a
mother myself. I couldn't help it, my boy—I
couldn't help it.

The second shot of the unerring rifleman was
aimed at a hapless contraband, who had been sent

out to the end of a gun by the enemy, to see that the ball did not roll out before the gunner had time to pull the trigger. Crack ! went the deadly weapon of the sharpshooter, and down went the unhappy African—to his dinner.

" Ah !" says Villiam, skeptically, " do you think you hit him, Ajack ?"

" Truelie, stranger," responded the unmoved marksman, sententiously. " He will die at twenty minutes past three this afternoon."

Sick of this dreadful slaughter, my boy, I turned from the spot with Villiam, and presently overtook the general of the Mackerel Brigade, who was seated on a fence by the roadside, trying to knock the cork out of a bottle with a piece of rock. We saluted, and went on to the camp.

Sharpshooters, my boy, are a source of much pain to hostile gunners, and if one of them should happen to put a bullet through the head of navigation, it would certainly cause the tide to fall.

Yours, take-aimiably,

ORPHEUS C. KERR.

LETTER XLIII.

CONCERNING MARTIAL LITERATURE: INTRODUCING A DIDACTIC POEM
BY THE "ARKANSAW TRACT SOCIETY," AND A BIOGRAPHY OF
GARIBALDI FOR THE SOLDIER.

WASHINGTON, D. C., May 7th, 1862.

SOUTHERN religious literature, my boy, is admir-
ably calculated to improve the morals of race-courses,
and render dog-fights the instruments of wholesome
spiritual culture.

On the person of a high-minded Southern Confederacy captured the other day by the Mackerel pickets,
I found a moral work which had been issued by the
Arkansaw Tract Society for the diffusion of religious
thoughts in the camp, and was much improved by
reading it. The pure-minded Arkansaw chap who
got it up, my boy, remarked in pallid print, that
every man "should extract a wholesome moral from
everything whatsomedever," and then went on to say
that there was an excellent moral in the beautiful
Arkansaw nursery tale of

THE BEWITCHED TARRIER.

Sam Johnson was a cullud man,
  Who lived down in Judee;
He owned a rat tan tarrier
  That stood 'bout one foot three;
And the way that critter chawed up rats
  Was gorjus for to see.

One day this dorg was slumberin'
  Behind the kitchen stove,
When suddenly a wicked flea—
  An ugly little cove—
Commenced upon his faithful back
  With many jumps to rove.

Then up arose that tarrier,
  With frenzy in his eye,
And waitin' only long enough
  To make a touchin' cry,
Commenced to twist his head around,
  Most wonderfully spry.

But all in vain; his shape was sich,
  So awful short and fat—
And though he doubled up hisself,
  And strained hisself at that,
His mouth was half an inch away
  From where the varmint sat.

The dorg sat up an awful yowl
  And twisted like an eel,
Emitting cries of misery
  At ev'ry nip he'd feel,
And tumblin' down and jumpin' up,
  And turnin' like a wheel.

But still that most owdacious flea
    Kept up a constant chaw
Just where he couldn't be scratched out
    By any reach of paw,
But always half an inch beyond
    His wictim's snappin' jaw.

Sam Johnson heard the noise, and came
    To save his animile;
But when he see the crittur spin—
    A barkin' all the while—
He dreaded hiderfobia,
    And then began to rile.

"The pup is mad enough," says he,
    And luggin' in his axe,
He gev the wretched tarrier
    A pair of awful cracks,
That stretched him out upon the floor,
    As dead as carpet-tacks.

MORAL.

Take warnin' by this tarrier,
    Now turned to sassidge meat;
And when misfortin's flea shall come
    Upon your back to eat,
Beware, or you may die because
    You can't make both ends meet.

The Arkansaw Tract Society put a note at the
bottom of this moral lyric, my boy, stating that the
"wicked flea here mentioned is the same varmint
which is mentioned in Scripture as being so bold;
'the wicked flea, when no man pursueth but the
righteous, is as bold as a lion.'"

Speaking of literature, my boy, I am happy to say

that the members of the Mackerel Brigade have been inspired to emulate great examples by the biographies of great soldiers which have been sent to the camp for their reading by the thoughtful women of America. For instance, here we have the

LIFE OF GENERAL GARIBALDI.

BY THE NOBLEST RUM 'UN OF THE MALL.

CHAPTER I.

HIS BIRTH.

At that period of the world's history when the Past immediately preceded the Present, and the Future was yet to come, there existed in a small town of which the houses formed a part, a rich but respectable couple. Owing to a combination of circumstances, their first son was a boy of the male gender, who inherited the name of his parents from the moment of his birth, and who is the subject of our story. When he was about five hours old, his male parent said to him :

" My boy, do you know me ?"

In an instant the eyes of the child flashed Jersey lightning, he ceased sucking his little fistesses, his hair would have stood on end if there had been any on his head, and he exclaimed in tones of thunder-r-r :

" *Viva Liberte et Maccaroni !*"

Mr. Garibaldi instantly clasped the little cherubim

to his stomach, while Mrs. Garibaldi waved the tri-colored flag above them both, and requested the chambermaid to bring her a little more of that same burning-fluid, with plenty of sugar in it.

Thus was Garibaldi ushered into the world; and the burning fluid is for sale by all respectable druggists and grocers throughout the country, with S. O. P. on the wrapper.

CHAPTER II.

HIS EDUCATION.

On arriving at years of indiscretion, our hero began to display a tendency to " seven-up," Old Sledge, and other card-inal virtues, calculated to fit him for playing his cards right in future years. Just about this time, too, his parents resolved to send him to school, and it is as the young scholar we must now regard him.

Behold him, then, at his tasks, in a red shirt amputated at the neck, and two yellow patches (the badge of Sardinia) flaming from the background of his seat of learning. He readily mastered the Greek verbs and roots, comprehended liquorice root, studied geography, etymology, sycorax, and mahogany; could decline to conjugate the verb toby, and quickly knew enough about algebra to prove that X plus Y, *not* being equal to Z, is *minus* any dinner at noon, and *plus* one of the tightest applications of birch that

ever produced the illusion of a red-hot stove in immediate contact with the human body.

CHAPTER III.

GARIBALDI GOES TO SEA.

Just before the breaking-out of the rebellion at
Rome, the trade in garlic and domestic fleas took a
sudden start, and the Po was crowded with vessels
of all nations—especially the halluci-nations. One
day, young Garibaldi was in the act of stabbing a
barrel of molasses to the heart with a quill, on Pier
4, P. R. (Po River), when he was descried by the
captain of a fishing-smack, detailed by Government
to watch the motions of the English fleet.

" Boy, ahoy !" says the Captain.

The future liberator of Italy dropped his murder-
ous quill, wiped his nose with a pine shaving, and
answered, in trumpet-tones :

" You're another !"

So delighted was the captain with this noble reply,
that he flogged the whole starboard watch at the gun-
wales, ordered a preventer backstay on the kedge-an-
chor, leaped ashore to where Garibaldi was standing,
and offered to make him familiar with the seas, and a
second Cæsar. Garibaldi replied that he had already
been half-seas over, but would not object to another
cruise. He said he had traveled half-seas over, " on
his face," and would now travel the other half on a

vessel. He went. The vessel proved to be a vessel of wrath, and Garibaldi became so familiar with the cat-o-nine-tails, that he soon *mused* upon a plan for deserting the ship.

CHAPTER IV

HE FIGHTS FOR ROME.

All seas are liable to commotions, hence it is not strange that the Holy See encountered a storm about the time that it occurred. For some weeks, certain pure spirits had been fomenting the small beer of civil war, and in spite of vaticanation, it broke out at last, and was a rash proceeding. Garibaldi was sent for by the Goddess of Liberty to lead the insurrectionary forces, while the liberty of the goddess was endangered by the leadership of the commander of the French troops aiding the Pope. Our hero had but a handful of patriots on hand and on foot to fight with him ; but he determined to struggle to the last and perish in the attempt, even though he should lose his life by it. The Frenchman had an immense array of tried soldiers on the *qui vive* and on horseback ; but Garibaldi was not dismayed, and kept his courage up to the "sticking" point by hoping for aid. Alas ! the only aid they received was lemonade and cannonade—but not a brigade. They fought with the French, and were whipped like blazes. *Hinc illa slacryma !*

CHAPTER V.

GARIBALDI IN AMERICA.

After wandering about Italy as an exile for some months, the bold patriot came to America and opened a cigar shop. The writer remembers entering his shop one day to purchase a genuine meerschaum, and discovering, afterwards, that it was made of plaster of Paris, and smelt—when heated—like ancient sourkrout flavored with lamp-oil. Garibaldi also sold the finest Habana cigars ever made on Staten Island, one brand of which was so strong in its integrity that it once defeated dishonesty, thus :

One night, while Garibaldi was praying for his beloved Italy, at the house of a friend, a burglar broke into his store, with the intention of robbing it. The scoundrel broke open the till, took out all the city money (he refused to take anything but current funds), and then broke open a box of the cigars strong in their integrity, intending to have a quiet smoke before he left. Alas ! for him.

When Garibaldi opened the store in the morning, he found the burglar laying on his back, with a cigar in his mouth, and *too weak to move!* In the attempt to smoke the cigar, he had drawn his back bone clear through until it caught on his breast bone, and the back of his head was just breaking through the roof of his mouth, when the patriot found him. He was taken to the police-office, and discharged by the first alderman that came along. Such is life !

When the Emperor of France commenced his war with Austria, Garibaldi suddenly appeared at one of the elbows of the Mincio, and having passed around the Great Quadrilateral, headed a select body of Alpine shepherds, and charged the Austrians more than they could pay. All the world knows how that war ended. The emperors of France and Austria signed a treaty by which each was compelled to go back to his own country, tell his subjects that it was "all right," and set all the wise men of the nation to discover what he had been fighting about. Sardinia was not asked to give an opinion. About this time Garibaldi was left out in the cold.

CHAPTER VI.

OUR HERO IN SICILY.

As we look abroad upon the vast nations of the earth, and remember that if they were all destroyed, not one of them would be left, the mind involuntarily conceives an idea, and becomes conscious of the pregnant fact, that "what is to be will be, as what has been, was." So when we look upon families, the thought forces itself upon us that if there were no births there would be no children : without fathers there could be no mothers ; and if the entire household should be swept away ·by disease, they would cease to live. So it is also, when we look upon an individual. Our intellect tells us that if he dies in infancy he will not live to be a man ; and if he never does anything, he will surely do nothing.

This metaphysical line of thought is particularly natural in the case of Garibaldi. Look at him as he now stands, with one foot on Sicily and the other in a boot. Had he not been educated, he would have been uneducated ; had he not gone to sea he would never have been a sailor ; had he not fought for Rome, he would have laid down arms in her cause ; were he not now fighting for Italian independence, he would be otherwise engaged !

Thus the aspect presented by Garibaldi throughout his career, leads our thoughts into all the deep meanderings of the German mind, and teaches us to perceive that " whatever is, is right," as whatever is not, is wrong.

Enraged at the impotent conclusion of the French-and-Austrian war, Garibaldi determined to prosecute hostilities on his own individual curve. In consequence of the high price of ferriage on the Mincio, he moved down toward Palermo, and there called to his standard all Italians favorable to the immediate emancipation of Sicily and the removal of all duties on Maccaroni. Immediately the wildest enthusiasm raged among the friends of freedom. Six patriots attacked the fortress of Messalina, and were immediately placed in prison, with chains around their necks, and Tupper's poems in their pockets.

By degrees, Garibaldi made ready to capture Palermo ; he laid in a stock of cannon and woólen stockings, he harangued his warriors, and told them the day was theirs if they won it ; he invited all the reporters to a banquet. Then he went and took Palermo.

How did he take it ?

I know not ; there are more things in heaven and earth than are dreamed of in ordinary philosophy : all I know is, that he took Palermo.

Having brought my history down to this point, I deem it proper to pause in my task until the future shall have revealed what takes place hereafter ; and the past shall have ceased to interfere so outrageously with the present, that its limits can only be distinguished through the bottom of a tumbler. Liberty is the normal condition of the Italian, and while Garibaldi leads, the cry will be : "Liberty or death, with a preference for the former." Already the day-star of freedom gilds the horizon of beautiful Naples, and if it should not happen to be proved a comet by some evil-minded astronomer, Italy may yet be as free as New York itself, and pay a war-tax of not more than some millions a year.

This finely-written life of the great Italian patriot

had such an effect upon the Mackerels, my boy, that they all wished to *live* like Garibaldi—hence, they are in no hurry to die for their country.

Lives of great men all remind us, my boy, that we may make our lives sublime ; but I never read one yet, that gave instructions for making our deaths sublime—to ourselves.

Yours, for continued respiration,

ORPHEUS C. KERR.

LETTER XLIV.

SHOWING HOW THE GREAT BATTLE OF PARIS WAS FOUGHT AND WON
BY THE MACKEREL BRIGADE, AIDED AND ABETTED BY THE IRON-
PLATED FLEET OF COMMODORE HEAD.

WASHINGTON, D. C., May 10th, 1862.

I HAVE just returned, my boy, from witnessing one
of the most tremendous battles of modern times, and
shall see star-spangled banners in every sunset for
six months to come.

Hearing that the Southern Confederacy had evacu-
ated Yorktown, for the reason that the Last Ditch had
moved on the first of May to a place where there
would be less rent from our cannon, I started early
in the week for the quarters of the valorous and sanguinary Mackerel Brigade, expecting that it had gone
toward Richmond for life, liberty, and the pursuit of
happiness.

On reaching the Peninsula, however, I learned that
the Mackerel " corpse dammee" had been left behind
to capture the city of Paris in co-operation with a
squadron.

Reaching the stamping-ground, my boy, I beheld
a scene at once unique and · impressive. Each indi-

vidual Mackerel was seated on the ground, with a sheet of paper across his knees and an ink-bottle beside him, writing like an inspired poet.

I approached Captain Villiam Brown, who was covering some bare spots on his geometrical steed Euclid, with pieces scissored out of an old hair-trunk, and says I :

" Tell me, my noble Hector, what means this literary scene which mine eyes behold ?"

" Ah !" says Villiam, setting down his glue-pot, " we are about to engage in a skrimmage from which not one may come out alive. These heroic beings," says Villiam, " are ready to die for their country at sight, and you now behold them making their wills. We shall march upon Paris," says Villiam, " as soon as I hear from Sergeant O'Pake, who has been sent to destroy a mill-dam belonging to the Southern Confederacy. Come with me, my nice little boy, and look at the squadron to take part in the attack."

This squadron, my boy, consisted of one twenty-eight-inch row-boat, mounting a twelve-inch swivel, and commanded by Commodore Head, late of the Canal-boat Service. It is iron-plated after a peculiar manner. When the ingenious chap who was to iron-plate it commenced his work, Commodore Head ordered him to put the plates on the *inside* of the boat, instead of outside, as in the case of the Monitor and Galena.

"What do you mean?" says the contractor.

"Why," says the commodore, "ain't them iron plates intended to protect the crew?"

"Yes," says the contractor.

"Well, then, you poor ignorant cuss," says the commodore, in a great passion, "what do you want to put the plates on the outside for? The crew won't be on the outside—will it? The crew will be on the inside—won't it? And how are you going to protect the crew on the inside by putting iron plates on the outside?"

Such reasoning, my boy, was convincing, and the Mackerel Squadron is plated inside.

While I was contemplating this new triumph of American naval architecture, and wondering what they would say about it in Europe, an orderly rode up and handed a scrap of paper to Villiam.

"Ha!" says Villiam, perusing the message, and then passing it to me, "the veteran O'Pake has not deceived the United States of America."

The message was directed to the General of the Mackerel Brigade, my boy, and read as follows:

"GENERAL :—*In accordance with your orders, I have destroyed the mill d—n.*   O'PAKE."

"And now," says Villiam, returning his canteen to his bosom and pulling out his ruffles, "the United States of America will proceed to capture Paris with great slaughter. Let the Brigade form in marching order, while the fleet proceeds around by water, after the manner of Lord Nelson."

The Mackerel Brigade was quickly on the march, headed by the band, who played an entirely new version of "Hail Columbia" on his key bugle. Tramp, tramp, tramp! and we found ourselves in position before Paris.

MAP OF THE WORLD, SHOWING THE POSITION OF THE MACKEREL BRIGADE AT THE GREAT BATTLE OF PARIS.

Paris, my boy, was a city of two houses previous to the recent great fire, which destroyed half of it, and we found it fortified with a strong picket-fence and counterscarp earthworks, from the top of which frowned numerous guns of great compass.

The Mackerel Brigade was at once formed in line-of-battle-order—the line being not quite as straight as an ordinary Pennsylvania railroad—while the fleet menaced the water-front of the city from Duck Lake.

You may not be able to find Duck Lake on the maps, my boy, as it is only visible after a heavy rain.

Previous to the attack, a balloon, containing a Mackerel chap, and a telescope shaped like a bottle, was sent up to reconnoitre.

" Well," says Villiam to the chap when he came down, " what is the force of the Confederacy ?" ·

The chap coughed respectfully, and says he :

" I could only see one Confederacy, which is an old woman !"

" Scorpion !" says Villiam, his eyes flashing like the bottoms of two reversed tumblers, " I believe you to be an accursed abolitionist. Go instantly to the rear," says Villiam, fiercely, "and read the Report of the Van Wyck Investigating Committee."

It was a terrible punishment, my boy, but the example was needed for the good of the service.

The Orange County Howitzers now advanced to the front, and poured a terrible fire in the direction of a point about half way between the nearest steeple and the meridian, working horrible carnage in a flock of pigeons that happened to be passing at the time.

"Splendid, my glorious Prooshians!" says Vil_
liam, just escaping a fall from his saddle by the con-
vulsive start of Euclid, that noble war-horse having
been suddenly roused from a pleasant doze by the
firing—"Splendid, my artillery darlings. Only," says
Villiam, thoughtfully, "as the sun is a friendly
power, don't aim at him so accurately next time."

Meantime, Company 3, Regiment 5, had advanced
from the right, and were just about to make a spendid
bayonet-charge, by the oblique, over the picket-fence
and earthwork, when the concealed Confederacy suddenly opened a deadly fire of old shoes, throwing the
Mackerels into great confusion.

Almost simultaneously, a large potato struck the
fleet on Duck Lake on the nose, so intensely exciting
him that he incontinently touched off his swivel, to
the great detriment of the surrounding country.

This was a critical moment, my boy; the least
trifle on either side would have turned the scale, and
given the victory to either party. Villiam Brown had
just assumed the attitude in which he desired Frank
Leslie's Illustrated Artist to draw him, when a familiar domestic utensil came hissing through the lurid
air from the rebel works, and exploded in two pieces
at his feet.

"Ha!" says Villiam, eyeing the fragments with
great pallor, "they have commenced to throw shell."-

In another moment that incomparable officer was

at the head of a storming party; and as the fleet opened fire on the cabbage-patch in the rear of the enemy's position, an impetuous charge was precipitated in front.

Though met by a perfect hail of turnips, stove-covers, and kindling-wood, the Mackerels went over the fence like a fourth-proof avalanche, and hemmed in the rebel garrison with walls of bayonets.

" Surrender to the Union Anaconda and the United States of America," thundered Villiam.

" You're a nasty, dirty creetur," responded the garrison, who was an old lady of venerable aspect.

" Surrender, or you're a dead man, my F. F. Venus," says Villiam, majestically.

The old lady replied with a look of scorn, my boy, walked deliberately toward the road, and when last seen was proceeding in the direction of Richmond under a green silk umbrella and a heavy press of snuff.

Now it happened, just after we had formally taken possession of the city, while the band was playing martial airs, and the fleet winding up his chronometer, that the General of the Mackerel Brigade made his appearance on the field, and was received with loud cheers by those who believed that he brought their pay back with him.

" My children," says the general, with a paternal smile, " don't praise me for an achievement in which all have won such imperishable laurels. I have only done my jooty."

This speech, my boy, made a great impression upon me on account of its touching modesty. War, my boy, is calculated to promote an amount of bashful modesty never equaled except in Congress, and I have known brigadiers so self-deprecatory that they lived in a state of perpetual blush—especially at the ends of their noses.

Yours, inadequately,

ORPHEUS C. KERR.

‴LETTER XLV.

EXEMPLIFYING THE INCONSISTENCY OF THE CONSERVATIVE ELEMENT,
AND SETTING FORTH THE MEASURES ADOPTED BY CAPTAIN VILLIAM
BROWN IN HIS MILITARY GOVERNMENT OF PARIS.

WASHINGTON, D. C., May 18th, 1862.

SUFFER me, my boy, to direct your attention to
the Congress of our once distracted country, which is
now shedding a beautiful lustre over the whole nation,
and exciting that fond emotion of admiration which
inclines the human foot to perform a stern duty.
"Congress," says Captain Samyule Sa-mith, nodding
to the bar-keeper, and designating a particular bottle
with his finger—"Congress," says he, "is a honor
and a ornament to our bleeding land. The fortunes
of war may fluctuate, the rose may fade ; but Congress
is ever stable. Yes," says Samyule, in a beautiful
burst of enthusiasm, softly stirring the Oath in his
tumbler with a toothpick, "Congress is stable—in
short, a stable full of mules."

The Conservatives from the Border States, my boy,
look upon the Southern Confederacy as a brother,
whom it is our duty to protect against the accursed
designs of the fiendish Abolitionists, who would make

this war one of bloodshed. They ignore all party feeling, support the Constitution as it was, in contra-distinction to what it is, and object to any Confisca-tion measure calculated to irritate our misguided brothers and sisters in that beautiful land where

> The suitor he goes to the planter so grand,
>   And " Give me your daughter," says he,
> " For each unto other we've plighted our loves—
>   I love her and so she loves me,"
>   Says he,
>   " And married we're wishing to be."

> The planter was deeply affected indeed,
>   Such touching devotion to see ;
> " The giving I couldn't afford ; but I'll sell
>   Her for six hundred dollars to thee,"
>   Says he,
>   " Her mother was worth that to me."

Which I quote from a sweet ballad I recently found among some rebel leave-ings at Yorktown.

These conservative patriots, my boy, remind me of a chap I once knew in the Sixth Ward. A high moral chap, my boy, and full of venerable dignity. One night the virtuous cuss doing business next door to him, having just got a big insurance on his stock, and thinking himself safe for a flaming speculation, set fire to his own premises and then called " Murder " on the next corner. Out came the whole Fire Department, only stopping to have two fights and a scrimmage on the way, and pretty soon the water was pouring all over every house in the street except the one on fire. The high moral chap stuck his head out of the window, and says he :

" This here fire ain't in my house, and I don't want no noise around this here residence."

Upon this, some of our gallant firemen, who had just been into a fashionable drinking-shop not more than two blocks off, to see if any of the sparks had got in there, called to the chap to let them into his house, so that they might get at the conflagration more easily.

" Never !" said the chap, shaking his nightcap convulsively ; I didn't set fire to Joneses, and I can't have no Fire Department running around my entries."

" See here, old blue-pills," says one of the firemen, pleasantly, " if you don't let us in, your own crib will go to blazes in ten minutes."

But the dignified chap only shut down the window and went to bed again, saying his prayers backwards. I would not accuse a noble Department of violence, my boy, but in about three minutes there was a double back-action machine standing in that chap's front entry, with three-inch streams out of all the back windows. The fire was put out with only half a hose company killed and wounded, and next day there was a meeting to see what should be done with the incendiary when he was caught. The high moral chap was at that meeting very early, and says he :

"Let me advise moderation in this here unhappy matter. I feel deeply interested," says the chap, with tears ; "for I assisted to put out the conflagration by permitting the use of my house by the firemen. I almost feel," says the genial chap, "like a fellow fire-man myself."

At this crisis, a chap who was assistant engineer, and also Secretary to the Board of Education, arose, and says he :

"What are yer coughin' about, old peg-top ? Didn't me and the fellers have to cave in your door with a night-key wrench—sa-a-ay ? What are yer gassin' about, then ? *You* did a muchness—*you* did ! Yes—slightually—*in* a horn. Now," says the gallant fireman, with an agreeable smile, "if you don't jest coil in yer hose and take the sidewalk very sudden, it'll be my duty, as a member of the Depart-ment, to bust yer eye."

I commend this chaste and rhetorical remark, my boy, to the attention of Border State Conswervatives.

Since the occupation of Paris by the Mackerel Brigade, affairs there have been administered with great intellectual ability by Captain Villiam Brown, who has been appointed Provisional Governor, to govern the sale of provisions.

The city of Paris, my boy, as I told you lately, is

laid out in one house at present ; and since the discovery, that what were at first supposed to be Dahl-
gren guns by our forces were really a number of old
hats with their rims cut off, laid in a row on top of
the earthworks, the democracy have stopped talking
about the General of the Mackerel Brigade for next
President.

The one house, however, was a boarding-house ;
and though all the boarders left at the approach
of our troops, it was subsequently discovered that all
of them save one, were good Union men, and were
brutally forced to fly by that one Confederate miscreant. When Villiam heard of the fate of these
noble and oppressed patriots, my boy, he suffered a
tear to drop into the tumbler he had just found, and
says he :

"Just Hevings ! can this be so ? Ah !" says
Villiam, lifting a bottle near by to see that no rebel
was concealed under it, " I will issue a proclamation
calculated to conciliate the noble Union men of the
sunny South, and bring them back to those protect-
ing folds in which our inedycated forefathers folded
theirselves."

Nobody believed it could be done, my boy—nobody
believed it could be done ; but Villiam understood
his species, and issued the following

PROCLAMATION.

The Union men of the South are hereby informed that the United States of America has reasserted hisself, and will shortly open a bar-room in Paris. Also, cigars and other necessaries of life. By order of

CAPTAIN VILLIAM BROWN, Eskevire.

" There," says Villiam, " the human intelleck may do what violence might fail to accomplish. " Ah !" says Villiam, " moral suasion is more majestik than an army with banners."

In just half an hour after the above Proclamation was issued, my boy, the hum of countless approaching voices called us to the ramparts. A vast multitude was approaching. It was the Union men of the South, my boy, who had read the manifesto of a beneficent Government, and were coming back to take the Oath—with a trifle of sugar in it.

How necessary it is, my boy, that men intrusted with important commands—generals and governors responsible for the pacification and welfare of misguided provinces—should understand just how and when to touch that sensitive chord in our common nature which vibrates responsively when man is invited to take something by his fellow-man.

Scarcely had Villiam assumed his office and suppressed two reporters, when there were brought before him a fugitive contraband of the color of old meerschaum, and a planter from the adjacent county, who claimed the slave.

"It's me—that's Misther Murphy—would be afther axing your riverence to return the black crayture at once," says the planter; "for its meself that owns him, and he runn'd away right under me nose and eyes as soon as me back was turned."

"Ah!" says Villiam, balancing a tumbler in his right hand. "Are you a Southerner, Mr. Murphy?"

"Yaysir," says Mr. Murphy, "it's that I am, intirely. Be the same token, I was raised and born in the swate South—the South of Ireland."

"Are you Chivalry?" says Villiam, thoughtfully.

"Is it Chivalry!—ah, but it's that I am, and me father before me, and me childers that's afther me. If Chivalry was praties I could furnish a dinner to all the wur-ruld, and have enough left to fade the pigs."

"Murphy is a French name," says Villiam, drawing a copy of Vattel on International Law from his pocket and glancing at it, "but I will not dispute what you say. You must do without your contraband, however; for slavery and martial law don't agree together in the United States of America."

"Mr. Black," says Villiam, gravely, turning to the emancipated African, "you have come to the right shop for freedom. You are from henceforth a freeman and a brother-in-law. You are now your own master," says Villiam, encouragingly, "and no man has a right to order you about. You are in the full enjoyment of Heving's best gift—Freedom !. Go and black my boots."

The moral grandeur of this speech, my boy, so affected the Southern planter that he at once became a Union man, took the Oath with the least bit of water in it, and asked permission to have his own boots blacked.

I have been deeply touched of late, my boy, by the reception of a present from the ladies of Alexandria. It is a beautiful little dog, named Bologna (the women of America think that Bologna is the goddess of war, my boy), shaped like a door-mat rolled up, and elegantly frescoed down the sides in white and yellow. The note accompanying the gift was all womanly.

" Accept," it said, " this slight tribute, as an index of the feelings with which the American women regards the noble volunteer. Wear this gift next your heart when the fierce battle rages ; but, in the meantime, give him a bone."

Bologna is a pointer, my boy—a Five-Pointer.

As a dead poet expresses it, Woman is "Heaven's noblest, best, and last good gift to man ;" and I assure, you, my boy, that she is just the last gift he cares about.   Yours, in bachelordliness,

ORPHEUS C. KERR.

LETTER XLVI.

WHEREIN IS SHOWN HOW THE GENERAL OF THE MACKEREL BRIGADE
FOLLOWED AN ILLUSTRIOUS EXAMPLE, AND VETOED A PROCLAMA-
TION. ALSO RECORDING A MILITARY EXPERIMENT WITH RELIABLE
CONTRABANDS.

WASHINGTON, D. C., May 20th, 1862.

REJOICE with me, my boy, that I have got back
my gothic steed, Pegasus, from the Government chap
who borrowed him for a desk. The splendid architectural animal has just enough slant from his backbone to his hips to make a capital desk, my boy ;
and then his tail is so handy to wipe pens on. In a
moment of thirst he swallowed a bottle of ink, and
some fears were entertained for his life ; but a gross
of steel pens and a ream of blotting paper, immediately administered, caused him to come out all write.
In a gothic sense, my boy, the charger continues to
produce architectural illusions. He was standing on
a hill-side the other day, with his rear-elevation toward the spectators, his head up and ears touching at
the top, when a chap, who has been made pious by
frequent conversation with the contrabands, noticed
him afar off, and says he to a soldier, " What church

is that I behold in the distance, my fellow-worm of the dust?" The military veteran looked, and says he, "It does look like a church; but it's only a animated hay-rack belonging to the cavalry."

"I see," says the pious chap, moving on ; "the beast looks like a church, because he's been accustomed to steeple-chases."

I have also much satisfaction in the society of my dog, Bologna, my boy, who has already become so attached to me that I believe he would defend me against any amount of meat. Like the Old Guard of France, he's always around the bony parts thrown ; and, like a *bon vivant*, is much given to whining after his dinner.

The last time I was at Paris, my boy, this interesting animal made a good breakfast off the calves of the General of the Mackerel Brigade's legs, causing that great strategetical commander to issue enough oaths for the whole Southern Confederacy.

"Thunder!" says the General, at the conclusion of his cursory remarks, "I shall have the hydrophobia and bite somebody. It's my opinion," says the General, hastily licking a few grains of sugar from the spoon he was holding at the time, "it's my opinion that I shall go rabid as soon as I see water."

"Then you're perfectly safe, my conquering hero," says I ; "for when *you* see water, the Atlantic Ocean will be principally composed of brandy pale."

Speaking of Paris, it pains me, my boy, to say, that Captain Villiam Brown's Proclamation for the conciliation of southern Union men has been repudiated by the General of the Mackerel Brigade.

" Thunder !" says the General, taking a cork from his pocket in mistake for a watch-key, " it's against the Constitution to open a bar so far away from. where Congress sits."

And he at once issued the following

" PROCLAMATION.

" Whereas, There appears in the public prints what presumptuously pretends to be a proclamation of Captain Villiam Brown, Eskevire, in the words following, to wit :

' PROCLAMATION.

' The Union men of the South are hereby informed that the United States ·of America has· reasserted hisself, and will shortly open a bar-room in Paris. Also, cigars and other necessaries of life.

' By order of
' CAPTAIN VILLIAM BROWN, Eskevire.'

" And whereas, the same is producing much excitement among those members from the Border States who would prefer that said bar-room should be nearer Washington, in case of sickness. Therefore, I, General of the Mackerel Brigade, do proclaim and declare that the Mackerel Brigade cannot stand this sort of thing, and that neither Captain Villiam Brown nor any other commander has been authorized to declare free lunch, either by implication or otherwise, in any State : much less in a state of intoxication, of which there are several.

"To persons in this State, now, I earnestly appeal. I do not argue : I beseech you to mix your own liquors. You cannot, if you would, be blind to the signs of the times, when such opportunity is offered to see double. I beg of you a calm and immense consideration of them (signs), ranging, it may be, above personal liquor establishments. The change you will receive after purchasing your materials will come gently as the dues from heaven—not rending nor wrecking anything. Will you not embrace me ? May the extensive future not have to lament that you have neglected to do so.

"Yours, respectfully, the

"GENERAL OF THE MACKEREL BRIGADE."

[Green seal.]

When Villiam read this conservative proclamation, my boy, he looked thoughtfully into a recently-occupied tumbler for a few moments, and then says he :

"There's some intelleck in that. The general covers the whole ground. Ah!" says Villiam, preparing, in a dreamy manner, to wash out the tumbler with something from a decanter, "the general so completely covers the whole ground sometimes, that the police departmink is required to clear it."

I believe him, my boy.

The intelligent and reliable contrabands, my boy, who have come into Paris from time to time, with valuable news concerning all recent movements not taking place in the Confederacy, were formed lately by Villiam, into a military company, called the Sambory Guard, Captain Bob Shorty being deputed to drill them in the colored-manual of arms. They were dressed in flaming red breeches and black coats, my boy, and each chaotic chap looked like a section of stove-pipe walking about on two radishes.

I attended the first drill, my boy, and found the oppressed Africans standing in a line about as regular as so many trees in a maple swamp.

Captain Bob Shorty whipped out his sleepless sword, straightened it on a log, stepped to the front, and was just about to give the first order, when, suddenly, he started, threw up his nose, and stood paralyzed.

"What's the matter, my blue and gilt?" says I.

He stood like one in a dream, and says he :

"'Pears to me I smell something."

"Yes," says I ; "'tis the scent of the roses that hangs round it still."

"True," says Captain Bob Shorty, recovering, "it does smell like a cent ; and I haven't seen a cent of my pay for such a long time, that the novelty of the odor knocked me. Attention, company !"

Only five of the troops were enough startled by this sudden order, my boy, to drop their guns, and only four stooped down to tie their shoes. One very reliable contraband left the ranks, and says he :

" Mars'r, hadn't Brudder Rhett better gub out the hymn before the service commence ?"

" Order in the ranks !" says Captain Bob Shorty, with some asperity, " Attention, Company !—Order Arms !"

The troops did this very well, my boy, the muskets coming down at intervals of three minutes, bringing each man's cap with them, and pointing so regularly toward all points of the compass, that no foe could possibly approach from any direction without running on a bayonet.

" Excellent !" says Captain Bob Shorty, with enthusiasm. " Only, Mr. Rhett, you needn't hold your gun quite so much like a hoe. Carry arms !"

Here Mr. Dana stepped out from the ranks, and says he :

" Carrie who, mars'r ?"

" Go to the rear," says Captain Bob Shorty, indignantly. " Present Arms !"

If Present Arms means to stick your bayonet into the next man's side, my boy, the troops did it very well.

" Splendid !" says Captain Bob Shorty. " Shoulder Arms—Eyes Right—Double-quick, March !   On to Richmond !"

The troops obeyed the order, my boy, and haven't been seen since.   Perhaps they're going yet, my boy.

Company 3, Regiment 5, Mackerel Brigade, started for an advance on Richmond yesterday, and by a forced march got within three miles of it.   Another march brought them within five miles of the place ; and the last despatch stated that they had but ten miles to go before reaching the rebel capital.

Military travel, my boy, is like the railroad at the West, where they had to make chalk marks on the track to see which way the train was going.

Yours, on time,

ORPHEUS C. KERR.

LETTER XLVII.

INTRODUCING A POEM BASED UPON AN IDEA THAT IS IN VIOLET—A POEM FOR WHICH ONE OF THE WOMEN OF AMERICA IS SOLELY RESPONSIBLE.

WASHINGTON, D. C., May 24th, 1862.

ONE of the Northern women of America, my boy, has sent me a note, for the express purpose of expressing her hatred of the Southern Confederacy. She says, my boy, that the Confederacy is a miserable man, only fit for pecuniary dishonesty; and that even the gentle William Shakspeare couldn't help revealing the peculiar failing of the Floydulent section when he spoke so feelingly of

"The sweet South,
That breathes upon a bank of Violets,
Stealing and giving odor."

A fair hit, my boy—a fair hit; and sorry should I be to let the sweet South breathe upon any kind of a bank in which I had a deposit.

Speaking of violets; the woman of America sent one of those pretty flowers in her note; and, as I looked upon it, I thought how fit it was to be

THE SOLDIER'S EPITAPH.

The woodlands caught the airy fire upon their vernal plumes,
  And echoed back the waterfall's exultant, trilling laugh,
And through the branches fell the light in slender golden blooms
  To write upon the sylvan stream the Naiad's epitaph.

On either side the sleeping vale the mountains swelled away,
  Like em'ralds in the mourning ring that circles round the world
And through the flow'r-enamel'd plain the river went astray,
  Like scarf of lady silver'd o'er around a standard furled.

The turtle wooed his gentle mate, where thickest hung the boughs,
  While round them fell the blossoms plucked by robins' wanton bills;
And on its wings the zephyr caught the music of his vows,
  To waft a strain responsive to the chorus of the hills.

'Twas in a nook beside the stream where grapes in clusters fell,
  And twixt the trees the swaying vines were lost in leafy showers,
That fauns and satyrs, tamed to rest beneath the noonday spell,
  Gave silent ear and witness to the meeting of the flowers.

The glories of the fields were there in summer's bright array,
  The virgins of the temple vast where Noon to Ev'ning nods,
To crown as queen of all the rest whose bosom should display
  The signet of a mission blest, the cipher of the gods.

The royal Lily's sceptred cup besought an airy lip,
  The Rose's stooping coyness told the bee was at her heart,
While all the other sisters round, with many a dainty dip,
  Sought jewels hidden in the grass, and waved its spears apart.

" We seek a queen," the Lily said, " and she shall wear the crown
  Who to the Mission of the Blest the fairest right shall prove;
For unto her, whoe'er she be, has come in sunlight down
  The badge of Nature's Royalty, from angel hands above.

" I go to deck the wreath that binds a fair, imperial brow,
  Whose whiteness shall not be the less that mine is purer still;
For though a band of sparkling gems is set upon it now,
  'Twill be the fairer that the Church in me beholds her will."

" I claim a loyal suitor's touch," the Rose ingenuous said,
  " And he will choose me when he seeks the bow'r of lady fair,
To match me, with a smile, against her cheek's betraying red,
  And place me, with a kiss, within the shadows of her hair."

And next the proud Camellia spoke : " Where festal music swells,
  And solemn priest, with gown and book, a knot eternal ties,
I go to hold the vail of her who hears her marriage-bells,
  And pledges all her life unto the Love that never dies."

The Laurels raised their glowing heads, and into language broke :
  " 'Tis ours to honor gallant deeds that awe a crouching world ;
We rest upon the warrior's helm when fades the battle's smoke,
  And bloom perennial on the shield that back the foeman hurled."

And other sisters of the field, the woodland, and the vale,
  Each told the story of her work, and glorified her quest ;
But none of all the noble ones had yet revealed the tale
  That taught them from the gods she wore the signet in her breast.

At length the zephyr raised a leaf, the lowliest of the low,
  And there, behold a Violet the Spring let careless slip ;
Beyond its season blooming there where newer beauties grow,
  Enshrined like an immortal thought that lives beyond the lip.

" We greet thy presence, little one," the graceful Lily said,
  And quivered with a silent laugh behind her snowy screen,
" Upraise unto the open sun thy modest little head ;
  For here, perchance, in thee at last the Flow'rs have found their
    queen."

A tremor shook the timid flower, and soft her answer came :
  " 'Tis but a simple duty left to one so small as I ;
And yet I would not yield it up for all the higher fame
  Of nodding on a hero's helm, or catching beauty's eye.

" I go to where an humble mound uprises in a field,
  To mark the place of one whose life was lost a land to save ;
Where bannered pomp no birth attests, nor marbled sword nor shield ;
  I go to deck," the Violet said, " a simple soldier's grave."

There fell a hush on all the flowers; but from a distant grove
　　Burst forth the anthem of the birds in one grand peal of praise;
As though the stern old Forest's heart had found its early love,
　　And all of earth's sublimity was melted in its lays!

Then, as the modest flower upturned her blue eyes to the sun,
　　There fell a dewdrop on her breast as shaken from a tree;
The lowliest of the sisterhood the godlike Crown had won;
　　For hers it was to consecrate Truth's Immortality.

The woodlands caught the airy fire upon their vernal plumes,
　　And echoed back the waterfall's exultant, trilling laugh;
And through the branches fell the light in slender golden blooms,
　　To sanctify the Violet, the Soldier's Epitaph.

I asked the General of the Mackerel Brigade, the other day, what kind of a flower he thought would spring above my head when I rested in a soldier's sepulchre? and he said "A cabbage!" my boy—he said "A cabbage!"　　Yours, inversely,

　　　　　　　　　　　　　　ORPHEUS C. KERR.

LETTER XLVIII.

TREATING CHIEFLY OF A TERRIBLE PANIC WHICH BROKE OUT IN
PARIS, BUT SUBSEQUENTLY PROVED TO BE ONLY A NATURAL EF-
FECT OF STRATEGY.

WASHINGTON, D. C., June 1st, 1862.

IT is my belief—my solemn and affecting belief, my
boy, that our once distracted country is destined to
be such a great military power hereafter, that an
American citizen will be distinguishable in any part of
the world by his commission as a brigadier. Even Congressmen will answer to the command of " Charge—
mileage !" and it is stated that sons of guns in every
variety are already being born at the West—sons of
" Pop" guns, my boy.

The last time the General of the Mackerel Brigade
was here, he was so much pleased with the high state
of strategy developed at the War Office, that he
visited all the bar-rooms in Washington, and ordered
the tumblers to be at once illuminated.

" Thunder !" says the general to Colonel Wobert
Wobinson, of the Western Cavalry, as they were
taking measures to prevent any possible mistake by

seeing the enemy double, " this war is making great tacticians of the whole nation, and if I wanted my sons to become Napoleons, I'd put them into the War Office for a week. My sons ! my sons !" says the general hysterically, motioning for a little more hot water, " why are you not here with me in glory, instead of remaining home there, like ripe plums on the parent tree."

"Plums ! plums !" says Colonel Wobinson, thoughtfully. " Ah ! I see," says the colonel, pleasantly, " your sons are damsons."

The general eyed the speaker with much severity of countenance, my boy, and says he :

" If *you* have any sons, my friend, they are probably fast young men, and take after their father—at the approach of the enemy."

The general is rather proud of his sons, my boy, one of whom wrote the following, which he keeps pinned against the wall of his room :—

POOR PUSSY.

We count mankind and keep our census still,
   We count the stars that populate the night;
But who, with all his computation, can
   Con catty nations right?

In all the lands, in zones of all degrees,
   No spot im-puss-able is known to be;
And sure, the ocean can't ignore the Cat,
   Whose capital is C.

Despise her not; for Nature, in the work
  Of making her, remembered human laws,
And gave to Puss strange gifts of human sort;
  Before she made her paws:

First, Puss is like a soldier, if you please;
  Or, like a soldier's officer, in truth;
For every night brings ample proof she is
  A fencer from her youth.

A model cosmopolitan is she,
  Indifferent to change of place or time;
And, like the hardy sailor of the seas,
  Inured to every climb.

Then, like a poet of the noble sort,
  Who spurns the ways of ordinary crews,
She courts the upper-storied attic salt,
  And hath her private mews.

In mathematics she eclipses quite
  Our best professors of the science hard,
When, by her quadrupedal mode, she shows
  Her four feet in a yard.

To try the martial simile once more:
  She apes the military drummer-man,
When, at appropriate hours of day and night,
  She makes her ratty plan.

She is a lawyer to the hapless rat,
  Who strives in vain to fly her fee-line paws,
Evading once, but to be caught again
  In her redeeming claws.

Then turn not from poor Pussy in disdain,
  Whose pride of ancestry may equal thine;
For is she not a blood-descendant of
  The ancient Catty line?

Speaking of strategy, my boy, you will remember that Company 3, Regiment 5, Mackerel Brigade, started for an advance on Richmond last week, and were within ten miles of that city. Subsequently they made another forced march of five miles, leaving only fifteen miles to go ; and on Tuesday, a messenger came in from them to Captain Villiam Brown, with the intelligence that the advance was already within twenty-five miles of the rebel head-quarters.

" Ha !" says Villiam, " the Confederacy is doomed; but I must curb the advancing impetuosity of these devoted beings, or they'll be in Canada in a week. I think," says Villiam, calculatingly, " that a retreat would bring us to the summer residence of the Southern Confederacy in less time."

Here another messenger came in from the Richmond storming party, and, says he :

". The advance on Richmond has failed in consequence of the shoes furnished by the United States of America."

" Ah !" says Villiam, hastily setting down a goblet.

" Yes," says the chap, mournfully, " them air shoes has demoralized Company 3, which is advancing back to Paris at double-quick. Them shoes," says the chap, " which was furnished by the sons of Revolutionary forefathers by a contractor, at only twenty-five dollars a pair for the sake of the Union, has caused a fatal mistake. They got so ragged with being exposed to the wind, that when Company 3 hastily put them on for an advance on Richmond, they got the heels in front and have been going in the wrong direction ever since."

" Where did you leave your comrades ?" says Villiam.

" At Joneses Court House," says the chap.

" Ah !" says Villiam, " is that a healthy place ?"

" No," says the chap, " it's very unhealthy—I was drunk all the time I was there." .

" I see," says Villiam, with great agitation, " my brave comrades are in a tight place. Let all the newspaper correspondents be ordered to leave Paris at once," says Villiam to his adjutants, " and we'll take measures for a second uprising of the North."

When it became generally known, my boy, that Company 3, Regiment 5, Mackerel Brigade, were falling back across Duck Lake, there was great agitation in Government circles, and the general of the Mackerel Brigade prepared to call out all persons capable of bearing arms.

" The Constitution is again in danger," says the general, impulsively, " and we must appeal to the populace."

" Ah !" says Villiam, " it would also aid our holy cause to call out the women of America. For the women of America," says Villiam, advisedly, " are capable of baring arms to any extent."

"No!" says the general. "Woman's place in this
war is beside the couch of the sick soldier. Thunder!" says the general, genially, "it's enough to make
us fonder of our common nature to see the devotion
of women to the invalid volunteer. As I was passing through the hospital just now," says the general,
feelingly, "I saw a tender, delicate woman acting
the part of a ministering angel to a hero in a hard
ague. She was fanning him, my friend—she was
fanning him."

"Heaven bless her!" says Villiam, with streaming
eyes ; "and may she never be without a stove when
she has a fever. I really believe," says Villiam, glowingly, "that if woman found her worst enemy, even,
burning to death, she would heap coals of fire upon
his head."

Villiam's idea of heaping coals of fire, my boy, is
as literal as was the translation of Enoch.

On learning of the repulse from Richmond, all the
Southern Union men of Paris commenced to remember that the rebels are our brethren, and that this
war was wholly brought about by the fiendish abolitionists.

"Yes!" says a patriotic chap from Accomac, sipping the oath loyally, "the Abolitionists brought
this here war about, and I have determined not to
support it. Our slaves read the *Tribune*, and have
learned so much from military articles in that paper

that the very life of the South depended upon separation."

In fact, my boy, notwithstanding the efforts of Captain Villiam Brown to tranquillize public feeling by seizing the telegraph office and railroad depot, telegraphing to everybody he knew for reënforcements, the excitement was steadily increasing, until word came from Company 3, Regiment 5, Mackerel Brigade, that no enemy had been in sight at all.

When the intelligence was brought to the General of the Mackerel Brigade, and as soon as the band had finished serenading him, he called for a fresh tumbler, and says he :

" I may as well tell you at once, my children, that this whole matter is simply a part of my plan for bringing this unnatural war to a speedy termination. Company 3 retired by my design, and—and—in fact, my children," says the general, confidingly, " it's something you can't understand—it's strategy."

Perhaps it was, my boy—perhaps it was ; for there is more than one reason to believe that strategy means military shoes with the heels in front.

Yours, cautiously,
ORPHEUS C. KERR.

LETTER XLIX.

NOTING THE ARCHITECTURAL EFFECTS OF THE GOTHIC STEED, PEGASUS,
AND DESCRIBING THE MACKEREL BRIGADE'S SANGUINARY ENGAGE-
MENT WITH THE RICHMOND REBELS.

WASHINGTON, D. C., June 8th, 1862.

ONCE more, my boy, the summer sun has evoked long fields of bristling bayonets from the seed sown in spring tents, and the thunder of the shower is echoed by the roar of the scowling cannon. Onward, right onward, sweeps the Sunset Standard of the Republic, to plant its Roses and its Lilies on the soil where Treason has so long been the masked reaper ; to epitaph with its eternal Violet the honored battle-graves of the heroic fallen, and to set its sleepless Stars above the Southern Cross in a new Heaven of Peace.

In my voyage down the river, to witness the great battle for Richmond, I took my frescoed dog, Bologna, and my gothic steed, Pegasus. The latter architec-tural animal, my boy, has again occasioned an optical mistake. Being of a melancholy turn, and partaking somewhat of the tastes of the horrible and sepulchral German Mind, the gothic charger has peregrinated

much in a churchyard near Washington, frequently
standing for hours in that last resting-place, lost in
profound mortuary contemplation, to the great admiration of certain vagrant crows in the atmosphere.
On such occasions, my boy, his casual pace is, if possible, rather more *requiescat in "pace"* than on ordinary marches. I was going after him in company
with a religious chap from Boston, who is going down
South to see about the contrabands being born again,
when we caught sight of Pegasus, in the distance.
The sagacious architectural stallion had just ascended
the steps leading into the graveyard, my boy, and
presented a gothic and pious appearance. The religious chap clutched my arm, and says he :

"How beautiful it is, my fellow-sinner, to see that
simple village church, resting like the spirit of Peace
in the midst of this scene of war's desolation."

"Why, my dear Saint Paul," says I, "that's my
gothic steed, Pegasus."

"Ahem !" says he. "You must be mistaken,
my poor worm ; for I can see half way down the
aisle."

"The perspective," says I, "is simply the perspective between the hind legs of the noble creature, and
his rear elevation deceives you."

"Well," says the religious chap, grievously, "if
you ever want to do anything for the missionary
cause, my poor lost lamb, just skin that horse and

and let me have his frame for a numble chapel, wherein to convert contrabands."

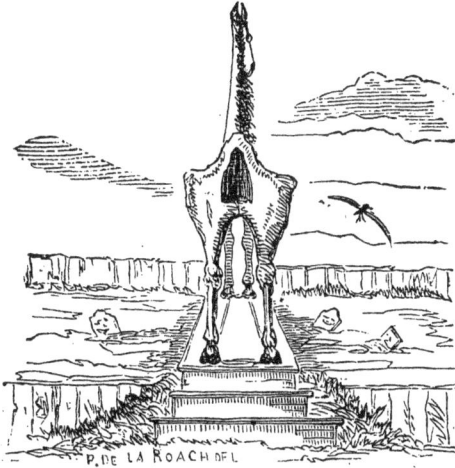

REQUIESCAT IN "PACE."

ARCHITECTURAL VIEW OF THE GOTHIC STEED, PEGASUS—REAR ELEVATION.

On my way down the Potomac to Paris, my boy, with Pegasus and the intelligent dog Bologna, I met Commodore Head, of the new iron-plated Mackerel fleet, who was taking his swivel Columbiad to a blacksmith, to have the touch-hole repaired. The Commodore met with a great disappointment at Washington, my boy. He ordered the great military painter, Patrick de la Roach, to paint him a portrait of Secretary Welles, Cabinet size. When the picture came home, my boy, it was no larger than a twenty-five-cent piece, frame and all ; and the portrait was hardly perceptible to the naked eye.

" Wedge my turret !" says the Commodore, in his iron-plated manner, " I wouldn't give a Galena for such a picture as that. What did you make it so small for, you daubing cuss ?"

" Didn't you want it Cabinet size ?" says the artist.

" Batter my plates ! of course I did," says the Commodore.

" Well," says the artist, earnestly, " if you ever attended a Cabinet meeting, you'd know that that is exactly the Cabinet size of the Secretary of the Navy."

The Commodore related this to me, my boy, in the interval of naval criticisms on the gothic Pegasus, whom he pronounced as incapable of being hit at right angles by a shell as the Monitor. " Explode my hundred-pounder !" says the Commodore, admiringly, " I don't see any flat surface about that oat-crushing machine. Perforate my armor, if I do !"

A great battle was going on upon the borders of Duck Lake when we reached Paris, my boy, and on ambling to the battle-field with my steed and my dog, I found the Mackerel Brigade blazing away at the foe in a thunder-storm and vivid-lightning manner.

Captain Villiam Brown, mounted on the geometrical steed Euclid, to whom he had administered a pinch of Macaboy to make him frisky—was just re-

ceiving the answer of an orderly, whom he h&f sent
to demand the surrender of a rebel mud-work in
front.

"Did you order the rebel to surrender his incendiary establishment to the United States of America?" says Villiam, majestically returning his canteen
to his bosom.

"I did, sire," says the Orderly, gloomily.

"What said the unnatural scorpion?" says Villiam.

"Well," says the Orderly, "his reply was almost
sarcastic."

"Ha!" says Villiam, "what was't?"

"Why," says the Orderly, sadly, "he said that if
I didn't want to see a dam fool, I'd better not go into
a store where they sold looking-glasses."

"Ah!" says Villiam, nervously licking a cork,
"that *was* sarcastic. Let the Orange County Howitzers push to the front," says Villiam, excitedly,
"and we'll shatter the Southern Confederacy. Hello!"
says Villiam, indignantly, "Who owns that owdacious dog there?"

I looked, my boy, and behold it was my frescoed
canine, Bologna, who was innocently discussing a
bone right in the track of the advancing artillery. I
whistled to him, my boy, and he loafed dreamily
toward me.

The Orange County Howitzers thundered forward,
and then hurled an infernal tempest of shell and can-

ister into the horizon, taking the roofs off of two barns, and making twenty-six Confederate old maids deaf for life. At the same instant, Ajack, the Mackerel sharpshooter, put a ball from his unerring rifle through a chicken-house about half a mile distant, causing a variety of fowl proceedings.

"Ah !" says Villiam, critically, "the angels will have to get a new sky, if the artillery practice of the United States of America keeps on much longer."

Meantime Company 2, Regiment 5, Mackerel Brigade, was engaging the enemy some distance to the right, under Captain Bob Shorty ; and now there came a dispatch from that gallant officer to Villiam, thus :

"*The Enemy's Multiplication is too much for my Division. Send me some more Democrats.*
"CAPTAIN BOB SHORTY."

"Ah !" says Villiam, "the Anatomical Cavalry and the Western Centaurs are already going to the rescue. Blue blazes !" says Villiam, cholerically, "Why don't that blessed dog get out of the way ?"

I looked, my boy, and, behold ! it was my frescoed canine, Bologna, calmly reasoning with a piece of army beef, in the very middle of the field. I whistled, my boy, and the intelligent animal floated toward me with subdued tail.

The obstruction being removed, the Anatomicals

and the Centaurs charged gloriously under Colonel Wobert Wobinson, and would have swept the Southern Confederacy from the face of the earth, had not the fiendish rebels put a load of hay right in the middle of the road. To get the horses past this object was impossible, for they hadn't seen so much forage before in a year.

"Ah!" says Villiam, contemplatively, "I'm afraid cavalry's a failure in this here unnatural contest. Ha!" says Villiam, replacing the stopper of his canteen, and quickly looking behind him, "What means this spectacle which mine eyes observe?"

A cloud of dust opened near us, and we saw Captain Samyule Sa-mith rushing right into headquarters, followed by Company 6, having an aged and very reliable contraband in charge.

"Samyule, Samyule," says Villiam, fiercely, "expound why you leave the field with your force, at this critical period in the history of the United States of America?"

"I'm supporting the Constitution," says Samyule, breathlessly, "I'm a conservative, and——." Here Samyule tumbled over something and fell flat on his stomach.

"By all that's blue!" says Villiam, frantically, "why the thunder don't somebody shoot that unnatural dog!"

I looked, my boy, and beheld it was my frescoed

canine, Bologna, who had run between the legs of the fallen warrior, with the remains of a captured Confederate chicken. I whistled, my boy, and the faithful creature angled towards me with mitigated ears.

" I'm supporting the Constitution," repeated Samyule, rising to his feet and examining a small, black bottle to see if anything had spilt, " I'm a conservative, and have left the field to restore this here misguided contraband to his owner, which is a inoffensive rebel. War," says Samyule, convincingly, " does not affect the Constitution."

" Ah !" says Villiam, " that's very true. Take the African chasseur to his proper master, and tell him that the United States does not war against the rights of man."

Now it happened, my boy, that the withdrawal of this force to carry out the Constitution, so weakened the Advance Guard, that the Southern Confederacy commenced to gain ground, and Villiam was obliged to form Company 3, Regiment 5, in line immediately, for a charge to the rescue. He got the splendid *corps* to leave the distillery where they were quartered, for a few minutes, and says he :

" There's beings for you, my nice little boy ! Here's veteran centurions for you."

" Yes," says I, admiringly. " I never saw so many red noses together before, in all my life."

"Ah !" says Villiam, dreamily, "there's nary red about them, except their noses. And now," says Villiam, "you will see me lead a charge destined to cover six pages in the future history of our distracted country."

"Soldiers of the Potomac !" says Villiam, drawing his sword, and hastily sharpening it on the left profile of his geometrical steed, "your comrades are engaging nine hundred and fifty thousand demoralized and routed rebels, and you are called upon to charge bayonets. Follow me."

Not a man moved, my boy. Many of them had families, and more were engaged to be married to the women of America. They were brave but not rash.

Villiam drew his breath, and says he : "The United States of America, born on the Fourth of July, 1776, calls upon you to charge bayonets, Come on, my brave flowers of manhood !"

Here a fearless chap stepped out of the ranks, and says he : "In consequence of the heavy dew which fell this morning, the roads is impassable."

Villiam remained silent, my boy, and drooped his proud head. Could nothing induce those devoted patriots to strike for the forlorn hope ? Suddenly, a glow of inspiration came over his face, he rose in his saddle like a flash, waved his sword toward the foe, and shouted—

"I know you now, my veterans ! The day is hot, yonder lies our road, and—my peerless Napoleons," said Villiam, frenziedly :

"COME AND TAKE A DRINK !"

In an instant I was blinded with a cloud of dust, through which came the wild tramp and fierce hurrahs of Company 3, Regiment 5, Mackerel Brigade. The appeal to their finer feelings had carried them by storm, and they charged like the double-extract of a compound avalanche. I was listening to their cheers as they drove the demoralized foe before them, when a political chap came riding post-haste from Paris, and says he :

"How many voters have fallen ?"

Before I could answer him, my boy, the triumphant Mackerels came pouring in, just in time to meet the General of the Mackerel Brigade, who had just rode up from a village in the rear, with an umbrella over his head to keep off the sun."

"My children," says the general, kindly, as their shouts fell upon his ears, "you have sustained me nobly this day, and we will enjoy the thanks of our grateful country together. I thank you, my children."

Here the political chap threw up his hat, and says he : "Hurroar for the Union ! My fellow-beings," says the political chap, glowingly, "I announce the idolized General of the Mackerel Brigade for President of the United States in 1865."

" Ah !" says Villiam—he would have said more, but at that moment his horse's legs became entangled in something, and both horse and rider went to grass. I looked, my boy, and behold, it was my frescoed dog Bologna, who had run against the geometrical steed of the warrior in pursuit of an army biscuit. I whistled, my boy, and the docile quadruped shrunk toward me with criminal aspect.

And so, the unblest cause of treason has received a decisive blow. The end approaches ; but I can't say which end, my boy—I can't say which end.

Yours, martially,

ORPHEUS C. KERR.

LETTER L.

REMARKING UPON A PECULIARITY OF VIRGINIA, AND DESCRIBING
COMMODORE HEAD'S GREAT NAVAL EXPLOIT ON DUCK LAKE, ETC.

WASHINGTON, D. C., June 15th, 1862.

EARLY in the week I trotted to the other side of
the river on my gothic steed Pegasus, and having lent
that architectural pride of the stud to a thoughtful
individual, who wished to make a sketch of his facade,
I took a branch railroad for a circuitous passage to
Paris, intending to make one stoppage on the way.
The locomotive was about two-saucepan power, my
boy, and wheezed like a New York Alderman at a
free lunch. First we stopped at a town composed of
one house, and that was a depot.

"What place is this?" says I to my fellow pas-
senger, who was the conductor, and was reading the
Tribune, and was swearing to himself. "It's Mul-
ligan's Court-House, the Capital of Sally Ann
County," says he, and again took out the bill I had
paid my fare with to see if it was good.

I took another branch road here, and we snailed
along to another town, composed of a wood-pile.

" What place is this ?" says I to my fellow-traveller, the brakeman. " It's Abednego Junction, the capital of Laura Matilda County," says he, sounding my quarter on his seal ring to make sure that it was genuine. Now, as London, the city I was going to, happened to the capital of Anna Maria County, my boy, I made up my mind that the sacred soil had as many metropolises as railways.

" Virginia," says a modern Southern giant of intellect, " is one grand embodied poem."

I believe him, my boy ; for, like a poem, Virginia appears to have a capital at the commencement of every line.

Reaching London, and brushing past a crowd of our true friends the contrabands, whose cries of anguish upon hearing that I had brought them no plum-pudding, were truly harrowing, I pushed forward to the new Union paper, the London Times, with whose editor I had business.

Just as I entered the office, my boy, there rushed out in great rage an exasperated southern Union man. Having no gun about the house to pick off our pickets as they came into town, he borrowed a barber's pole and stuck it out of the window, proclaimed himself an oppressed Unionist, had a meeting of his family to elect him to the United States Congress from Anna Maria County, and made a thrilling Union address to two contrabands from his back-stoop. He wound up this great speech, my boy, by saying :

" Young men, it is your duty to fight for the Union, which has caused us all so many tears. If any young man's wife would fain dissuade him, let him say to her, in the language of the poet,

> " 'I could not love thee, dear, so much,
> Loved I not Honor more !' "

This touching peroration was sent in manuscript to the London Times, and this is the way it appeared in that intellectual American journal :

" Young hen, it is your duty to fight for the Onion, which has caused us all so many tears. If any young man's wife would fain dissuade him, let him say to her, in the language of the poet :

> " 'I could not love thee, dear, so much,
> Loved I not Hannah. More.' "

When the southern Union man read this twistification, he put his paper where his wife couldn't see it (she being a very jealous woman), and went out to cowhide the editor. He cowhided him, by frantically placing the cowhide in the editor's hands, and then running his back repeatedly against the weapon. Typographical errors have a unique effect in reports of killed and wounded, my boy ; but they knock the Promethean blaze out of eloquence.

Having transacted my business with the editor, and

read a dispatch, just received from a Gentleman of Eminence, stating that Beauregard, who was at Oko-lonna, had a force of 120,000 men ; but that Halleck would probably succeeed in putting the entire 80,000 to flight before Beauregard could return from Rich-mond ; though it was currently reported that the rebels were sixty thousand strong, and General Pope must be expeditious if he wanted to capture the whole 10,000 before General Beauregard got back from the Shenandoah valley ; I turned to the editor, and says I :

" How does newspaper business pay now, my gifted Censor ?"

He sighed, as he shoved a demijohn further under his desk, and says he :

" There's only one newspaper in the world that pays now, sonny :

" What's that ?" says I.

" The Paris *Pays*," says he.

I left him immediately, my boy. Ordinary de-pravity don't affect me, for I have known several Congressmen in my time ; but I can't stand abnor-mal iniquity.

Arriving at Paris I found that a recent shower had made Duck Lake navigable, and Commodore Head was preparing his fleet to attack a secession squadron, which some covert rebel had built during the night for the purpose of annoying the Mackerels in Paris.

"Batter my plates!" says the commodore, cholerically, "I could capture that poor cuss easily, if I
only had a proper pilot."

As Duck Lake is only about four yards wide at a
freshet, my boy, your ignorance may suggest no sufficient reason for a pilot in such a case; but you are
no martial mariner, my boy.

Luckily the man for the place was at hand. On
Wednesday, a glossy contraband, in a three-story
shirt-collar, and looking like a fountain of black ink
with a strong wind blowing against it, came into Paris,
and surrendered to Captain Villiam Brown.

"Ha!" says Villiam, replacing the newspaper that
had just blown off from two lemons and a wicker flask
on the table, "what says our cousin Africa?"

"Mars'r Vandal," says the faithful black, earnestly,
"I hab important news to combobicate. I knows all
de secrets of de rebel Scratchetary of the Navy. True
as you lib, Mars'r Vandal, so help me gad, I'se de
coachman of de pirate Sumter."

"Ah!" says Villiam, cautiously, "tell me, blessed
shade, what has a coachman got to drive on board a
vessel?"

The true-hearted contraband modestly eyed a wonder of the insect kingdom which he had just removed
from his hair, and says he:

"I drove de ingine, mars'r."

That was enough, my boy. Having learned from

this intelligent creature what the rebel Secretary was going to have for dinner next Sunday, and what the Secretary's wife said in her letter to her mother, Villiam ordered him to act as pilot on the Mackerel Fleet.

And now let me draw a long breath before I attempt to describe that terrific and sanguinary naval engagement, which proved conclusively what Europe may expect, if Europe bother us with any more bigodd nonsense.

Having ballasted with mortar, my boy, to seem more naval, the unblushing commodore mounted his swivel-gun at the bow of the Mackerel Fleet, and selected for his gunner and crew a middle-aged Mackerel chap, whose great fondness for fresh fish made him invaluable for ocean service.

"Crack my turret!" says the commodore, as the Fleet pushed off amid the cheers of Company 4, Regiment 1, Mackerel Brigade; "I'll take that craft by compound fracture. Belay the starboard ram there, you salamander, and take a reef in the grating. Up with the signal—two strips of pig iron rampant, with a sheet of tin in the middle."

All this was splendidly performed by the crew, my boy, who trimmed the rudder, did the rowing, and tended the gun—all at once. The craft fairly flew through the water in the direction of the rebel craft, whose horse-pistol amidship still remained silent.

It was an awfully terrific and sublime sight, my boy. I shall never forget it, my boy, if I live till I perish.

The faithful colored pilot sat in the stern of the Fleet, examining some silver spoons which he had found somewhere in the Southern Confederacy, and we could see the noble old commodore mixing something that steamed in the fore-sheets.

Two seconds had now passed since our flotilla had started, and the hostile squadrons were rubbing against each other. We were expecting to see our navy go through some intricate manœuvre before boarding, when the Mackerel crew accidentally dropped a spark from his pipe on the touch-hole of the swivel; and bang! went that horrid engine of destruction, sending some pounds of old nails right square into the city of Paris.

Simultaneously, four-and-twenty foreign Consuls residing near Paris got up a memorial to Commodore Head, protesting against any more firing while any foreigners remained in the country, and declaring that the use of gunpowder was an outrage on civilized warfare and the rights of man. They tied a stone to this significant document and threw it to Commodore Head, who instantly put the Mackerel crew on half rations and forbid smoking abaft the big gun.

Meanwhile the enemy had wounded our brave pilot

on the shins with his oar, and exploded his horse-pistol in an undecided direction, with such dreadful concussion that every glass in Commodore Head's spectacles was broken.

It was at this dreadful crisis of the fight that the gay Mackerel crew leaned over the side of our fleet, placed one hand on the inside of the enemy's squadron, and with the other, regardless of the shower of old-bottles and fish-bones flying about him, deliberately bored a small hole, with a gimlet, through the bottom of the adversary. At about the same moment the commodore touched off the swivel-gun at the enemy's rudder, and threw one of his boots against the rear stomach of the rebel captain.

This sickening carnage might have lasted five minutes longer, had not the Confederate squadron sunk in consequence of the gimlet-hole. Down went the doomed craft of unblest treason, and in another moment the officer and crew of her were in the water, which reached nearly to their knees, imploring our fleet not to let them drown.

Oh, that sight! the thrilling yet terrifying and agonizing grandeur of that dreadful moment! shall I ever forget it—ever cease to hear those cries ringing in mine ears? I'm afraid not, my boy—I'm afraid not.

The Commodore rescued the sufferers from a watery grave; and having been privately informed by them that the South might be conquered, but never overcome, brought them ashore by the collars.

Need I describe how our noble old nautical sea-dog was received by the Mackerel Brigade? need I tell how the band whipped out his key-bugle and played all the triumphant airs of our distracted country, and several original cavatinas?

But, alas! my boy, this iron-plate business is taking all the romance out of the navy. How different is the modern from

THE ANCIENT CAPTAIN.

The smiles of an evening were shed on the sea,
    And its wave-lips laughed through their beardings of foam;
And the eyes of an evening were mirrored beneath
    The shroud of the ship and her home.

And as Time knows an end, so that sea knew a shore,
    Afar in a beautiful, tropical clime,
Where Love with the Life of each being is blent,
    In a soft, psychological Rhyme.

Oh, grand was the shore, when deserted and still
    It breasted the silver-mailed hosts of the Deep!
And like the last bulwark of Nature it seemed,
    'Twixt Death and an Innocent's sleep.

But grander it was to the eyes of a knight,
    When clad in his armor he stood on the sands,
And held to his bosom its essence of Life—
    An heiress of titles and lands.

Ah, fondly he gazed on the face of the maid!
    And blush-spoken fondness replied to his look;
While heart answered heart with a feverish beat,
    And hand pressed the hand that it took.

"Fair lady of mine," said the knight, stooping low,
  "Before I depart for the banquet of Death,
I crave a new draught from the fountain of Life,
  Whose waters are all in thy breath.

"The breast that is filled with thine image alone,
  May safely defy the dread tempest of steel;
For while all its thoughts are of love and of thee,
  What peril of Self can it feel?"

He paused; and the silence that followed his words,
  Was spread like a Hope, 'twixt a Dream and a Truth·
And in it, his fancy created a world
  Wrought out of the dreams of his youth.

Then shadows crept over the beautiful face
  Turned up to the sky in the pale streaming light,
As shadows sweep over the orient pearl,
  Far down in the river at night.

"You're going," she said, " where the fleets are in leash,
  Where plumed is a knight for each wave of the sea;
Yet all the wide Ocean shall have but One wave,
  One ship and One sailor for me!"

He left her, as leaveth the god of a dream
  The portals that close with a heavier sleep;
And then, as he sprang to the shallop in wait,
  The rowers pushed off in the Deep.

When a captain leaves his lady-fair nowadays, my
boy, he's not an economical man if he don't destroy
his life-insurance policy, and defer making his will.

Yours, navally,

ORPHEUS C. KERR.

LETTER LI.

GIVING DUE PROMINENCE ONCE MORE TO THE CONSERVATIVE ELE-
MENT, NOTING A CAT-AND-DOG AFFAIR, AND REPORTING CAPTAIN
BOB SHORTY'S FORAGING EXPEDITION.

WASHINGTON, D. C., June 23d, 1862.

NOT wishing to expire prematurely of inanity, my
boy, I started again last Sunday for Paris, where I
took up my quarters with a dignified conservative
chap from the Border States, who came on for the
express purpose of informing the Executive that
Kentucky is determined this war shall be carried on
without detriment to the material interests of the
South, otherwise Kentucky will not be answerable
for herself. Kentucky has married into the South,
and has relations there which she refuses to sacrifice.
What does the Constitution say about Kentucky?
Why, it don't say anything about her. "Which is
clear proof," says the conservative chap, violently,
"that Kentucky is expected to take care of herself.
Kentucky," says he, buttoning his vest over the
handle of his bowie-knife. "Kentucky will stand no
nonsense whatsomever."

I have much respect for Kentucky, my boy ; they play a good hand of Old Sledge there, and train up a child in the way he should go fifty better ; but Kentucky reminds me of a chap I once knew in the Sixth Ward. This chap hired a room with another chap, and the two were engaged in the dollar-jewelry business. Their stock in trade was more numerous than valuable, my boy, and a man couldn't steal it without suffering a most painful swindle ; but the two dilapidaries were all the time afraid of thieves ; and at last, when a gentleman of suspicious aspect moved into the lower part of the house, and flavored his familiar conversation with such terms as "swag," "kinchin," and "coppers," the second chap insisted upon buying a watch-dog. The first chap said he didn't like dogs, but if his partner thought they'd better have one, he would not object to his buying it. The second chap bought a sausagacious animal in white and yellow, my boy—an animal covered with bark that pealed off in large pieces all night long. The first chap found he couldn't sleep much, and says he :

"If you don't kill that ere stentorian beast we'll have to dissolve pardnership."

His partner took a thoughtful chew of tobacco, and says he :

"That intelligent dorg is a defending of your property as well as mine, and if we put up with his strains a little while longer, the chap down stairs will understand the hint and make friends."

With that the first chap flamed up, and says he :

"I sold a breast-pin to the chap down stairs the other day, and found out that he considers the dollar-jewelry business the same by nature as his own. I'm beginning to think we misjudged him, and I can't have no dog kept here to worry him. Our lease of these here premises don't say anything about keeping a dog," says the chap, reflectively, "nor our articles of pardnership, and I refuse to sanction the dog any longer."

So the dog was sent to the pound, my boy, and that same night the burglarious gentleman downstairs walked off with the dollar-jewelry, in company with the first chap, leaving the poor second chap to make himself uselessly disagreeable at the police-office, and set up an apple-stand for support.

Far be it from me, my boy, to say that certain Border States are like the first chap ; but if Uncle Sam should happen to be the second chap let him hold on to the watch-dog.

Speaking of dogs, I must tell you about a felis-itous canine incident that occurred while I was at Paris. Early one morning, the Kentucky chap and I were awakened by a great noise in the hall outside our door. Presently an aged and reliable contraband stuck his head into the room, and says he :

"I golly, mars'r, dar's a big fight goin' on in dis yar place."

At the word, my boy, we both sprang up and went to the door, from whence we beheld one of those occurrences but too common in this dreadful war of brother against brother.

Face to face in the hall stood my frescoed dog, Bologna, and the regimental cat Lord Mortimer, eyeing each other with looks of deadly hatred and embittered animosity. High in air curved the back of the enraged Mortimer, and his whiskers worked with intense wrath ; whilst the eloquent tail of the infuriated Bologna shot into the atmosphere like a living flag-staff.

"Oh-h-h ! How-now ?" ejaculated Bologna, throwing out his nose to reconnoitre the enemy's first line.

" 'Sdeath !—'Sdeath !" hastily retorted Mortimer, skirmishing along in his first parallel with spasmodic clawing.

And now, my boy, commenced a series of scientific manœuvres that only Russell, of the *London Times*, could describe properly. Lord Mortimer advanced circularly to the attack in four columns, affrighting the air with horrid yells of defiance ; and I noticed, with a feeling of mysterious awe, that his eyes had turned a dreadful and livid green, whilst an expression of inexpressible bitterness overspread his countenance.

Fathoming the enemy's plan at a glance, Bologna presented his front and rear divisions alternately, to distract the fire of the foe ; and then, by a rapid and skillful flank movement, cut off a portion of Lord Mortimer's tail from the main body.

This reminded me of General Mitchell's tactics, my boy.

Here the conservative Kentucky chap wanted to stop the fight. Says he :

"Mortimer will be forever alienated if he loses any more of his tail. I protest against the dog's teeth," says he ; "for they'll render future reconciliation between the two impossible. Let him use his paws alone," says the conservative chap, reasoningly, "and he won't injure Mortimer's constitution so much.

"You're too late with your talk about conciliation, my noble Cicero," says I. "It's the cat's nature to show affection for his young ones, even, by licking them, and Mortimer will never be convinced that Bologna cares for him until he has been soundly licked by him."

"Ah—well," says the Kentucky chap, vaguely, "let hostilities proceed."

Finding that the enemy had cut off a portion of his train in the rear, Mortimer quickly massed his four columns and precipitated them upon the head of Bologna's two front divisions, succeeding in destroying a bark half launched, and driving him back four feet.

" Hurroar for Mortimer !" says the Kentucky chap ; and then he burst into the Conservative Virginia National Anthem :

" John Smith's body lies a-mouldering in the grave,
  'Twas him that Pocahontas risked her father's wrath to save;
  And unto old Virginia certain Chivalry she gave,
      That still go scalping on !"

" Calm your exultation, my impulsive Catiline," says I, " and behold the triumph of Bologna."

Undaunted by the last claws of the foe's argument, my boy, the frescoed dog hurled back the torrent of invasion, and, with a howl of triumph, charged headlong upon Mortimer's works, routing the foe, who retreated under cover of a cloud of fur.

I looked at the conservative Kentucky chap, my boy, and I could see by his expression that it would be useless for me to ask of him a contribution toward rewarding Bologna with a star-spangled kennel. He still felt neutral, my boy

I had intended to remain in Paris all the week ; but on receiving a telegraphic dispatch from the General of the Mackerel Brigade to attend a Strawberry Festival he was about to give in this city, I hastened hither. For I am very fond of the gay and festive strawberry, my boy, on account of its resemblance to one of the hues in our distracted banner.

The Strawberry Festival was given in an upper room at Willard's, and the arrangement of the fruit would have provoked an appetite in a marble statue. At short intervals around the table were strawberries in fours, supported by pedestals of broken ice, which was kept in position by a fluid of pleasing color, and walled in by a circular edging of thin glass. Strips of lemon and oranges garnished the rich fruit, and from their midst sprang up a dainty mint plant, and a graceful hollow straw.

When the festival was in full operation, my boy, the General of the Mackerel Brigade arose to his feet, and waved his straw for silence. Says he :

" My children, though this strawberry festival is ostensibly for the purpose of encouraging fruit culture by the United States of America, it has yet a deeper purpose. The democratic party," says the general, paternally, "is about to be born again, and it is time to make preparation for the next Presidential election in 1865. I must go to Albany and Syracuse, and see the State Conventions ; after which I must attend to the re-organization of the party in New York city. Then I go to Pennsylvania to do stump duty for a year ; and from thence, to—"

Here a serious chap, who had taken rather too much Strawberry Festival, looked up, and says he :

" But how about the war all that time ?"

" The war !—the war !" says the general, thoughtfully. "Thunder !" says the general, with such a start that he spilt some of his Festival, "I'd really forgotten all about the war !"

"Hum !" says the serious chap, gloomily, "you're worth millions to a suffering country—*you* are."

"Flatterer !" says the general blandly.

"Yes," says the chap, "you're worth millions— with a hundred per cent off for cash."

In vino veritas is a sage old saying, my boy, and I take it to be a free translation of the Scripture phrase, "In spirit and in truth."

Our brigadiers are so frequently absent-minded themselves, my boy, that they are not particularly absent-minded by the rest of the army.

Upon quitting the Strawberry Festival I returned post-haste again to Paris, where I arrived just in time to start with Captain Bob Shorty and a company from the Conic Section of the Mackerel Brigade on a forag- ing expedition. We went to look up a few straw- beds for the feeding of the Anatomical Cavalry horses, my boy, and the conservative Kentucky chap went along to see that we did not violate the Constitution nor the rights of man.

"It's my opinion, comrade," says Captain Bob Shorty, as we started out—"it's my opinion, my Union ranger, that this here unnatural war is getting worked down to a very fine point, when we can't go out for an armful of forage without taking the Constitution along on an ass. I think," says Captain Bob Shorty, " that the Constitution is as much out of place here as a set of fancy harness would be in a drove of wild buffaloes."

Can such be the case, my boy—can such be the case ? Then did our Revolutionary forefathers live in vain.

Having moved along in gorgeous cavalcade until about noon, we stopped at the house of a First Family of Virginia who were just going to dinner. Captain Bob Shorty ordered the Mackerels to stack arms and draw canteens in the front-door yard, and then we entered the domicil and saluted the domestic mass-meeting in the dining-room.

" We come, sir," says Bob, addressing the venerable and high-minded Chivalry at the head of the table, " to ask you if you have any old straw-beds that you don't want, that could be used for the cavalry of the United States of America."

The Chivalry only paused long enough to throw a couple of pie-plates at us, and then says he :

" Are you accursed abolitionists ?"

The conservative Kentucky chap stepped hastily forward, and says he :

No, my dear sir, we are the conservative element."

The Chivalry's venerable wife, who was a female Southern Confederacy, leaned back a little in her chair, so that her little son could see to throw a tea-cup at me, and says she :

" You ain't Tribune reporters—be you ?"

" We were all noes and no ayes. Quite a feature in social intercourse, my boy.

The aged Chivalry caused three fresh chairs to be placed at the table, and having failed to discharge the fowling-piece which he had pointed at Captain Bob Shorty, by reason of dampness in the cap, he waved us to seats, and says he :

" Sit down, poor hirelings of a gorilla despot, and learn what it is to taste the hospitality of a Southern gentleman. You are Lincoln hordes," says the Chivalry, shaking his white locks, "and have come to butcher the Southern Confederacy ; but the Southern gentleman knows how to be courteous, even to a van-dal foe."

Here the Chivalry switched out a cane which he had concealed behind him, and made a blow at Cap-tain Bob Shorty.

" See here," says Bob, indignantly, " I'll be—"

" Hush !" says the conservative Kentucky chap, agitatedly, " don't irritate the old patriarch, or future amicable reconstruction of the Union will be out of the question. He is naturally a little pro-voked just now," says the Kentucky chap, sooth-ingly, " but we must show him that we are his friends."

We all sat down in peace at the hospital board, my boy, only a few sweet potatoes and corn-cobs being thrown by the children, and found the fare to be in keeping with the situation of our distracted country—I may say, war-fare.

"In consequence of the blockade of the Washington Ape," says the Chivalry, pleasantly, "we only have one course, you see; but even these last-year's sweet potatoes must be luxuries to mercenary mud-sills accustomed to husks."

I had just reached out my plate, to be helped, my boy, when there came a great noise from the Mackerels in the front door-yard.

"What's that?" says Captain Bob Shorty.

"O, nothing," says the female Confederacy, taking another bite of hoe-cake, "I've only told one of the servants to throw some hot water on your reptile hirelings."

As Captain Bob Shorty turned to thank her for her explanation, and while his plate was extended, to be helped, the aged Chivalry fired a pistol at him across the table, the ball just grazing his head and entering the wall behind him.

"By all that's blue," says Captain Bob Shorty, excitedly, "now I'll be—"

"Be calm—now, be calm," says the conservative Kentucky chap, hastily, "don't I tell you that it's only natural for the good old soul to be a little provoked ?   If you go to irritate him, we can never live together as brethren again."

Matters being thus rendered pleasant, my boy, we quickly finished the simple meal ; and as Captain Bob Shorty warded off the carving-knife just thrown at him by the Chivalry's little son, he turned to the female Confederacy, and says he :

"Many thanks for your kind hospitality ; and now about that straw bed ?"

The Virginia matron threw the vinegar-cruet at him, and says she :

"My servants have already given one to your scorpions, you nasty Yankee."

"Of course," says the venerable Chivalry, just missing a blow at me with a bowie-knife, "of course, your despicable Government will pay me for my property !"

"Pay *you!*" says Captain Bob Shorty, hotly, "now I'll be—"

"Certainly it will, my friend," broke in the conservative Kentucky chap, eagerly, "the Union troops come here as your friends ; for they make war on none but traitors."

As we left the domicil, my boy, brushing from our coats the slops that had just been thrown upon us from an upper window, I saw the Chivalry's children training a fowling-piece from the roof, and hoisting the flag of the Southern Confederacy on one of the chimneys.

And will it be possible to regain the love of these noble people again, my boy, if we treat them constitutionally? We shall see, my boy, we shall see.

Yours, for further national abasement,

ORPHEUS C. KERR.

LETTER LII.

DESCRIBING, AMONG OTHER THINGS, A SPECIALITY OF CONGRESS, A
VENERABLE POPULAR IDOL, AND THE DIFFICULTIES EXPERIENCED
BY CAPTAIN SAMYULE SA-MITH IN DYING.

WASHINGTON, D. C., June 25th, 1862.

How beautiful is Old Age, my boy, when it neither
drinks nor swears. There is an oily and beneficent
dignity about fat Old Age which overwhelms us with
a sense of our crime in being guilty of youth. I
have at last been introduced to the Venerable Gammon, who is all the time saying things ; and he is a
luscious example of overpowering Old Age. He is
fat and gliding, my boy, with a face that looks like a
full moon coming out of a sheepskin, and a dress
indicating that he may be anything from a Revolutionary Forefather to the patriarch of all the Grace
Church sextons. I can't find out that he ever did
anything, my boy, and no one can tell why it is that
he should treat everybody in office and out of it in
such a fatherly and fatly condescending manner ;
but the people fairly idolize him, my boy, and he is
all the time saying things.

When I was introduced to the Venerable Gammon

he was beaming benignantly on a throng of adoring
statesmen in the lobby of Congress, and I soon discovered that he was saying things.

"Men tell us that this war has only just commenced," says the Venerable Gammon with fat pro-
fundity, "but they are wrong. *War is like a stick,
which has two ends—the end nearest you being the*
BEGINNING."

Then each statesman wanted the Venerable Gammon to use *his* pocket-handkerchief; and five-and-
twenty desperate reporters tore passionately away to
the telegraph office to flash far and wide the comforting remarks of the Venerable Gammon.

Are we a race of unsuspecting innocents, my boy,
and are we easily imposed upon by shirt-ruffles and
oily magnitude of manner? I believe so, my boy—I
believe so.

Speaking of Congress; I attended one of its sittings
the other day, my boy, and was deeply edified to observe its manner of legislating for our happy but distracted country.

The "Honorable Speaker" (*né* Grow) occupied the
Chair.

Mr. PODGERS (republican, Mass.) desired to know
if the tax upon Young Hyson is not to be moderated?
Speaking for his constituents he would say that the
present rate was entirely too high to suit any grocer—

Mr. STAGGERS (conservative, Border State) wished

to know whether this body intended to legislate for
white men or niggers ? His friend, the pusillanimous
scoundrel from Massachusetts, chose to oppose the tax
on Young Hyson because—to use his own words—it
would not " suit a negro, sir—"

Mr. PODGERS thought his friend from the Border
State was too hasty. The phrase he used was *" any
grocer."*

Mr. STAGGERS withdrew his previous remark. We
were fighting this war to secure the Constitution and
the pursuit of happiness to the misguided South, and
he accepted his friend's apology.

Mr. FIGGINS (democrat, New Jersey) said that he
could not but notice that everything all the Honorable gentlemen had said during this session was a
fatal heresy, destructive of all Government, degrading
to the species, and an insult to the common sense of
his (Figgins') constituents. His constituents de-
manded that Congress should set the country at
rights before Europe. It would appear that at the
least imperious sign from Europe, the American knee
grows—

Mr. JUGGLES (con., Border State) desired to inquire
of the House whether the great struggle in which we
are now engaged is for the benefit of the Caucasian
race or the debased African ? His friend, the puling
idiot from New Jersey, had seen fit to remark that
the American negroes—

Mr. FIGGINS denied that he had spoken at all of negroes. He was about to say, that at the slightest behest of Europe "the *American knee grows flexible to bend.*"

Mr. JUGGLES wished it to be understood that he was satisfied with his Honorable friend's explanation. He would take something with the Honorable Gentleman immediately after adjournment.

Mr. CHUNKY (rep., New Hampshire) was anxious to inquire whether it was true, as stated in the daily papers, that General McDowell had been ordered to imprison all the Union men within his lines on suspicion of their being Secessionists, and place a guard over the property of the Secessionists, on suspicion of their being Union men? If so, he would warn the Administration that it was cherishing a viper which would sting it:

> " The rose you deftly cull-ed, man,
>   May wound you with its thorn,
>   And—"

Mr. WADDLES (Union, Border State) protested against the decency of a Constitutional body like Congress being insulted with the infamous and seditious abolition doggerel just quoted by his friend, the despicable incendiary from New Hampshire. We were waging this war solely to put down treason, and not to hear a rose, the fairest of flowers, mentioned in the same breath with the filthy colored man—

Mr. Chunky was sorry to observe that his Honorable friend had misunderstood his language. The line he had used was simply this :

"The rose you deftly *cull-ed, man.*"

Mr. Waddles was glad that his valued friend from New Hampshire had apologized. He had only taken exception to what he considered a fatal heresy.

That was enough for me, my boy, and I left the hall of legislation ; for I sometimes become a little wearied when I hear too much of one thing, my boy.

I mentioned my impression to the Venerable Gammon, and says he :

"Congress is the soul of the nation. Congress," says the Venerable Gammon, with fat benignity, "*is something like a wheel, whose spokes tend to tire.*"

He said this remarkable thing in an overtowering way, my boy, and I felt myself to be a crushed infant before him.

Early in the week, I took my usual trip to Paris, and found Company 3, Regiment 5, Mackerel Brigade, making an advance from the further shore of Duck Lake, for sanitary reasons. It was believed to be detrimental to the health of the gay Mackerels to be so near a body of pure water, my boy, for they were not accustomed to the element.

"Thunder !" says the general, brushing off a small

bit of ice that had adhered to his nose, "they'll be drinking it next."

Captain Samyule Sa-mith was ordered to command the advance ; but when he heard that the Southern Confederacy had two swivels over there, he was suddenly taken very sick, and cultivated his bed-clothes.

When the news of the serious illness of this valiant officer got abroad, my boy, there was an immediate rush of free and enterprising civilian chaps to his bedside.

One chap, who was an uncombed reporter for a discriminating and affectionate daily press, took me aside, and says he :

"Our paper has the largest circulation, and is the best advertising mejum in the United States. As soon as our brother-in-arms expires," says the useful chap, feelingly, "just fill up this printed form and send it to me, and I will mention you in our paper as a promising young man."

I took the printed form, my boy, which I was to fill up, and found it to read thus :

"BIOGRAPHICAL SKETCH OF THE LATE ———.

"This noble and famous officer, recently slain at the head of his ——— (I put the word 'bed' in this blank, my boy), was born at ——— on the — day of — -, 1776, and entered West Point in his — year. He won immortal fame by his conduct in the Mexican

campaign, and was created brigadier-general on the
— of ——, 1862."

These printed forms suit the case of any soldier, my
boy ; but I didn't entirely fill this one up.

Samyule was conversing with the chaplain about
his Federal soul, when a tall, shabby chap made a
dash for the bedside, and says he to Samyule :

"I'm agent for the great American publishing
house of Rushem & Jinks, and desire to know if you
have anything that could be issued in book-form after
your lamented departure. We could make a handsome 12mo book," says the shabby chap, persuadingly,
"of your literary remains. Works of a Union
Martyr—Eloquent Writings of a Hero—Should be
in every American Library—Take it home to your
wife—Twenty editions ordered in advance of publication—Half-calf, $1.—Send in your orders."

Samyule looked thoughtfully at the publishing
chap, and says he :

"I never wrote anything in my life."

"Oh !" says the shabby chap, pleasantly, "anything will do—your early poems in the weekly journals—anything."

"But," says Samyule, regretfully, "I never wrote
a line to a newspaper in all my life."

"What !" says the publishing chap, almost in a
shriek—"never wrote a line to a newspaper ?   Gen-

tleman," says the chap, looking toward us, suspic-
iously, "this man can't be an American." And he
departed hastily.

Believing, my boy, that there would be no more
interruptions, Samyule went on dying; but I was
called from his bedside by a long-haired chap from
New York. Says the chap to me :

"My name is Brown—Brown's Patent Hair-Dye,
25 cents a bottle. Of course," says the hirsute chap,
affably, " a monument will be erected to the memory
of our departed hero. An Italian marble shaft, standing on a pedestal of four panels. Now," says the
hairy chap, insinuatingly, "I will give ten thousand
dollars to have my advertisement put on the panel
next to the name of the lamented deceased. We can
get up something neat and appropriate, thus :

> WE MUST ALL DIE;
>
> BUT
>
> **BROWN'S DYE IS THE BEST.**

"There !" says the enterprising chap, smilingly,
" that would be very neat and moral, besides doing
much good to an American fellow-being."

I made no reply, my boy ; but I told Samyule
about it, and it excited him so that he regained his
health.

"If I can't die," says the lamented Samyule, "without some advertising cuss's making money by it, I'll defer my visit to glory until next season."

And he got well, my boy—he got well.

I was talking to the chaplain about Samyule's illness, and says the chaplain :

"I am happy to say, my fellow-sinner, that when our beloved Samyule was at the most dangerous crisis, he gave the most convincing proof of realizing his critical condition."

"How ?" says I, skeptically.

"Why," says the chaplain, with a Christian look, "when I told our beloved Samyule that there could be little hope of his recovery, and asked him if his spiritual adviser could do anything to make his passage easier, he pressed my hand fervently, and besought me to see that he was buried *with a fan in his hand.*"

Can it be, my boy, that the soul of a Mackerel will need a fan in another world ?   Let us meditate upon this, my boy—let us meditate upon this!

Yours, seriously,

ORPHEUS C. KERR.

www.ingramcontent.com/pod-product-compliance
Lightning Source LLC
Chambersburg PA
CBHW031124090426
42738CB00008B/960